Sue Kay & Vaughan Jones

with Jon Hird & Philip Kerr

Inside Out

Student's Book

MACMILLAN

1 Images

1 Work with a partner. Look at each of the following images of the twentieth century and note down as much information as you can. Use the following headings.

What?   Where?   Who?   Importance?

Discuss your notes with other members of the class.

2 Test your years! Match the pictures in 1 with the years in the box. (There are four more years than you will actually need.) Then check your answers on page 136.

| 1965 | 1969 | 1973 | 1977 | 1981 | 1989 | 1990 | 1997 |

3 🔲 01 We asked four people to talk about their most memorable image of the twentieth century. Listen and decide which of the images in 1 each person is talking about.

4 Complete what each person said in the listening in 3 with an appropriate verb structure. Listen again and compare your answers with the recordings. Discuss any differences between your answers and the recordings.

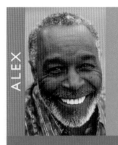

ALEX

It was the highlight of my whole life because, when I was a kid I always (1) _____ (think) – I hope I (2) _____ (live) long enough to see a man on the moon. So when it (3) _____ (happen) – I don't know how old my son was, but I said to him, 'Sit down and watch all of this – this is one of the most momentous things that (4) _____ (ever happen) in your life.'

BETH

What (1) _____ (annoy) me is that people think punk was just a fashion. For me, it was much more than that – it was a way of life. I mean, how long do you think it (2) _____ (take) to do that make-up and hair? It (3) _____ (take) about four hours a day just getting dressed!

CHRIS

What I found most amazing about that day was that he (1) _____ (spend) twenty-seven years in prison, and yet he looked as if he (2) _____ (just step) out for a walk with his wife, as if it was something he (3) _____ (do) every day of his life.

DEBRA

I was only a kid and I (1) _____ (watch) television, when a newsflash (2) _____ (come on), and I saw these crowds of people climbing on this wall. I had no idea what was going on and I actually (3) _____ (think) something terrible (4) _____ (happen). Then I realised people were laughing and celebrating. I (5) _____ (never hear) of the Berlin Wall before that night.

5 Write down five years that have been or will be significant …
- in your own life • in the history/future of your country

Work with a partner. Tell each other about the years you have chosen. Find out as much information as you can.

Close up

Verb structures **1** Choose the most appropriate verb structure for the sentences below.

a) **I've been knowing / I've known / I know** Alice since I was a child.
b) **I had / I've had / I used to have** breakfast with Ben this morning.
c) **I'm talking / I've been talking / I was talking** to Cathy just before the lesson started.
d) **I like / I'm liking / I'd like** Dan a lot – he's one of my best friends.
e) **I've learnt / I've been learning / I'm learning** English for about the same number of years as Erica.
f) **I've gone / I've been / I've been going** out to dinner with Frank lots of times.
g) **I've already met / I already met / I'd already met** Gina before I joined this class.
h) **I was having / I used to have / I'd have** a friend called Harry, but we've lost touch with each other.

2 Replace the names in the sentences in 1 to make the sentences true for you. Read your partner's sentences and find out as much information as you can about each person mentioned in their sentences.

Auxiliary verbs

1 Use the correct forms of *be*, *have* and *do* to complete the questions (a–h). Then match the questions with the answers (1–8).

a) _____ you ever won a competition?
b) _____ anyone in your family speak English fluently?
c) _____ you going out tonight?
d) _____ you given a lot of toys when you were a child?
e) _____ you think you'll ever go to South Africa?
f) _____ you studied English at another school before this one?
g) _____ you sleep long enough last night?
h) _____ anyone ever told you what beautiful eyes you've got?

1 No, no one has. But thanks for the compliment!
2 No, I've got to revise for my exam.
3 No, but I once did a course at university.
4 Yes, my father does.
5 Yes, I'm going there next year.
6 No, I didn't. In fact, I could do with a nap now!
7 Yes, I was very spoiled!
8 No, I haven't. I've come second though.

2 Work with a partner. Ask the questions in 1. Give true answers.

So & neither

1 ◉ 02 Listen to a conversation between two people and note down things they've got in common. Why does the conversation stop?

2 From your notes in 1 use the sentence frame below to make as many true sentences as you can about the man and the woman.

The man _____ , and so _____ the woman.
and neither/nor

For example: *The man is American, and so is the woman.*

3 Listen again and check your sentences.

4 Work with a partner. Use the following sentence beginnings to write statements which are true for you and which you believe are also true for your partner. Find at least two ways to finish each sentence beginning. You will need your sentences in 5. Do not speak to your partner yet.

For example: *I was born in 1975. I was born in hospital. I was born in Mexico City.*

a) I was born …
b) I'm not keen on …
c) I'm …
d) I used to …
e) I've got …
f) I can't …
g) I've never been to …
h) I'd like to …
i) I hardly ever go …

5 Use the sentences you have written in 4 to play *Bingo!*

Instructions

a Copy the Bingo card onto a separate piece of paper.

b With a partner, take it in turns to read out one of your sentences from 4. If your partner can answer with one of the responses on the Bingo card, you can cross out the square. If your partner can't use one of the responses because what you say is not true for them, you must wait for your next go to try another sentence.

c The aim of the game is to be the first person to cross out all the squares on the card.

So was I.	Nor do I.	So have I.
So would I.	Nor am I.	So did I.
Neither have I.	So am I.	Neither can I.

Question tags & short answers

1 Read the following extracts from the conversation in 1 in the previous section. Replace each underlined word or expression with one of the question tags or short answers in the box.

> Neither was I   Yes, I do   so did I   aren't you   so am I   Yes, I am   don't you

a) 'Sorry, but you're American, <u>right</u>?' '<u>Right</u>.' 'Oh, <u>me too</u>.'
b) 'But you like London, <u>right</u>?'
c) 'I wasn't a very good student.' '<u>Me neither</u>.'
d) 'What year did you graduate?' '1989.' 'That's weird, <u>me too</u>.'
e) 'Do you remember Mrs Rivers?' 'The math teacher? <u>Sure</u>.'

Language reference p8

2 🔈 03 Use the tags in the box to complete the questions. Then listen and check your answers.

> will you   haven't they   is it   do they   shall we   aren't I

a) Everybody's arrived, _____ ?
b) Nobody likes her, _____ ?
c) Just leave me alone, _____ ?
d) I'm late again, _____ ?
e) That's not really true, _____ ?
f) Let's have a drink, _____ ?

3 Work with a partner and make up a short dialogue which includes three of the tag questions in 2.

Sounding interested

Intonation which starts at a high level can make a speaker sound interested. Flat intonation can make a speaker sound bored.

1 🔈 04 Read and listen to the following short conversations. Tick (✓) the responses which sound interested, and cross (✗) those that don't. The first one has been done for you.

a) 'I don't remember my first day at school.'
   'Don't you? I do.' ✓
b) 'I've seen all of Madonna's films.'
   'Have you? I think she's so boring.' ☐
c) 'Can you remember your first kiss?'
   'Yes, I can. Can you?' ☐
d) 'I loved punk music.'
   'Did you? I really hated it.' ☐
e) 'I'll never forget the death of Princess Diana.'
   'Neither will I. It was so sad, wasn't it?' ☐

2 Work with a partner. Practise the conversations in 1, but make all your responses sound interested.

3 Complete the sentences below in a way that is true for you. In pairs, say your sentences to each other and give short responses like those above. Sound as interested as you can.

a) I'll never forget my first …
b) Can you remember …
c) I loved …
d) I've never been to …
e) I don't like …
f) I've never …
g) My favourite … is …
h) I always …

Language reference: verb structures & auxiliary verbs

Verb structures

English combines present or past time with the simple, continuous or perfect aspect to form different tenses.

Present verb structures

You use the present simple mainly to talk about habits and routines or things that are always true.
*I usually **go** to bed around midnight.*
*Pictures **say** more than words.*

You can use the present continuous to talk about activities that are in progress now, or to describe changing situations.
*I**'m learning** Japanese as well as English.*
*The world's climate **is getting** warmer.*

Note that some verbs are not normally found in continuous forms. You will find more information about these verbs in unit 6.

You can use the present perfect to talk about present situations which started in the past and that are continuing now, or which exist because of a completed past event, or which happened at an indefinite time in the past.
*I**'ve been taking** English classes since last year.*
*Look, she**'s changed** her hairstyle.*
*We**'ve seen** Madonna in concert nine times!*

Past verb structures

You use the past simple to fix events and situations in the past.
*Nelson Mandela **was** in prison for twenty-seven years.*
*He **was released** in 1990.*

You usually use the past continuous in contrast with the past simple to talk about activities that were in progress when something happened.
*He **was driving** to London when the accident **happened**.*

You use the past perfect to show clearly that one past event happened before another past event.
*The film **had started** when I arrived.*

You can use both *would* and *used to* to refer to regular or repeated past actions.
*When she was at school, she **used to** get up before six o'clock and **would** always have tea for breakfast.*

You can also use *used to* – but not *would* – to refer to past states or situations.
*I **used to** have a motorbike but I sold it a few years ago.*

You will find a review of future verb structures in unit 12.

Auxiliary verbs

The auxiliary verbs *be*, *have* and *do* are used to form different verb structures. They are also used with *so* and *neither/nor* in question tags and in short answers.

So & neither

You use *so* to mean 'also' in the structure *So + auxiliary + subject*.
*'I'm American.' '**So** am I.'*
*'I've been to New York.' '**So** has my sister.'*
*'He fell in love.' '**So** did she.'*

You use *neither* or *nor* to mean 'also not' in the same structure.
*'I don't like warm beer.' '**Neither** do I.'*
*'I didn't use to like biology.' '**Nor** did I.'*
*'I can't swim.' '**Neither** can my brother.'*

Both *so* and *neither* are used to show agreement between speakers. Note what happens when there is disagreement between speakers.
'I'm Irish.' 'I'm not.' (NOT ~~'I'm not Irish.'~~)
'He hasn't got a car.' 'She has.' (NOT ~~'She's.'~~)
'I didn't see the match.' 'We did.' (NOT ~~'We'd.'~~)

Question tags & short answers

You usually use a negative question tag with a positive statement, and a positive question tag with a negative statement.

+	–	–	+

*You're Irish, **aren't you**? | You're not Irish, **are you**?*
*It's cold today, **isn't it**? | It isn't cold today, **is it**?*

You use *they* to refer to *somebody*, *anybody*, *everybody* and *nobody*.
***Somebody** must have called earlier, mustn't **they**?*

You use a positive question tag after *never*, *hardly*, *little*.
*He **never** gives up, **does** he?*

You can use *will/would* or *can/can't/could* after imperatives.
***Get** me some milk from the shops, **would** you?*

Other cases:
***Let's** go out for dinner, **shall** we?*
***There**'s no time left, **is there**?*
***Nothing** can go wrong, **can it**?*

To answer *Yes/No* questions you can use the structure *Yes* or *No* + subject + auxiliary.
'Have you been working?' 'Yes, I have. / No, I haven't.'

Image queue

1 What do you know about Madonna? What did she look like the last time you saw a picture or a video of her?

2 Read the article and put Madonna's different 'looks' (*a–i*) in the order they are mentioned. <u>Underline</u> the parts of the article which describe the photos.

Material girl
TO GEISHA GIRL

The look is pure subservience. The white-painted face, with lips like a red gash, is framed by a dead straight curtain of dark glossy hair. It is the stark image of
5 a geisha that stares into the camera. So it is difficult to believe that this is Madonna … the woman who sums up feisty independence in the post-feminist era … posing as a silent, submissive geisha girl.
10 But to take Madonna at face value is to misunderstand one of the most complex and intensely clever female stars of the past two decades.

She is the mistress of reinvention. And
15 behind every change of image – always total, always perfect down to the last detail – is a carefully thought-out strategy to get the attention that she wants.

From the moment the Detroit convent
20 girl hitch-hiked to New York twenty years ago with a burning ambition to be the world's most famous woman, she has shown an amazing talent for transformation.
25 She was named the new face of Max Factor make-up – quite an achievement at the age of forty. But the singer almost certainly has her eye on her next film role. It is no coincidence that Steven Spielberg
30 is looking for a woman for his film adaptation of Arthur Golden's best-selling novel, *Memoirs of a Geisha*. And if her new geisha look is part of Madonna's campaign to secure the part,
35 who can blame her? It has paid off before.

She desperately wanted the role of Eva Peron in the film *Evita*, so she showed director Alan Parker she was the perfect choice by adopting an uncanny
40 resemblance to the Argentinian president's wife.

Madonna has always been a brilliant consolidator of trends, picking up on an existing look and making it her own. When
45 she first bounced into the charts in 1984

with hits such as *Holiday*, it was as a trashy punk with torn tights and big bangles.

Material Girl in 1985 was not just a clever pastiche on Marilyn Monroe's
50 *Diamonds Are a Girl's Best Friend*. The platinum blond hair, furs and glitzy jewellery she wore for the video so entranced actor Sean Penn that he was determined to have her. Another example
55 of Madonna dressing for results.

By 1989, when her marriage to Penn formally ended, she had already moved on and was involved with Warren Beatty. For a short time, she dressed like the gangster's
60 moll she played in their joint movie venture, *Dick Tracy*, in which she played Breathless Mahoney … a role she took so seriously that she was prepared to put on weight for it.

When the Beatty romance ended, she
65 turned to Jean-Paul Gaultier for space-age outfits with tight corsets and menacing conical bra tops.

At the 1995 MTV Music Video Awards she adopted the Brigitte Bardot look with
70 black eyeliner and loose hair falling over her shoulders.

When Madonna was expecting her daughter, Lourdes, in 1996 she completely vanished from view. It wasn't until Lourdes
75 was nine months old that she emerged as an Earth Mother, wearing pretty dresses and hardly any make-up.

Then at forty, she moved into the Indian mystic phase … and nine months later her
80 hair, which has been almost every colour under the sun, is now back to its natural dark brown, cut in a bob.

What has drawn Madonna to the persona of the geisha, one of the most
85 notorious symbols of pre-feminist woman, virtually imprisoned in the service of men?

Only time will tell, but one thing is certain … this geisha is being used in the service of only one person. Madonna
90 herself.

(Based on an article in *The Mail on Sunday*)

3 Read the article again and answer the questions.

a) Why might it be surprising to see Madonna posing as a geisha girl?
b) Why shouldn't you take Madonna at face value?
c) Why does Madonna keep reinventing herself?
d) What is the real reason for Madonna's geisha look?
e) How did Madonna get the part of Eva Peron in the film *Evita*?
f) How does Madonna 'consolidate trends'?
g) What helped Madonna attract her first husband, Sean Penn?
h) Why did Madonna put on weight for the film *Dick Tracy*?
i) How many more times has Madonna changed her image since *Dick Tracy*?
j) Which of these words does *not* describe Madonna: *scheming, intensely clever, innocent, complex, calculating, ambitious*?

What is your own opinion of Madonna?

Lexis **1** Complete the following statements using words from the text about Madonna.

a) I usually take people at ____ value and then regret it. (line 10)
b) I have no ____ ambitions, but I'd quite like to earn a lot of money. (line 21)
c) I have an amazing ____ for wasting time, particularly when I need to do something urgently. (line 23)
d) I'm always disappointed when I see a film ____ of a novel I've read. (line 31)
e) When I was at school I ____ my work very seriously. (line 62)
f) I've recently ____ a new look. (line 69)

2 Are any of these sentences true for you? Compare your answers with a partner.

Anecdote Think about your favourite living famous person. You are going to tell a partner about them. Choose from the list below the things you want to talk about. Think about what you will say and what language you will need.

☐ Is it a man or a woman?
☐ What are they famous for?
☐ Are they a singer, actor, politician or something else?
☐ What do you particularly like about them?
☐ How long have you been a fan?
☐ When did you first become aware of them?

☐ Did they look any different then from how they look now?
☐ What do they look like now?
☐ How old are they?
☐ Are they married?
☐ Do you know where they live?
☐ Are they world famous?
☐ Have you ever seen them in real life?

Kylie Minogue

You are what you wear

Charles   Rick   Alan   Matt

1 Look at the photographs. What kind of images do you think the four men are trying to project and why?

2 ▭ 05 Listen to a journalist for the mens' fashion magazine, *CHAPS*, stopping the four men in the street and asking them about their self-images. Compare their answers to your ideas in 1.

3 Rewrite the second part of the questions below with the exact word order the journalist uses. Use contractions where necessary.

a) I'd like to know | what clothes about say your you .

b) Would you say | image about your you care ?

c) Could you tell me | image you trying are what achieve to ?

d) Would you say that | of you fashion are aware ?

e) I'd like to know | appearance your whether life affects your .

f) Could you tell me | last bought thing what was the you ?

g) Do you mind telling me | wear what go to out evening in the you ?

h) I'd just like to know | clothing if of is item live there you without an couldn't .

4 Listen again and check your answers.

5 Do you identify with any of the people in the photographs? Do you know any men who try to project similar images?

6 Work with a partner. Take it in turns to ask each other some of the questions in 3.

Close up

1 The journalist for *CHAPS* magazine used indirect questions with the men who
she stopped in the street. Refer to 3 in the previous section and change the journalist's
indirect questions to direct questions using the beginnings below.

a) What do …
b) Do you …
c) What image are …
d) Are you …
e) Does your appearance …
f) What was …
g) What do …
h) Is there …

2 Compare the direct questions in 1 to the indirect questions used by the journalist, and
discuss the following questions.

a) What is the difference in word order between direct and indirect questions?
b) Can you use the auxiliaries *do/does/did* in indirect questions?
c) When do you use *if* and *whether* in indirect questions?

3 Correct the mistakes in the following sentences.

a) Do you know how much does she weigh?
b) I'd like to know how old was she when she joined *The Spice Girls*.
c) I want to know if has she got any pets.
d) Have you any idea what does she think of Madonna?
e) Could you tell me who are her favourite designers?

f) Do you know why did he shave his head?
g) I'd like to know if has he got any tattoos.
h) Could you tell me which football club does he play for?
i) Have you any idea which position does he play in?
j) I want to know what is his star sign.

4 What do you know about Victoria Beckham and David Beckham? Work with a partner.
Student A turn to page 136. Student B turn to page 138. Student A is going to find out
some information about Victoria Beckham by asking Student B questions *a–e* in 3 above.
Student B is then going to find out some information about David Beckham by asking
Student A questions *f–j* in 3 above.

5 Take it in turns to ask and answer three more questions about Victoria Beckham and
David Beckham.

David, Brooklyn and Victoria
Beckham

Language reference: indirect questions

Indirect questions are often used when you want to be more polite or tentative, because, for
example, you are starting a conversation with someone you don't know or you are asking a
sensitive personal question. The word order is the same as in normal statements: subject +
verb. In *Wh-* questions you use the same question word. In *Yes/No* questions you use *if* or
whether.

Question frame		Subject	Verb
Do you mind telling me	what	the time	is, please?
Would you mind showing me	how	this	works, please?
Do you have any idea	when	they	are arriving?
I'd like to know	where	she	buys (her shoes).
Could you tell me	who	they	have invited?
I was wondering	if/whether	you	could help me.
What time	do you suppose	they	will get here?
What	does he think	he	is doing?

Getting to know you – inside out!

Play the game in small groups. You will need a dice and counters.

1 Place your counters on the square marked START and throw the dice.
2 The first player to throw a six starts the game.
3 The first player throws the dice and moves their counter along the board according to the number on the dice.
4 When you land on a square, answer the question or ask somebody else, according to the instruction on the square. If you land on a square marked ASK ANY QUESTION!, you can choose any question on the board and ask any other player. Alternatively, you can make up your own question and ask any other player.
5 Players then play in turns, moving around the board.
6 If a player doesn't want to answer a question, they are allowed to pass and miss a turn.
7 The game continues until the first player reaches the square marked FINISH.

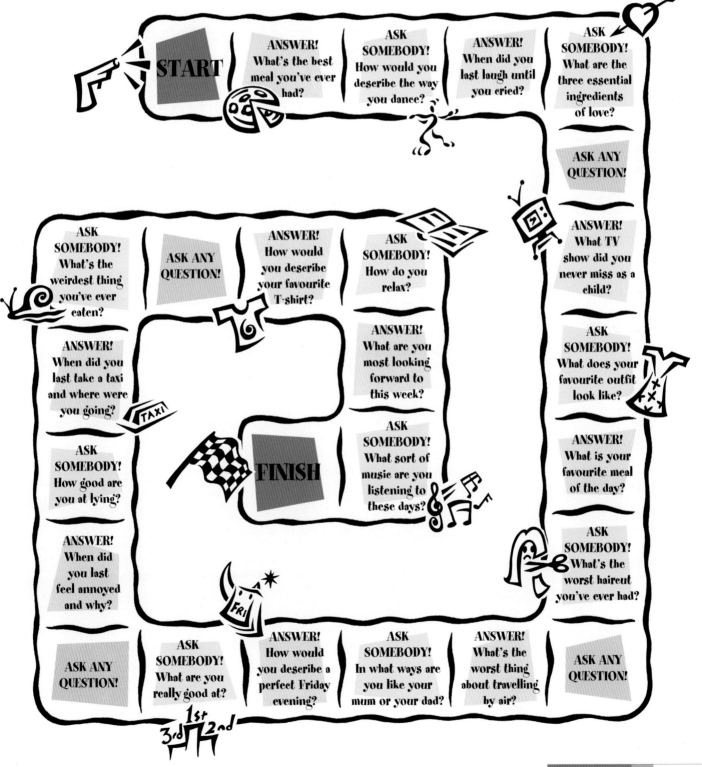

2 Family

Alex and his dad | Kayleigh and her mum | Gina and her mum

Reading 1 Look at the three photographs. They show Alex, Kayleigh and Gina, each with one of their parents. Answer the questions.

a) What do you think the parents' jobs or hobbies are?
b) How do you think these teenagers feel about their parents? Choose from the adjectives in the box.

> amused (by)   impatient (with)   annoyed (with)   satisfied (with)
> irritated (with)   proud (of)   embarrassed (by)   angry (with)
> humiliated (by)   fed-up (with)

c) Tell your partner about a time when you have had any of the feelings above about your parents.

2 Read the article on the opposite page about Alex, Kayleigh and Gina and decide which of the teenagers you would *least* like to be.

3 Test your memory! Without looking again at the article, put the names *Alex, Kayleigh* or *Gina* into the appropriate boxes to complete these sentences.

1 _____
a) would have liked to have vanished when her mum embarrassed her.
b) attempts to escape from her mum as quickly as possible.
c) 's mum forces her to hug her in front of the crowd.

2 _____
d) 's mum enjoys getting a lot of attention.
e) hates people noticing her.
f) 's mother succeeds in staying slim.

3 _____
g) really didn't want his friends to find out about his father's job.
h) 's dad forced him to participate in the performances.
i) was never interested in his father doing a boring job.

Problem Parents

(Adapted from *The Sunday Mirror Magazine*)

Alex Courtley finds it difficult to see the funny side of his father's job. His father, Paul, is better known to his fans as Corky the Clown.

Alex says: My dad couldn't have become Corky at a worse time – it was about ten years ago, and I was at the age where I knew what it was like to feel really, really embarrassed.

At first I dreaded my friends finding out what he did, but eventually everyone at school got to hear about it, and they nicknamed me Corky Junior. But the worst times were when he took me to children's parties and made me join in the act. He used to pay me a bit of money, but nothing could compensate for the humiliation.

My dad is always clowning around. He's a total exhibitionist, the loudest person I know. He sings out loud when we go shopping and he's always whistling. He's also been on television quite a lot and he's done adverts.

I used to wish he wasn't Corky, but I never wanted him to have a boring, ordinary job, like an accountant.

Kayleigh Rolls is thirteen years old, a difficult age to have an embarrassing parent. Her mum is the club mascot for Cardiff City Football Club.

Kayleigh says: Even though she wears a bird costume, everyone knows it's our mum underneath. She has to wear a really silly Bluebird costume and fool around to entertain the crowd.

Once, she went over to my maths teacher who was in the crowd and shook his hand. Then she took her bird head off and said, 'I'm Kayleigh's mum!' I just wanted the ground to open up and swallow me. I'm one of the ball girls for the club, and our mum loves to chase me around the ground. I try to run away as fast as I can, but sometimes she catches me and makes me cuddle her in front of the whole crowd.

She does cause us a lot of embarrassment, but life is never dull, and she's our mum, and I think we're lucky to have her.

Gina Clark cannot believe that her mother, a singing and piano tutor by day, is a Cher look-a-like in her spare time.

Gina says: Everyone round here knows my mum as Cher, but it's a nightmare if she's performing at a club when I'm there, because a lot of people look at me while she's doing her act, and we're so different. She loves being in the limelight, whereas I can't stand being the centre of attention. Cher is known for her outrageous clothes, and so Mum's got some incredible little see-through, all-in-one black body stockings in lace that cost a fortune. I find it embarrassing to see her in her Cher costumes, but at least when she's not Cher, she looks more normal in jeans and casual stuff. I have to admit, my mum is gorgeous, and she manages to stay in shape without spending a fortune on cosmetic surgery.

---

4 Rewrite the sentences in 3 with the verb patterns and expressions used in the article. Refer to the article to check your sentences. The first one has been done for you.

a) ____ want / ground / open up / swallow *Kayleigh wanted the ground to open up and swallow her.*

b) ____ try / run away / fast

c) ____ make / cuddle / front / crowd

d) ____ love / be / limelight

e) ____ can't stand / be / centre of attention

f) ____ manage / stay / shape

g) ____ dread / friends / find out / father / do

h) ____ make / join in / act

i) ____ never want / father / have / boring job

5 In the article Kayleigh describes a time when 'she wanted the ground to open up and swallow her'. Work with a partner and describe a time when you felt very embarrassed.

Close up

Language reference p18

Verb +
***to*-infinitive**

1 Look at the three sentences below. Do the verbs in the sentences correspond to verb pattern A or verb pattern B?

a) Kayleigh **tries** to run away as fast as she can.
b) Alex's dad **forced** him to participate in the performances.
c) Gina's mum **manages** to stay in shape.

Pattern A He (VERB) to go. (subject + verb + *to*-infinitive)
Pattern B He (VERB) her to go. (subject + verb + object + *to*-infinitive)

2 Work with a partner. Decide if the verbs in the box fit most naturally into verb pattern A or verb pattern B. What do you notice about *expected*, *wanted* and *would like*?

> aimed encouraged expected hoped reminded wanted allowed would like
> decided

3 Copy the diagram below into your notebooks and put the verbs in the box in the appropriate places.

> arranged helped taught intended can't afford attempted offered invited
> ordered paid refused warned (not) planned preferred urged

```
              arranged          helped           taught

     Pattern A                                          Pattern B
```

make* & *let **4** Read these two sentences. How do the verb patterns with these two verbs differ from the verb patterns with the verbs in 1, 2 and 3?

a) When I was fourteen, my father always **made** me come home by eleven o'clock.
b) However, my mother **let** me stay out till midnight.

5 Some parents were asked what 'rules' they would apply to teenagers. The beginnings and ends of their responses have been mixed up. Rewrite the sentences according to what you think they actually said. (In some cases various combinations are possible.)

a) We wouldn't let them   keep their rooms tidy.
b) We'd expect them   smoke in the house.
c) We'd make them   go out late at the weekend.
d) We wouldn't let them   take their studies seriously.
e) We'd tell them not   to respect their elders.
f) We'd warn them not   to keep fit.
g) We'd let them   hitch-hike by themselves.
h) We'd make them   to take drugs.
i) We'd encourage them   to play their music too loud.
j) We'd ask them not   to do well at school.
k) We'd want them   to believe everything they hear.

Discuss your sentences with a partner. Do you agree with the parents' 'rules'?

Verb + -ing form

1 Complete the sentences using the -ing forms of the verbs in the box. You can use each verb only once.

talk	study	buy	borrow	have	embarrass	iron

a) I don't mind my friends _____ my books.
b) When I've finished _____ , I want to go travelling.
c) I've considered _____ my own flat but I can't afford to.
d) My mother keeps _____ me in front of my friends.
e) I never waste time _____ my clothes: someone else does it for me!
f) Now I've got a job, I miss _____ lots of free time.
g) My family always avoids _____ about politics.

2 Are any of the sentences in 1 true for you or your partner? Discuss your sentences.

Verb + preposition structures

1 🔲 06 Eva lived with an English family for a few weeks. Put her account of her stay in the correct order. Then listen and check your answer.

(*1*) a) I knew that there were a lot of things I would have to get used

( ) b) on talking about the weather all the time. Nor did they approve

( ) c) about the reserved British character. I'd heard that they objected

( ) d) to the family for the few weeks I was there.

(*2*) e) to when I decided to go to England and stay with a family. But I was looking forward

( ) f) in making me feel at home, and I felt as if I belonged

( ) g) of, and we never had English breakfast or tea at five. But they succeeded

( ) h) of the charming English country cottage I would be staying in. I was a bit worried

( ) i) of hugging or kissing, apparently. So imagine my surprise when my English family welcomed me with a big hug and then asked me

( ) j) to talking about anything personal but insisted

( ) k) about my family, my work and even my boyfriend. They didn't live in the country cottage I'd dreamt

( ) l) to having egg and bacon for breakfast and tea at five o'clock. I was also dreaming

2 Things turned out better than expected for Eva. Work with a partner and describe a time when things turned out better than expected for you.

3 Study the examples, and then complete the sentences to make true statements.

verb	preposition	-ing form
I've always dreamt	*of*	*visiting the USA.*
I don't approve	*of*	*people smoking in class.*

I've always dreamt of ...
I don't approve of ...
I always insist on ...
I don't object to ...
I worry about ...
I've never succeeded in ...

Discuss your sentences with a partner.

Language reference: verb patterns

Verbs followed by the *to*-infinitive

1   The following verbs *don't* typically take an object before the *to*-infinitive: *aim, arrange, attempt, can't afford, decide, hope, intend, manage, offer, plan, refuse, seem, tend, try.*
    She **manages to stay** in shape.
    We **tend to go** on camping holidays.

2   The following verbs *sometimes* take an object before the *to*-infinitive: *expect, help, pay, prefer, want, would like.*
    I **wanted to go out** but I couldn't afford to.
    I **wanted her to go out** with me, but she said she was busy.

3   The following verbs *usually* take an object before the *to*-infinitive: *allow, encourage, force, invite, order, remind, teach, urge, warned (not).*
    My father **taught me to swim** when I was five.
    My parents **allowed me to go** to the party.

Make & let

After *make* and *let* you use the infinitive without *to*.

She **makes me cuddle** her.
(NOT *... makes me to cuddle*)

They **let me have** my own beliefs.
(NOT *... let me to have ...*)

Verbs followed by the *-ing* form

You use the *-ing* form after the following verbs: *avoid, can't stand, consider, detest, dislike, don't mind, dread, enjoy, fancy, finish, keep, miss, spend/waste time.*
My mother **keeps embarrassing** me.
I **can't stand being** the centre of attention.

You will find more about verbs followed by both the *to*-infinitive and the *-ing* form in unit 5.

Verb + preposition structures

You use the *-ing* form after verb + preposition structures: *accuse someone of, apologise for, approve of, believe in, blame someone for, concentrate on, congratulate someone on, consist of, dream about/of, forgive someone for, insist on, look forward to, object to, prevent someone from, rely on, specialise in, succeed in, think of, worry about.*
Gina's mother **succeeds in staying** slim.
I **look forward to hearing** from you.

There is a comprehensive listing of verb patterns on page 141.

Single vowel sounds

There are twelve single vowel sounds in English. Look at the phonetic symbols and the example words on page 143.

1   ▣ 07 Listen to these sayings about family and friendship. Write the phonetic symbols for the parts of the words which are underlined. The first one has been done for you.

   a) Ch<u>a</u>rity beg<u>i</u>ns at home.   (9) /æ/   (1) /ɪ/
   b) Bl<u>oo</u>d is thicker than w<u>a</u>ter.
   c) Home is where the h<u>ea</u>rt is.
   d) B<u>ir</u>ds of a f<u>ea</u>ther fl<u>o</u>ck together.
   e) T<u>wo</u>'s company, thr<u>ee</u>'s a crowd.
   f) One g<u>oo</u>d turn deserves anoth<u>er</u>.

2   Match the sayings in 1 with their meanings below.

   1   If someone does you a favour, you should do them a favour in return.
   2   People of the same character often stay together.
   3   Look after your family and friends first.
   4   Two people can be happy together. A third can get in the way.
   5   Wherever your loved-ones are, that's where your home is.
   6   Family relationships are the most important.

3   Which of the sayings do you like best? Discuss your choice with a partner.

Meeting the parents

Work in groups. Which of the following points do you think parents would consider important / not important in their son or daughter's future partner? Do you think the same points would be important for the son or daughter?

They should …

- [ ] have good table manners.
- [ ] be clean and smartly dressed.
- [ ] be from a good family background.
- [ ] be kind.
- [ ] be good-looking.
- [ ] be a non-smoker.
- [ ] be about the same age as the son/daughter.

- [ ] have good academic qualifications.
- [ ] like children.
- [ ] have a good job / good job prospects.
- [ ] be from the same social class.
- [ ] have the same religion as the son/daughter.
- [ ] be wealthy / have wealthy parents.
- [ ] be the same nationality as the son/daughter.

Listening

1 🔲 08 Listen to an interview with Sarah's parents about how they feel about meeting their daughter's boyfriend, Andy, for the first time. Decide whether the following are true or false.

a) Sarah has had a lot of boyfriends.
b) Her parents have met all of them.
c) They don't think most of Sarah's boyfriends are good enough for her.
d) Sarah ended a relationship with a man called Jeremy when she found out her parents didn't like him.
e) Sarah's parents think that Andy is a serious boyfriend.

Sarah and Andy   Sarah's parents

2 Choose the *to*-infinitive or the *-ing* form to complete these sentences from the conversation in 1. Then listen again and check your answers.

a) We're looking forward **to meet** / **meeting** Andy at last.
b) It's difficult **to know** / **knowing** with Sarah really – she changes boyfriends like other people change their socks.
c) I think it's essential for him **to come** / **coming** from the same kind of background.
d) It's very important for him **to have** / **having** some kind of qualifications.
e) He needs to **be** / **being** a strong character to stand up to Sarah.
f) She'd soon go off somebody who lets her **do** / **doing** what she wants all the time.
g) The poor chap is unlikely **to last** / **lasting** very long.

3 🔲 09 Listen to the interviewer asking Andy how he feels about meeting Sarah's parents. Decide whether the following are true or false.

a) Andy thinks Sarah's parents may disapprove of him.
b) He works as a DJ.
c) He's going to wear a suit.
d) He's going to take Sarah's mum some chocolates.
e) It was Andy's idea to meet Sarah's parents.

4   Complete these sentences from the conversation in 3 with the appropriate verb patterns. Then listen again and check your answers.

a)   How do you feel about ____ (meet) Sarah's parents?
b)   I'm worried about ____ (make) a bad impression.
c)   It's easy for me ____ (hide) behind my music decks at work.
d)   I'm not very good at ____ (make) conversation.
e)   Well, I gave up ____ (study) to become a DJ.
f)   How are you going to try ____ (make) a good impression?
g)   Because Sarah fancies ____ (go) to London for the day, and she feels like ____ (have) Sunday lunch at home.

Lexis   All the verbs in the box come from the conversations in 1 and 3 in the previous section. Use these verbs to replace the verbs underlined in the sentences below. You may have to change the form of the verbs.

give up	go out with	get on with	go for	stand up to	go off

a)   I find it easy to be friends with people of all ages and from all walks of life.
b)   When I'm depressed, I tend to lose interest in my food.
c)   I've never dated anybody who's got red hair.
d)   One of my colleagues is a bit of a bully, but I usually manage to defend myself against her.
e)   I used to have piano lessons, but I got bored with them and stopped.
f)   I tend to be attracted to brunettes rather than blondes.

Are any of the statements true for you? Discuss with a partner.

Anecdote   Think about a couple that you know very well. You are going to tell a partner about them. Choose from the list below the things you want to talk about. Think about what you will say and what language you will use.

☐ Who are they?
☐ How do you know them?
☐ When and where did they meet each other?
☐ How old were they when they met?
☐ Did they start going out together straight away or were they just friends to begin with?
☐ Do you think their parents approved of their choice of partner?
☐ Why do you think they were attracted to one another?
☐ What personal qualities make them compatible?
☐ What are they doing now?
☐ When was the last time you saw them?

Close up

1 On a piece of paper write three sentences about yourself using ideas from the table.

For example: *I find it boring to discuss politics with my parents.*

It's	difficult		to look at photographs of myself as a child.
It isn't	embarrassing easy	for me	to talk about my relationship with my parents. to discuss politics with my parents.
I find it	boring	—	to see my parents dancing.
	irritating		to annoy my sisters and brothers.
	amusing		to visit relatives.

2 Fold your piece of paper and give it to your teacher. Then take a piece of paper with sentences written by another student and ask questions to find out which student it belongs to. Use the following question structure.

Do you find it **adjective**   *to*-**infinitive clause**
Do you find it   *embarrassing*   *to see your parents dancing?*

3 Test your adjective + preposition structures! Complete these sentences with prepositions from the box. You can use each preposition only once.

for   in   on   at   with   of   to   about

a) Were there any school subjects you were particularly hopeless ____ ?
b) If you could be famous, what would you like to be famous ____ ?
c) What sort of music are you keen ____ ?
d) Which of the following are you most afraid ____ : spiders, heights, the dark?
e) Is there anything you're allergic ____ ?
f) What kind of sports are you interested ____ ?
g) Who was the last person you got angry ____ ?
h) Are you optimistic ____ the future?

4 Work with a partner. Ask and answer the questions in 3.

Language reference: adjective structures

Adjective + *to*-infinitive

An adjective can be followed by a *to*-infinitive in the following structure.
*It's **difficult to know** with Sarah.*
*The poor chap is **unlikely to last** very long.*

Adjective + *for* + object + *to*-infinitive

If you need to mention a specific person or type of person, use *for* + object between the adjective and the *to*-infinitive.
*It's important **for him** to have some qualifications.*
*It's easy **for me** to hide at work.*
Note: You don't say: ~~For me~~ *it's easy to hide at work.*

Adjectives + dependent prepositions

Many adjectives are followed by a particular preposition. Here is a list of some of the more common ones.
certain about   optimistic about   serious about
good at   hopeless at   useless at
famous for   late for   ready for
covered in   interested in   lacking in
afraid of   fond of   proud of
dependent on   keen on   reliant on
accustomed to   allergic to   used to
angry with   compatible with   fed up with

Do come in

Register **1** Read the two conversations: the first between Sarah and Andy; the second between Sarah's parents and Sarah and Andy. Choose from the alternatives to complete the conversations in the most appropriate way. The first one has been done for you.

1 a) The door's open   b) Do come in
2 a) thank you – that's very kind of you   b) cheers – that's great
3 a) How's it going   b) How are you
4 a) totally shattered   b) absolutely exhausted
5 a) What've you been up to   b) What's the matter
6 a) relax   b) chill out
7 a) Do you want   b) Would you prefer
8 a) I don't mind   b) Whatever
9 a) no idea   b) I'm afraid I don't know
10 a) rather old   b) on its last legs

Sarah arrives at Andy's flat and knocks at the door.

Sarah: Hello!
Andy: Hiya. (1) _(a)_ !
Sarah: Here, I remembered to bring you that CD.
Andy: Oh, (2) _____ .
Sarah: (3) _____ ?
Andy: All right. I'm (4) _____ .
Sarah: Why? (5) _____ ?
Andy: Nothing – it's just that I didn't finish work until five o'clock this morning.
Sarah: Oh right. Well, you'd better just (6) _____ this evening. (7) _____ to watch telly, or shall I go and get a video?
Andy: (8) _____ .
Sarah: Do you know what's on telly tonight?
Andy: Oh, (9) _____ . Rubbish as usual, I should think.
Sarah: Oh dear, you're in a bad mood. You're not nervous about meeting my parents, are you?
Andy: No – why should I be? But I am a bit worried about the long drive – my car's (10) _____ .
Sarah: Oh well, let's worry about that tomorrow. Come on – make me a nice cup of tea.

Sarah and Andy arrive at Sarah's parents' house.

Mum: Hello. Welcome. (1) _(b)_ .
Sarah: Mum, Dad, this is Andy.
Mum and Dad: Nice to meet you.
Andy: Nice to meet you. These are for you – Sarah says they're your favourites.
Mum: Oh (2) _____ . And (3) _____ , darling?
Sarah: I'm (4) _____ , actually.
Mum: Oh dear. (5) _____ ? Have you been working too hard.
Sarah: Oh no, nothing like that – it's just a long drive, isn't it?
Mum: Yes, of course. You must sit down and (6) _____ , both of you. (7) _____ coffee or tea, Andy?
Andy: (8) _____ . Whatever's easiest.
Dad: How many miles is it exactly?
Andy: Oh, (9) _____ . The journey's taken us five and a half hours, but my car is (10) _____ .
Dad: Oh yes, I always take the A420, followed by the A34, except during the summer when I tend to avoid motorways and go through Winchester on the backroads.
Mum: Well, we're not going to talk about roads all day, are we? Now Andy, what exactly do you do? Sarah tells us you're in the music industry …

2 🔊 10 Listen to each conversation and check your answers to 1. How long do you think Sarah and Andy will continue going out together?

3 Work in groups. Imagine someone you know is going to meet their girlfriend's/boyfriend's parents for the first time. Discuss what advice you would give.

4 Work with a partner. Choose one of the following situations and act out a conversation using appropriate language from 1.

Situation 1: You are a foreign student arriving at your English host family's house for the first time.
Situation 2: You are at a friend's house. Your friend has had a bad day at work and needs cheering up.

Correspondence

1 Work with a partner and discuss these questions.

   a) Have you (or anybody you know) ever had a penfriend?
   b) How long did you/they have one for?
   c) Did you/they ever meet this penfriend?

2 Read this letter from Ling Chun to her penfriend, Hanna West. What do you notice about the letter?

14 Jalan Hajijah
Changi
Singapore

21st April 2000

123 Clifton Crescent
Bristol BR1 3HT
England

Dear Hanna,

(1) With reference to your letter of the 12th April, (2) I would be pleased to accept your offer of becoming your new penfriend.

First of all (3) I should apologise for the delay in replying to your letter, but (4) I have been extremely busy with work. (5) Moreover, my best friend (6) separated from her boyfriend recently, and (7) consequently I have spent a lot of time trying to cheer her up.

(8) I would be grateful if you could tell me more about you, your family, what kind of music you enjoy, what you do in your free time and (9) any other relevant information.

(10) Personally, I'm from quite a big family. (11) It consists of three children – two girls and a boy. I'm number three in the family and only I live at home now with my parents. My elder sister has just had a baby, and my brother got married last year.

(12) I regret to inform you that I haven't got an up-to-date photograph of us all together, but (13) I enclose a photo of me and my sister taken at my brother's wedding. I've put our names (14) on the reverse side so you know who's who.

(15) Incidentally, I agree with what you say about e-mail. It's very convenient, but perhaps it's not the best way for me to improve my English, because nobody bothers about punctuation or spelling!

(16) In conclusion, (17) I am delighted to be in touch with you and (18) I look forward to hearing from you again as soon as possible.

(19) Yours truly,

Ling

Ling Chun

(20) Enc: 1 photograph

3 The underlined words and expressions (1–20) make the letter very formal. Replace these words and expressions with more informal language (a–t).

   a) I've been up to my eyes in work
   b) By the way,
   c) anything else you think I should know about you.
   d) PS Hope you like the photo!
   e) As for me,
   f) Also
   g) Love,
   h) I can't wait to hear from you again
   i) I'd love to hear
   j) I'm afraid
   k) here's
   l) Thank you for your letter which I received on
   m) I'm really sorry I haven't written back sooner,
   n) There are three of us
   o) so
   p) Anyway
   q) I'd love to be
   r) I'm really pleased
   s) split up
   t) on the back

Are there any other things in the letter that you would change in order to make it more informal?

4 Write a letter introducing yourself to a penfriend. Include information about the following:
   • your family
   • your work/studies
   • the place where you live
   • what you would like to know about your penfriend

5 Exchange letters with another student in the class and write a reply, answering his or her questions.

3 Money

(Based on an article in *The Independent on Sunday*)

Reading

1 Read the article and explain the links between the following.

a) John Sutter – a private empire – disillusion
b) James Marshall – a sawmill – half a pea
c) President James Polk – the gold rush – the 'Forty-Niners'

GOLD FEVER

IN 1848, when gold was discovered in California, John Sutter was already one of the wealthiest people in the state. By 1850 he was a ruined man.

5 A private empire

Sutter was a Swiss immigrant who came to California in 1839, intent on building his own private empire. At that time, the state was a distant outpost that only a handful of Americans
10 had seen. San Francisco had just a few hundred residents. Sutter built a fort, and soon he had 12,000 head of cattle and hundreds of workers.

By the mid-1840s, more and more Americans were trickling into California by
15 wagon and ship. Sutter welcomed the newcomers: he saw them as subjects for his new kingdom. But he had no idea that the trickle would become a flood, a deluge of humanity that would destroy his dream.

20 Discovery

At the beginning of 1848, Sutter sent James Marshall and about twenty men to the American River to build a sawmill. It was nearly complete when a glint of something caught Marshall's eye.
25 Later he wrote, '*I reached my hand down and picked it up; it made my heart thump, for I was certain it was gold. The piece was about half the size and shape of a pea. Then I saw another.*'

The 'Forty-Niners'

30 By the end of the year, whispers of a gold strike had drifted eastward across the country – but few easterners believed it until President James Polk made a statement to Congress on December 5th 1848. The discovery, he declared, was a fact.
35 Within days 'gold fever' descended on the country.

The news was telegraphed to every village, to every town. Hundreds of thousands of people, almost all of them men, began to prepare for the
40 epic journey west. They sold possessions, mortgaged farms, borrowed money, and banded together with others from their towns to form joint stock companies. They said their goodbyes and streamed west – thousands of young adventurers
45 willing to take a chance on gold: a year of pain in return for a lifetime of riches. They were called 'Forty-Niners' because they left home in 1849. When they would return was another matter entirely.
50 By early 1849, gold fever was an epidemic. By the end of 1850, Sutter's grand empire had completely collapsed. Sutter did not have gold fever. He wanted an agricultural empire and refused to alter his vision. In the new California,
55 he was simply in the way. The Forty-Niners trampled his crops and tore down his fort for the building materials. Disillusioned, he eventually left the state. The man who had had the best opportunity to capitalise on the discovery of gold
60 never even tried.

2 Which words would you use to describe: a) John Sutter; b) one of the Forty-Niners?

> risk-taker visionary farmer opportunist businessman dreamer
> entrepreneur conservative

3 🔊 11 Listen to and read the article again. Then put the lines of this summary in the correct order.

(   ) a)   a fortune. John Sutter, on whose land gold was discovered, had
(*1*) b)   The gold rush is the story of thousands of ordinary people willing to take
(   ) c)   a chance on gold in the hope that they might make
(   ) d)   a statement in Congress declaring that the discovery was a fact, it created
(   ) e)   a sensation, and thousands of adventurers poured into California.
(   ) f)   no idea of the impact gold would have. When President Polk made

Lexis

1 This table shows the verb + noun collocations from the summary in 3 in the previous section. Use the nouns and noun phrases in the box to make more collocations. (In some cases more than one answer is possible.)

a) take	a chance
b) made	a fortune
c) had	no idea
d) created	a sensation

> money a risk an atmosphere a mess of his exams a think about it sense
> advantage of the hotel facilities the right conditions a go at skiing

2 Choose five collocations and use them to write sentences about yourself.

For example: *I was twenty-one before I had a go at skiing for the first time.*

Listening

1 🔊 12 Sam Brannan was one of the first to make a fortune from the gold rush. Listen to his story. Discuss the significance of the pictures with a partner.

Sam Brannan

2 Match the beginnings (*a–g*) with the ends of the sentences (*1–7*). Then listen again and check.

a) During the gold rush, Sam Brannan became
b) When gold was discovered in 1848, he owned
c) He recognised a gap in the market and bought up all
d) Having cornered the market, he ended up
e) He became the first
f) However, Brannan lost his fortune and his health
g) In the end California's first millionaire

1 died an unnoticed death.
2 one of the most successful businessmen in California.
3 with more gold than the gold diggers.
4 the only store between San Francisco and the goldfields.
5 because of alcoholism.
6 the picks, shovels and pans he could find.
7 gold rush millionaire.

A Forty-Niner with a bottle of liquor,
a pick, a prospecting pan and a shovel

Time is money

Metaphor

1 What do these words all have in common? Check them in your dictionary if you need to.

> deluge   drift   flood   stream   trickle

2 The words in the box in 1 can be used metaphorically to describe movement (*Movement = water.*). For example, in *Gold fever* the author writes: ... *Americans were **trickling** into California*. Here, *trickling* means 'moving in tiny numbers'. Use the words in 1 to complete these extracts from *Gold fever* so that they fit the definitions in brackets. (You may need to change the form of some of the words.) Then look back at the text on page 24 to check your answer.

    a) ... the ____ (*movement of a tiny number*) would become a ____ (*movement of a large number*), a ____ (*rapid movement of a large number*) of humanity.

    b) ... whispers of a gold strike had ____ (*moved steadily but with random changes of direction*) eastward ...

    c) They said their goodbyes and ____ (*moved steadily and rapidly in the same direction*) west.

3 Read the conversation between Martha and her dad. Use the words in the box to complete some expressions which show *Time = money* and *Ideas = food*.

> spend   half-baked   spare   profitably   food   running out   chewing
> wasting   digest   valuable   worth

Martha: Morning!

Dad: You're in a good mood today. Any particular reason?

Martha: Yes, there is actually.

Dad: What – in love again?

Martha: No – I've decided to become a millionaire.

Dad: You've decided to become a millionaire. I see. And how exactly do you propose to do that?

Martha: Well, if you can (1) ____ **a couple of minutes**, I'll tell you.

Dad: Martha, you know how (2) ____ **my time** is ...

Martha: Oh, Dad, I promise you it will be (3) ____ **your while**.

Dad: Okay – but just five minutes or else I'll be late for work.

Martha: Right. I've got this idea for a website ...

Dad: Oh come on, you're (4) ____ **your time** if you think you can make money out of the Internet. All the best ideas have been used up. You should be **using your time** more (5) ____ getting a proper job ...

Martha: All right, all right. Look, I promise you it's not some (6) ____ **idea**. It's something I've been (7) ____ **over** for the last few weeks. Please just have a look at these plans, then tell me what you think.

Dad: Hm, hm, yes, interesting. There's certainly (8) ____ **for thought** here. How are you going to find the money to do it?

Martha: Ah, well, um, I was rather hoping you might help me. Oh will you?

Dad: Well, I can't tell you until I've had time to (9) ____ **all this information**. But you've certainly got a good idea. It's very original.

Martha: But **we're** (10) ____ **of time**. If we don't do it very soon, somebody else will.

Dad: Yes, you could be right. Look, I've got to go now, but as soon as I get back from work I'll (11) ____ **the rest of the evening** looking at it. Have you told anybody else your idea?

Martha: No, not yet.

Dad: Well, don't ... I think you've really got something here.

4 🔲 13 Listen and check your answers.

5 Do you agree with the following? Discuss with a partner.

    a) E-mail is great because it saves time.

    b) Don't rush decision-making. Always take time to chew things over.

    c) Everybody should spend at least one year living in a foreign country.

    d) Going to the gym is a huge waste of time.

    e) The difficulty with exams is that you always run out of time.

    f) Always think things through carefully. Half-baked ideas are no good to anyone.

    g) It's best to read serious books. They give you food for thought.

    h) As people get older, they tend to use their time more profitably.

Close up

Articles

Language reference p28

1 ▱▱ 14 Complete the following texts with *a*, *an* or *the*, where they are necessary. Then listen and check your answers.

a) A tourist in (1) ____ Africa was walking by the sea when he saw (2) ____ man in (3) ____ simple clothes dozing in a fishing boat. It was (4) ____ idyllic picture, so he decided to take a photograph. The click of (5) ____ camera woke (6) ____ man up. (7) ____ tourist offered him (8) ____ cigarette. 'The weather is great. There are plenty of (9) ____ fish. Why are you lying around instead of going out and catching more?'

(10) ____ fisherman replied: 'Because I caught enough this morning.'

'But just imagine,' (11) ____ tourist said. 'If you went out there three times every day, you'd catch three times as much. After about (12) ____ year you could buy yourself (13) ____ motor-boat. After (14) ____ few more years of (15) ____ hard work, you could have (16) ____ fleet of (17) ____ boats working for you. And then …'

'And then?' asked the fisherman.

'And then,' (18) ____ tourist continued triumphantly, 'you could be calmly sitting on the beach, dozing in (19) ____ sun and looking at (20) ____ beautiful ocean.'

(Based on a short story by Heinrich Böll)

b) There was (1) ____ young lady from (2) ____ Niger,
Who smiled as she rode on (3) ____ tiger.
They came back from (4) ____ ride
With (5) ____ lady inside
And (6) ____ smile on (7) ____ face of (8) ____ tiger.
(Edward Lear)

2 Here are some general rules for using articles. Find an example of each rule in the texts in 1.

a) Don't use articles (*a/an*, *the*) with most proper nouns.
b) Don't use the indefinite article (*a/an*) with plurals or uncountable nouns.
c) Use the indefinite article (*a/an*) to introduce new information.
d) Use the definite article (*the*) to refer to specific things which have already been mentioned.
e) Use the definite article (*the*) to refer to things that you know the listener or hearer can identify.

3 Write three interesting statements, each of which combines a word from box A with a word from box B. Discuss your statements with a partner and the rest of your class.

For example:
Time is more important than money.   *Men are a mystery to women.*

A			
time	youth	wisdom	health
death	men	gold	music
war	humour		

+

B			
life	money	experience	love
women	peace	silver	
happiness	intelligence		

Schwa /ə/ Most unstressed vowels in English are pronounced using the schwa (/ə/) sound.

1 🔲 15 Read the sayings about money and <u>underline</u> the vowels that are pronounced using a schwa. Then listen and check. The first one has been done for you.

    a) Money makes th<u>e</u> world go round.
    b) There's no such thing as a free lunch.
    c) Put your money where your mouth is.
    d) In for a penny, in for a pound.
    e) Watch the pennies, and the pounds take care of themselves.
    f) The love of money is the root of all evil.

2 What do you notice about the pronunciation of short words like *a, the, as, for, of* and *your*?

3 Which of the sayings do you like the best? Discuss your choice with a partner.

Language reference: articles

Articles can be difficult to use correctly: the rules are many and complex. Here are some of the most important rules.

No article

You don't use articles with proper nouns such as places, people and companies.
*There was a young lady from **Niger**.*
***John Smith** had a job with **Microsoft** but now he's moved to **IBM**.*
Exceptions are when the article is part of a name (**The United States**, **The BBC**, **The Beatles**).

The indefinite article means 'one', so you don't use it with plurals or uncountable nouns.
*There are plenty of **ideas**. The love of **money** is the root of all evil.*
Note: In English, most abstract concepts are uncountable: *After a few years of **hard work** ...*
(You will find a list of common uncountable nouns on page 142.)

Indefinite article: introducing/categorising

When you first mention new people, places or objects etc., the most normal thing to do is to *introduce* them by saying what *category* they belong to. You use the indefinite article to show that this is what you are doing.
*There was **a young lady** from Niger*
*Who smiled as she rode on **a tiger**.*

Definite article: referring/identifying

When you *identify* something or *refer* to a *specific* thing, you use the definite article. This often happens for one of these two reasons.

1 Back reference:
  *They came back from **the ride***
  *With **the lady** inside*
  *And **the smile** on the face of **the tiger**.*
  The last three lines of the poem refer to things introduced in the first two. We now know which specific lady, tiger, ride and smile the poet is referring to.

2 Shared knowledge:
  *You could be calmly sitting on **the beach**, dozing in **the sun** and looking at **the ocean**.*
  It's obvious which beach, sun and ocean the tourist is talking about.

Back reference and shared knowledge can combine.
*He took **a photograph**. **The click** of **the camera** woke the man up.*
We know that to take a photograph you need a camera, and that most cameras go click when you take a picture.

Note: In general statements in English you don't usually use the definite article with plural or uncountable nouns.
Men are a mystery to women.   Time is money.

Money talks

'Dad, I need more pocket money.'

Lexis

1 Test your money expressions! Choose the correct option in the sentences below and say what each underlined money expression means. Refer to a dictionary if you need to.

a) They're quite an unusual couple. She earns a fortune as a lawyer. So when they had a baby, he gave up his job. Now <u>she's the main **breadwinner / breadbasket / breadmaker**</u>, while he stays at home to look after the children.

b) Last year I inherited some money from my grandmother, but I haven't spent it yet. <u>I'm saving **it for a wet day / a rainy day / a storm**</u>.

c) 'Have you got any wealthy friends?' 'No, <u>all my friends are **break / broken / broke**</u> like me.'

d) 'Did you hear about Alan winning £2,000 last week?' 'No! Lucky thing! What's he going to do with it?' 'Oh, you know Alan. He's already <u>**thrown it / flown it / blown it**</u> on a weekend in New York.'

e) You've been wearing the same suit for years. Don't you think <u>it's time you **bashed out / splashed out / rushed out**</u> on some new clothes?

f) 'Number 28's for sale.' 'How much for?' 'I don't know, but it's the biggest house in the street, and they've got a swimming pool, sauna and jacuzzi.' '<u>It must be worth **a fortune / a goldmine / a mountain**</u>.'

2 Tell your partner about …

a) a place where you'd enjoy blowing £2,000 in a weekend.
b) the kind of clothes you'd splash out on if you could afford to.
c) something you own that's worth a fortune.
d) the last time you didn't buy something because you were too broke.
e) the main breadwinner in your family.
f) somebody you know who's saving their money for a rainy day.

Listening & speaking

1 Match the questions and answers.

Questions
a) It's impossible to have too much money – do you agree?
b) Would you prefer fame or fortune?
c) Were you given or did you earn pocket money as a child?
d) What was the first thing you saved up for and bought yourself?
e) If you could buy yourself a skill, talent or change in your appearance, what would it be?
f) What can't money buy?

Answers
1 Happiness. I tend to think that once I have enough money to buy some new clothes or get a better car, then I'll be happy. But it never works out like that.
2 A set of toy soldiers. Not the plastic ones you get nowadays, but little metal ones, beautifully hand-painted. It took me nearly a year to save up for them. If I'd known that they would be valuable antiques today, I would've kept them. They'd probably be worth a fortune now.
3 Yes. If you have dreams, money makes them possible. Personally, I can't imagine having too much money. I'm always broke. Anyway, if I ever felt I had too much money, I'd give it away to charity.
4 Well, there are lots of things I'd like to be better at, but if I had to choose one, it would have to be football – I'd like to be a brilliant football player!
5 Being practical, I'd say fortune, but if I were single with no kids and no responsibilities, I'd go for fame.
6 I was given two shillings a week by my father, but on condition that I behaved myself. If I didn't behave well, I didn't receive it. Parents were much stricter in those days.

2 🔊 **16** Listen to the interview with Patti, Eric and Lee, and check your answers to 1.

3 🔊 **17** How do you think Patti, Eric and Lee would have answered the following two questions? Discuss with a partner, then listen and check.

a) Does it matter if a wife earns more than her husband?
b) If you were given £1,000 to save, spend or invest in just one day, what would you do with it?

4 Work with a partner or in small groups. Ask and answer the six questions in 1 and the two questions in 3.

Close up

Unreal conditionals

1 Match the *if*-clauses with the correct main clauses.

if-clauses
a) If you have dreams, …
b) If I ever felt I had too much money, …
c) If I'd known that they were valuable antiques, …
d) If I didn't behave well, …
e) If I were single with no kids and no responsibilities, …
f) If I had to choose one sport I couldn't live without, …

Main clauses
1 I didn't get any pocket money.
2 it would have to be football.
3 I'd give it away to charity.
4 I'd take a year out and go travelling.
5 I would've kept them.
6 money makes them possible.

Language reference p31

2 Work with a partner and discuss these questions.

a) All the sentences in 1 are *conditional sentences*. How many clauses do they have?
b) Two of the sentences in 1 are *real conditionals*, four are *unreal conditionals*. Which are the unreal conditionals?
c) Which *auxiliary verb* appears in the *main clause* of all the unreal conditionals in 1?
d) Look at the following sentences. What happens to the verb form in the *if*-clause in unreal conditionals? Write a rule.

Real situation	Unreal condition
I never feel I've got too much money.	*If I ever felt* I had too much money, I'd give some of it away.
We're not having a party.	*If we were having* a party, we wouldn't invite you!
You haven't done the job properly.	*If you'd (had) done* the job properly, we'd pay you.
I didn't know about her illness.	*If I'd (had) known* about her illness, I would have visited her.

3 What is the difference between these two sentences. Are they both grammatically correct? Is there any difference in meaning between the two sentences?

a) If I weren't so busy, I'd go to the gym more often.
b) If I wasn't so busy, I'd go to the gym more often.

4 Work in groups. Discuss the following situations.

If you governed your country …
a) where would you build your palace?
b) what laws would you change?
c) what new laws would you bring in?
d) what would you spend most money on?
e) what would you tax?
f) what would you ban?
g) who would you appoint as your ministers?
h) what would you have named after you?

5 Complete the sentences to make them true for you. Discuss your sentences with a partner.

a) If I'd been born in a different country …
b) If I'd been born a member of the opposite sex …
c) If I'd had famous parents …
d) If I'd started learning English earlier in my life …
e) If I'd listened to my parents advice when I was younger …
f) If I hadn't come to this English class today …

Language reference: unreal conditionals

Most conditional sentences have two clauses: the *if*-clause and the main clause.
1 The *if*-clause describes a condition: *If I were rich, …* It usually starts with the conjunction, *if*. (You'll find further information on *if*-clauses in unit 9.)
2 The main clause comments on the condition in the *if*-clause: *… I'd buy a yacht.*
The two clauses can be used in either order: *I'd buy a yacht if I were rich.* In writing, when the *if*-clause comes first, use a comma to separate it from the main clause:
If I were rich, I'd buy a yacht.

Types of conditional

Real conditionals are used to talk about real or possible events and situations.
If you see Max, can you give him this letter?
If it rained, we usually played indoors.

Unreal conditionals are used to talk about events and situations which are imaginary, untrue, impossible or unlikely.
If the world was flat, you would sail off the end.
If I were you, I'd give up smoking.

Backshifting

In the *if*-clause of an unreal conditional the tenses change. They *backshift*.

Backshift	Real situation	Unreal condition
present → past	I never **feel** I've got too much money … We're **not having** a party … You **haven't done** your homework …	If I ever **felt** … If we **were having** … If you'd (had) done …
past → past perfect	I **didn't know** …	If I'd (had) known …

In the main clause you can use any of the four past modal auxiliaries: *would, could, should* or *might*. The most useful of these is *would*.

With any of the four auxiliaries, you can use the simple form (*would do*), the continuous (*would be doing*) or the perfect (*would have done*), as appropriate.
If I ever felt that I had too much money, I'd give some to charity.
If we were having a party, we'd invite you.
If you'd done your homework, you wouldn't be having these problems.
If I'd known they were valuable antiques, I'd have kept them.

The perfect form is used when the main clause refers to the past.

If + was/were in unreal conditionals

In spoken and written English, you will find both *If I was* and *If I were (rich)*. Both are acceptable, though many people consider *were* to be more correct.

If	I you he/she/it we they	were	rich, … famous, … less busy, … better organised, … able to come, …

Note: *Were* is always used in the expression *If I were you*, which is used to give advice.

Treasured possessions

1 The four people in the pictures are holding treasured possessions. Why do you think their owners might think these possessions are special?

Armando Katie Heather Mike

2 🔊 18 Listen and match the possessions (*a–d*) with the notes about the stories (*1–4*).

a) Armando's typewriter
b) Katie's wedding ring
c) Heather's neck-warmer
d) Mike's mobile phone

1 mother – don't wear it – bedside table – remember – England
2 expensive – e-mail – addresses and numbers – three hundred people
3 father's – composer and storyteller – Peruvian jungle – ten years – wrote
4 saved life – avalanche – over face – mouth and nose – breathe

3 Listen again. Then work with a partner and try to reconstruct the stories using the notes in 2.

Anecdote Think about your most treasured possession. You are going to tell your partner about it. Choose from the following list the things you want to talk about. Think about what you will say and the language you will need.

☐ What is your most treasured possession?
☐ What's it made of?
☐ How old is it?
☐ How long have you had it?
☐ Did somebody give it to you or did you acquire it yourself?
☐ What special significance does it have?
☐ Did it belong to somebody else before?
☐ Does it remind you of a particular person? Who?
☐ Does it remind you of a time or an event in the past?
☐ What happened?
☐ Where do you keep your treasured possession?
☐ Do you wear it, carry it around with you or does it have a special place in your home?
☐ Who will you leave it to when you die?

A day in my very wealthy life

Linkers **1** Complete the text using appropriate linkers from the box. You can use each linker only once.

> as soon as   while   by the time   then
> when   as   during   until   after   just as

The first thing I did (1) _____ I woke up in my favourite house this morning was to admire the fabulous view from my bedroom window. **A** (2) _____ I did an hour's exercise with my personal fitness trainer (3) _____ my housekeeper prepared my breakfast. **B** (4) _____ a luxurious bath, I spent some time with my secretary and told her to send cheques to all the charities I support. **C** (5) _____ I was leaving the house, a special delivery arrived. It was a present from my secret admirer. **D**

I didn't get to the airport (6) _____ midday, so I instructed the pilot to use our fastest plane and take me to my favourite city. **E** (7) _____ the flight, I had a light lunch and looked at photographs of my last holiday. **F** (8) _____ we landed, I contacted a dear friend of mine who has just finished her latest film and arranged to meet her for dinner later. **G** I spent the rest of the afternoon doing what I love doing most. **H**

(9) _____ I met my friend at the restaurant, I was starving, so I ordered all my favourite things on the menu. **I** (10) _____ we were leaving the restaurant, I spotted somebody I'd always wanted to meet. **J** It was the perfect end to a perfect day.

2 Work with a partner. Take it in turns to read out the text in 1 and add the following details using your own ideas.

A Describe the view
B What did you have for breakfast?
C Which charities?
D What was the present?
E Which city?

F Describe your last holiday.
G Who is the friend?
H How did you spend the afternoon?
I What did you order?
J Who was it and what happened?

3 Write an account entitled *A perfect day*. Use all the linkers from the box in 1.

4 *Body*

Close up

Sympathy & advice

1 Read these conversations. Use the table to make sentences to describe the different body ailments.

I've got	a sore really bad a splitting a terrible dreadful a twisted	hangover. ankle. hay fever. throat. headache. sunburn.

A

Ann: Oh dear – you look like death warmed up! Heavy night last night?
Bob: Yeah – good party, but I feel terrible.
Ann: Oh well, if you hadn't drunk so much, you wouldn't be feeling so bad now, would you? Anyway listen, I'll give you my secret cure – get …

B

Chris: Why are you walking like that?
Dana: My ankle's killing me.
Chris: Oh dear, you poor thing. If you ask me, you need to …

C

Ed: Ugh! I can't swallow anything.
Fran: Oh yes, I know what you mean. I was the same last week. I could only eat ice cream!
Ed: So, what did you do?
Fran: Well, you could try this …

D

Greg: Don't touch my back!
Helen: Why? What's up?
Greg: I wanted to get a tan quickly so I didn't bother to put any suntan lotion on.
Helen: Oh well, it serves you right then, doesn't it?
Greg: It really stings.
Helen: Okay, take …

E

Ian: When did it start?
Jane: After I'd been playing computer games for about seven hours. I feel as if my head's going to explode!
Ian: Oh well, you've only got yourself to blame, haven't you?
Jane: I know, I know. But I've taken aspirin, and it hasn't worked.
Ian: Well, you could try …

F

Keith: Have you got a cold?
Lisa: No, I'm all right – I always get a streaming nose and red eyes at this time of the year.
Keith: That must be awful. If I were you, I'd …

Language reference p36

2 Look again at the conversations in 1. What advice do you think each friend gives? Work in pairs and complete the conversations with a suitable piece of advice.

3 🔊 19 Listen. Was the advice similar to your advice in 2?

Sounding sympathetic

1 Look at the following sentences from the conversations in the previous section. In each case, if the speaker is being sympathetic, mark the sentence with an *S*. If the speaker is being unsympathetic, mark the sentence with a *U*.

a) Oh well, if you hadn't drunk so much you wouldn't be feeling so bad now, would you?
b) Oh dear, you poor thing.
c) Oh yes, I know what you mean.
d) Oh well, it serves you right then, doesn't it?
e) Oh well, you've only got yourself to blame, haven't you?
f) That must be awful.

2 20 Listen to the sentences in 1. Mark the stressed words and try to remember the intonation used. Practise saying the sentences with a partner, trying to sound as sympathetic or unsympathetic as you can.

3 Work with a partner. Student A look at your problems on page 136. Student B look at your problems on page 138. Follow the instructions.

4 Have you ever had any of the problems in 3? What did you do about it? Tell your partner.

You're the expert

1 Work in small groups. Which of these statements do you agree with?

a) Regular exercise is essential for health and happiness.
b) Sport and exercise are boring and involve giving up things you enjoy.
c) The best way to avoid sports injuries is to avoid playing sports.
d) Regular visits to the doctor are the best way to avoid illness.
e) There's no gain without pain.

2 Do the quiz below. Then compare your answers with a partner.

body knowledge quiz

Your body is a marvellous machine. Understanding how to keep it in good working order by exercising properly will help keep it in shape for the rest of your life. Try this quiz to test your body knowledge.

1 What is the aerobic system?
  a an exercise video, record or tape
  b oxygen and carbon dioxide
  c the heart, lungs and blood circulation

2 The 'happy hormones' that are released during exercise are called …
  a endorphins
  b morphine
  c dolphins

3 A balanced diet should include
  a calories, fibre and sugar
  b carbohydrates, protein and fat
  c cereals, caffeine and glucose

4 Which of the following activities are best for keeping supple?
  a yoga, gymnastics and karate
  b rowing, horse-riding and jogging
  c walking, water-skiing and wind-surfing

5 To keep healthy you should exercise for at least …
  a one hour every day
  b twenty minutes three times a week
  c one hour three times a week

6 You build up stamina by …
  a drinking strong coffee
  b eating fruit
  c exercising regularly

(Based on a questionnaire in *The Sunday Times*)

3 21 Listen to Liz Hartley, an expert in health and nutrition and editor of *Health Today* magazine, and check your answers to 2.

Close up

1 Liz Hartley gives the following advice and recommendations. Complete the sentences from memory and then listen again to check your answers.

a) It's i____ to d____ aerobic exercise regularly.

b) It's a good i____ to d____ exercise when you're feeling run down or stressed.

c) You n____ to h____ a combination of carbohydrates, proteins and fats in your diet.

d) It's b____ not t____ include sugar and caffeine in your diet.

e) You d____ have t____ give them up completely, but you really o____ to____ down on them.

f) If we're talking about improving the suppleness of your body, then you definitely n____ to d____ something like yoga, where you get a lot of stretching.

g) One hour three times a week is fine, but you s____ overdo it.

h) It's n____ a g____ idea t____ get obsessed with it because that takes all the pleasure out of it.

i) D____ drink too much coffee. It's poison.

j) T____ not t____ take it all too seriously.

2 Work with a partner. Which piece of advice seems the most sensible? Which piece of advice would you find the most difficult to follow?

3 Read this letter to health expert, Liz Hartley. Work with a partner and note down some things you would suggest to the person who wrote the letter.

4 Write a reply to the letter. Use some of the phrases in the Language reference below.

Dear Liz

Ever since I booked my summer holiday last week I've been panicking. As a result of enjoying my food too much, slobbing out in front of the television and snacking all day in my boring job, I am really out of shape. There is no way I can go on the beach looking like this!

I've got two months to lose some weight and tone up, and I need your help.

Bearing in mind that I work from 9 to 5, five days a week in an office, what can you suggest?

Yours truly, Chris

Language reference: sympathy, advice & recommendations

Showing sympathy

You can use any of the following expressions to sympathise with someone.
Poor you.
Oh dear.
That must be awful.
I know what you mean.

If you are not sympathetic you can use the following.
Serves you right.
You've only got yourself to blame.
If you hadn't ... you wouldn't be ... now.

Giving advice & making recommendations

There are lots of ways of giving advice or making recommendations. The expression you use will normally depend on the formality of the situation.

Typical in conversation:
Have you tried + noun / -ing?
You could try + noun / -ing
If I were you, I'd ...
If you ask me, you should / you need to ...
Imperatives

Typical in written or more formal situations:
It's important (not) to ...
It's best (not) to ...
It's a good idea to ...

Body language

Idioms **1** 22 Read and listen to this conversation between two friends. <u>Underline</u> eight sections of the conversation that are different from what you hear on the recording.

Laura:	Hey, Phil, how are you doing?
Phil:	Oh hi Laura – not too bad thanks. How are you?
Laura:	Oh, extremely busy as usual. I'm on my way to my third meeting today. How's that lovely girlfriend of yours?
Phil:	Oh, we split up three weeks ago. She's on holiday with her new boyfriend.
Laura:	Oh no – trust me to say something to make you feel worse. I'm really sorry.
Phil:	No, it's okay. I need to talk about it.
Laura:	Who's her new boyfriend?
Phil:	It's her boss. You wouldn't know him. He's not from around here.
Laura:	What kind of work does he do?
Phil:	I don't know really. He seems to be involved in a lot of things. He owns several companies anyway, including the one Mandy was working for.
Laura:	Oh Phil, I don't know what to say.
Phil:	Yeah – it's hard. I mean, we were supposed to be going on holiday together in a couple of weeks.
Laura:	So, what are you going to do?
Phil:	I don't know – I haven't decided yet. I might go anyway, or I might not feel like it when the time comes. I don't know. I'll just have to see how I feel at the time.
Laura:	Look Phil, I'm afraid I've got to run – but if you need some sympathy, you know where to find me.
Phil:	Thanks, Laura – I'll be fine.

2 Replace the eight underlined phrases in 1 with the appropriate body idioms from the box.

> put my foot in it   a shoulder to cry on   not from this neck of the woods
> have his fingers in a lot of pies   up to my eyes in work   made up my mind yet
> get it off my chest   play it by ear

3 Listen again and check your answers to 2.

4 Work with a partner. Tell your partner about someone you know who …

   a) is up to their eyes in work at the moment.
   b) is always putting their foot in it.
   c) you talk to when you need to get something off your chest.
   d) doesn't come from this neck of the woods.
   e) has their fingers in a lot of pies.
   f) has difficulty making up their mind about things.
   g) likes to play things by ear.
   h) you go to when you need a shoulder to cry on.

5 Work with a partner. Decide who is Student A and who is Student B, and use a dictionary to find expressions using the following body parts.

Student A	**Student B**
nose brain hand eye	leg tongue head foot

6 Work together to write a conversation incorporating as many of the expressions in 5 as possible. Act out your conversation in front of the class.

Shape your body!

Reading & listening

1 Work with a partner. Ask and answer the following questions.

a) Do you know somebody who's always on a diet or has a strange diet?
b) Is there anything you won't or can't eat?
c) Is there anything you like eating or drinking that isn't good for you?

2 Read the information about six diets in the article below and find out which diet …

a) is based on the idea that the more you eat the thinner you get.
b) says that sweets don't make you fat.
c) allows you to eat cream.
d) has been translated into many different languages.
e) has unpleasant side effects.
f) doesn't allow you to eat fruit with your meal.

'It's simple. I buy all the diet plans, then I can't afford any food.'

Food **fads**

No-carbohydrate diet

■ **Premise:** High-carbohydrate diets, not fat, lead to weight gain. By replacing sugar, pasta, potatoes and bread with meat, vegetables and dairy products, you'll lose weight.
■ **Verdict:** Initial weight-loss is likely to be due to losing water rather than fat. It's difficult to eat more meat without eating more fat, which is linked to heart disease and cancer. You might be thinner, but your arteries won't be happy.

Hay diet

■ **Premise:** It's not what you eat, it's what you eat it with. Carbohydrates can't be digested in acid conditions, so shouldn't be eaten with protein. Mixing acid and alkaline is strictly forbidden, so fruit should never be allowed anywhere near a main meal.
■ **Verdict:** A mixture of foods is necessary for a healthy metabolism – vitamin C, for instance, helps the absorption of iron. Extremely fashionable but with debatable scientific basis.

F-plan diet

■ **Premise:** This is the original high-carbohydrate, low-fat plan, advocating lots of fruit and fibre. The 80s favourite has been translated into sixteen languages, and claims to be the best-selling diet ever.
■ **Verdict:** Common sense disguised as new scientific breakthrough.

Grapefruit diet

■ **Premise:** More energy is spent digesting grapefruit and other foods like celery than is contained in the food itself. The more you eat, logically, the thinner you get.
■ **Verdict:** Digesting food does burn calories, but in such tiny proportions, you would have to eat a vast amount to notice any difference.

Cabbage soup diet

■ **Premise:** By eating nothing but soup made from cabbage and a few other vegetables you can lose up to six kilos in a week.
■ **Verdict:** Most of the weight loss is due to water loss, not fat, and the weight returns when you move back on to solids. Unfortunate side effects have been reported.

System S diet

■ **Premise:** The way to get thin is to eat sugar-coated cereals, biscuits, chocolate and sugary soft drinks – 'not the villains they are made out to be'. It's a 'myth' that sweets make you fat and rot your teeth, so tuck into another bar of chocolate.
■ **Verdict:** Just ask a dentist.

(From The Guardian)

3 🔲 23 Listen to Sam and Catherine talking about a time when they dieted for a special occasion. Find out what the special occasion was in each case.

4 Listen again and make notes about Sam and Catherine, using the table below.

	wasn't allowed	was allowed	had to
Sam			
Catherine			

5 Which of the diets in 2 above are most similar to the diets Sam and Catherine followed?

6 Which of the six diets would you find the hardest to follow?

I will quit. Soon

1 You're going to read an article about giving up smoking. Think of …

a) three good reasons for giving up smoking.
b) three reasons why people smoke.
c) three different methods people use to give up smoking.

2 Read the article and find out …

a) the writer's reasons for wanting to give up smoking.
b) what he considers to be the advantages of smoking.
c) what method he has tried for giving up smoking.

Do you think he's likely to give up in the near future? Why / Why not?

I know it's bad for me, but I still can't stop

Three packs of cigarettes were lying there on the pavement. I hopped down from Yefim Shubentsov's office doorstep, picked them up and pocketed them. Later, in a bar, when I
5 opened the first pack, I found – to my delight – the twenty cigarettes intact.

I'm still at the bar, telephone in one hand and the cigarettes in the other. I'm dialling Shubentsov, who told me to call the moment I felt
10 the urge to smoke. I feel it, feel it even stronger than I felt Shubentsov's healing energy. That's saying something, since Shubentsov is known around the world for curing smokers of their nasty habit, using a mystical method. He transmits his
15 healing energy from his fingertips, he tells me – something he picked up from another bloke in Russia. 'I help you for free,' he told me in his muddy accent. 'Just call me whenever.'

I went to see Shubentsov because I think it's
20 time to stop. Time to stop because I'm getting old, and I can't keep doing this to myself. But here's the real problem. I should quit, but like a lot of you struggling with the same habit, I really don't want to. At least, not yet.

25 Smoking has been very good to me. Cigarettes have never let me down, never abandoned me on lonely, desperate nights. Smoking clears my head, helps me think. Smoking has started conversations, driven away annoying people.
30 Smoking helps me celebrate victories, get over losses, comfort the comfortless. It also chases away the mosquitoes.

I will quit. Soon. My body and my mind are demanding that I do, daily.
35 I claim to smoke for pleasure, but I realise that slowly, steadily, I'm losing control of this close,

special friend. I hate that. I realise it's not just a 'habit'. I'm hooked.

So here I am, attempting to give up again, at
40 Shubentsov's place. I've tried all the other quitting techniques available. Any time the urge to smoke strikes, he said, just call him immediately and he'll help. The funny thing is, I realise that I'm not phoning him to stop me from lighting up.
45 I'm phoning him so I can. If I call, I'll have done my part. Then I can smoke this cigarette. Besides, I know that at 9.30 on a Friday night, I'll get the answering machine. I do. 'The office is open from ten to four. Call me back then. This
50 machine does not take messages.'

I put the phone down and I can honestly say I'm relieved. You see, it's not Shubentsov's fault or anyone else's fault that I'm still smoking. It's mine.
55 Now if you'll excuse me, I'm going to smoke this cigarette. Whether I'll really enjoy it, though, is another story.

(Adapted from an article in *Men's Health Magazine*)

It takes a lot of strength to do this.

'Sidney still enjoys the occasional cigarette.'

3 Replace the underlined words and expressions with expressions from the text. You may have to change the grammar so that the sentence makes sense.

a) When I have a strong desire to eat chocolate, nothing else will do. (line 10)
b) I've learned a lot of new words and expressions from listening to pop music. (line 16)
c) I always find it very difficult to remember peoples' names when I'm at a party. (line 23)
d) My dog is my only friend – he never disappoints me. (line 26)
e) The last time I had a cold it took me ages to recover from it. (line 30)
f) I tell everyone that I go to the gym at least three times a week, but actually, I rarely go more than two or three times a month. (line 35)
g) I love Sherlock Holmes-type mysteries. I only need to read the first page and I can't stop. (line 38)
h) My dad still plays football, but he keeps on injuring himself. I think it's time for him to stop. (line 39)

Close up

Phrasal verbs

Language reference p41

1 Find the eleven phrasal verbs in the text in the previous section and underline them. Ten of them are transitive and so can take a direct object (for example: *put something down / get over something*). Which phrasal verb is intransitive? Check in a dictionary if you are not sure.

2 Complete the sentences using some of the phrasal verbs you have identified in 1 plus the pronouns *them*, *him* and *it*.

For example: *The writer saw three packs of cigarettes on the ground and ...* **picked them up.**

a) Shubentsov wasn't born with healing power in his fingertips, he ...
b) Smoking is the writer's friend because it never ...
c) Smoking is good for getting rid of annoying people – it ...
d) Smoking is good for getting rid of mosquitoes – it ...
e) Shubentsov's answering machine message advised everyone to ...
f) The phone was on the answer machine, so he ...

'James has given up smoking recently.'

3 Work with a partner. Discuss these questions about the phrasal verbs in 2 above.

a) Are they all transitive or intransitive?
b) Are they all separable or not separable?
c) If the direct object is a pronoun, where must you put it with phrasal verbs of this type?

4 Match the phrasal verbs in box A with synonyms in box B.

A

> it dawned on him   Step on it!   a feeling came over me   we're looking into it
> you can count on it   we saw through them

B

> a feeling affected me strongly   we weren't deceived by them
> we're investigating it   it became clear to him   you can depend on it   Hurry up!

5 Replace the underlined words or expressions in these jokes with phrasal verbs from box A in 4. You will need to change the form of the verbs. Explain why using the phrasal verbs makes the jokes funny.

a) A large hole has appeared in the wall of the local nudist camp. The police <u>are investigating it</u>.

b) 'Why are ghosts bad at telling lies?'
    'Because you <u>can't be deceived by them</u>.'

c) 'Waiter, Waiter, why is the food on my plate all squashed?'
    'Well, sir, you told me you were in a hurry, so I asked the cook to <u>hurry up</u>.'

d) 'Why is a pocket calculator reliable?'
    'Because you can always <u>depend on it</u>.'

e) 'Doctor, Doctor, I keep thinking I'm a bridge.'
    'What's <u>affected you so strongly</u>?'
    'Three cars, two buses and a bicycle.'

f) A man sat up all night wondering where the sun had gone to. The next morning it <u>became clear to him</u>.

'OK, everyone's gone – you can pick it up now.'

6 Work with a partner. Discuss these questions about the phrasal verbs in 5.

a) Are they all transitive or intransitive?
b) Are they all separable or not separable?
c) If the direct object is a pronoun, where must you put it with verbs of this type?

7 Check how your own dictionary shows you the difference between different types of phrasal verbs.

8 Write five true sentences about yourself using phrasal verbs from 1 and 4.

Language reference: phrasal verbs

The term 'phrasal verb' usually refers to all multi-word verbs, consisting of a verb + particle(s).

The meaning of phrasal verbs

Sometimes the meaning is obvious from the verb and the particle (*sit down, go away*).
Other times just the particle may help you work out the meaning (*sum up, do up, clean up, drink up, use up*, etc. 'up' = completing/finishing).
Most of the time though you should approach phrasal verbs like you do any other new lexical item: learn the exact meaning, notice how the word is used in context and frequently revise your examples.

The grammar of phrasal verbs

Phrasal verbs can be divided into four basic grammatical types.

1 verb + particle
Some phrasal verbs are intransitive and so do not take a direct object.
*Without any more help, we just can't **go on**.*
*The plane **takes off** at 3.55 this afternoon.*

2 verb + object + particle (SEPARABLE)
The biggest group of phrasal verbs are transitive. When the direct object is a noun, you can usually put it before or after the particle.
*She **picks** foreign languages **up** very quickly.*
*She **picks up** foreign languages very quickly.*

When the direct object is a pronoun, you must put it between the verb and the particle.
*I can honestly say that I've never **let** her **down**.*
(NOT ~~let down her~~ ...)
*I can't hear. **Turn** it **up**, will you?*
(NOT ~~Turn up it~~ ...)

3 verb + particle + object (NOT SEPARABLE)
With this type of phrasal verb you always put the direct object – noun or pronoun – *after* the particle.
*It took him a long time to **get over** the divorce.*
*I don't think he ever wants to **go through** it again.*

4 verb + particle + particle + object (NOT SEPARABLE)
Similar to type 3, you always put the direct object – noun or pronoun – *after* the second particle.
*I didn't **find out about** her boyfriend till after the party.*
*I don't know how she **puts up with** him.*

You will find a comprehensive listing of phrasal verbs on page 142.

5 *Ritual*

Football mad!

Lexis

1 Test your football vocabulary! Complete the questions with the words in the box.

match	support	won	colours
scored	lose	stadium	players

> **ritual** A **ritual** is **1.1** a religious service or other ceremony which involves a series of actions usually performed in a fixed order. **1.2** A way of behaving or of doing something which people or animals regularly follow when they are in a particular situation
>
> *(Collins Cobuild English Language Dictionary)*

a)   Which football team do you _____ ?
b)   What are your team's _____ ?
c)   Do any of your team's _____ play for a national team?
d)   What's the name of the _____ where your team plays?
e)   Did they win, draw or _____ their last game?
f)   Have they ever _____ a cup or a league title?
g)   Which player _____ the most goals last season?
h)   What's the best _____ you've ever seen?

2 If you are interested in football, answer the questions in 1. If you are not interested in football, find someone who is interested and ask them the questions.

3 What sort of behaviour would you expect from someone who is obsessed with football? Do you know anybody like this?

1 Read this extract from a novel called *Fever Pitch* by Nick Hornby. Which of the following sentences best describes the writer's attitude to football?

  a) He's interested in it.
  b) He really likes it.
  c) He's very keen on it.
  d) He's absolutely mad about it.

Nick Hornby

Nick Hornby is the author of three best selling novels about men, obsession and growing up: *Fever Pitch, High Fidelity* and *About a Boy.* He supports Arsenal and Cambridge United Football Clubs.

The sugar mouse ritual

What happened was, Chris Roberts bought a sugar mouse, bit its head off, dropped it in the Newmarket Road before he could get started on the body, and it got run over by a car. And that afternoon Cambridge United beat Orient 3–1, and a ritual was born.

5   Before each home game we all of us trooped into the sweet shop, purchased our mice, walked outside, bit the head off as though we were removing the pin from a hand grenade, and tossed the torsos under the wheels of oncoming cars. United, thus protected, remained unbeaten for months.

10   I know that I am particularly stupid about rituals, and have been ever since I started going to football matches, and I know also that I am not alone ... I can remember having to buy a programme from the same programme seller, and having to enter the stadium through the same turnstile.

15   There have been hundreds of similar bits of nonsense, all designed to guarantee victories for one or other of my two teams.
     I have tried 'smoking' goals in (Arsenal once scored as three of us were lighting cigarettes), and eating cheese-and-onion crisps at a certain point in the first half; I have tried not setting the video for

20   live games (the team seems to have suffered badly in the past when I have taped the matches in order to study the performances when I get home); I have tried lucky socks, and lucky shirts, and lucky hats, and lucky friends, and have attempted to exclude others who I feel bring with them nothing but trouble for the team.

25   Nothing (apart from the sugar mice) has ever been any good.

(Adapted from *Fever Pitch*, by Nick Hornby)

---

tossed (line 7): threw
torsos (line 8): bodies (without the heads)
turnstile (line 14): gate to a football stadium

---

2 How many rituals are mentioned in the text? Which ritual has been the most successful?

3 What do you think of the person in the text? Do you know anyone like him?

4 Work with a partner. What other examples of personal ritual can you think of? Think about the following situations.

  a) Before taking an exam
  b) Before a job interview
  c) Before taking part in a sporting competition
  d) Before leaving the house every morning
  e) Before setting off on a long trip
  f) Before going out on a Saturday night
  g) Before sitting down to start working or studying

Close up

Verbs +
to-infinitive
& *-ing* form

1 In the following texts Terry and Dawn talk about their passion for football. Complete each text with the *to*-infinitive or the *-ing* form of an appropriate verb in the box.

set believe equalize buy programme watch

I remember (1) _____ Man Utd against Bayern Munich in the Champions League final. I'll never forget Sheringham (2) _____ in the 89th minute. Then Solsjkar scored the winner two minutes later in injury time. It was incredible! With ten minutes to go I had already stopped (3) _____ it was possible to win, but Man Utd just never gave up!

If I've forgotten (1) _____ the alarm clock, it's always a rush. I have breakfast quickly, put on my Chelsea shirt and leave the house. I can walk to the ground from where I live, and I always stop (2) _____ a newspaper and get the latest team news. Three hours before kick off and the atmosphere is already building. It's a great day out – the best moment in the week. If I remember (3) _____ the video, then I can watch the whole match again when I get home. Magic!

Terry, Manchester United supporter, and Dawn, Chelsea supporter

2 🔊 24 Listen and check your answers.

3 Look at the texts again and decide which structure (*to*-infinitive or *-ing* form) you use to …

a) remember or (never) forget definite past events
b) remember or forget something you are supposed to do
c) say you have stopped something
d) say why you have stopped

Language reference p45

4 🔊 25 The following text is about another football supporter, Mark. Listen and underline the verb structures that he uses.

When I was about fourteen, I tried (1) **to go / going** to football matches for a while. All my friends did it, so I joined in just to be like them. I liked (2) **to think / thinking** I was one of the lads – you know how it is. I loved (3) **to be / being** part of a big crowd, but apart from that I was never really that interested, and as I got older I remember thinking what a waste of time it all was. Anyway, after my third season I stopped going.

But now, my nine-year-old son is football mad, so I've started going again. He likes (4) **to arrive / arriving** really early at the stadium to get a good place, so I'm spending more time there than ever! I love (5) **to see / seeing** his face when they score, but although I hate to admit it I can still think of at least a hundred things I'd rather be doing on a Saturday than standing around watching a football match.

Mark and Tim, Tottenham supporters

5 Look at the text in 4 again and find an example for each of the following concepts.

  a) try something and not be able to do it.
  b) try something and see what happens.
  c) describe how you feel about something.
  d) describe how you feel about something and imply that you think it's a good idea.

6 Complete these statements using an appropriate structure for the verbs given.

  a) I don't remember _____ (play) any dangerous games when I was a child.
  b) When I need to remember _____ (do) something important, I tie a knot in my handkerchief.
  c) I'll never forget _____ (tell) my first lie.
  d) I've never forgotten _____ (do) my English homework. Not once.
  e) I usually stop _____ (pick up) hitchhikers, whatever they look like.
  f) If I drink coffee in the evening, it stops me _____ (sleep).
  g) I tried _____ (windsurf) last summer and I really enjoyed it.
  h) I try _____ (learn) at least ten new English words every day, but I seem to forget most of them.
  i) I like _____ (keep) all my credit card receipts just in case the bank makes a mistake.
  j) I hate _____ (drive) at night, especially on country roads in the rain.

7 Are any of the statements in 6 true for you? Rewrite the sentences that are untrue and compare with a partner.

Language reference: verbs + *to*-infinitive & *-ing* form

to-infinitive or *-ing* form?

Many verbs are followed either by the *to*-infinitive (*he managed to pay, they taught her to ski*, etc.) or by the *-ing* form (*she enjoys reading, I miss hearing her voice*, etc.). You will find more information about these verbs in unit 2.

There is a small group of verbs which can be followed by both the *to*-infinitive *and* the *-ing* form. The meaning can change significantly depending on which form is used.

1 remember, forget
With the *to*-infinitive you can talk about actions somebody is/was supposed to do.
*I **remembered to buy** her a birthday card.*
*But I **forgot to post** it.*

With the *-ing* form you refer to definite events – things that people actually did.
*I **remember** meeting her in a bar.* = I met her and now I remember this meeting.
*I'll **never forget kissing** her for the first time.* = I kissed her and I'll never forget the kiss.
Note: *forget + -ing* form is usually only used with *never*.

2 stop
With the *-ing* form you are saying that an activity has stopped.
*She **stopped talking** to him after that last argument.*

With the *to*-infinitive you are giving the reason for stopping.
*She **stopped to tell** me about her boyfriend when I saw her in town.*

3 try
With the *to*-infinitive you try something but can't do it.
*I **tried to make** her understand my feelings, but she wouldn't listen.* = I didn't manage to make her understand.

With the *-ing* form you try something to see what the outcome will be.
*I **tried leaving** her messages, but she never replied.* = I managed to leave messages, but they didn't work.

Note: You can use *try + -ing* form as an alternative to *try + to*-infinitive in most cases.

4 like, love, hate
With the *to*-infinitive, you can imply that you think something is a good (or bad) idea to do.
*I **like to do** my tax returns early.*

With the *-ing* form you state your real feelings about something.
*I **hate doing** my tax returns.*

Note: *like, love*, etc. + *to*-infinitive can also be used to state your real feelings about something.
would + like/love/hate etc. is always followed by the *to*-infinitive.
*I'**d love to visit** China.*

Note: *Help, go on, come* and other verbs can also be followed by the *to*-infinitive or the *-ing* form (with a change in meaning).

You will find a comprehensive listing of verb patterns on page 141.

Anniversary night out

Lexis Chris and Shirley have been married for seven years, and today is their wedding anniversary. They have two children: Amy aged four, and Jack who's one. This evening, they've arranged a babysitter and they've gone out for a meal in a smart restaurant. Work with a partner. One of you is Chris and the other one is Shirley. Do the tasks.

a) Test your verb patterns! Complete Chris and Shirley's 'thoughts' using the *to*-infinitive or the *-ing* form of the verbs in brackets. Refer to the list of verb patterns on page 141 if necessary.

b) Compare your two stories. Is this going to be 'a night to remember'? Why / Why not?

c) Look at the verb patterns in each case and divide them into three groups.

Verbs + *to*-infinitive	Verbs + *-ing* form	Verbs + *to*-infinitive or *-ing* form
manage	*couldn't help*	*remember*

Chris is thinking ...	Shirley is thinking ...
1 I remember *bringing* (bring) Shirley here for our third date – it must be nearly ten years ago …	1 Oh dear, I hope I've remembered *to bring* (bring) the mobile phone. Oh good, here it is.
2 Yes, that was the evening I couldn't help ____ (tell) her that I loved her.	2 Oh no, I think I forgot ____ (tell) the babysitter what the number is. Jack hasn't been very well, and what if he wakes up ?
3 I'll never forget ____ (look) at Shirley that evening and thinking, 'This is the woman I want to marry.'	3 It's okay – she knows the name of the restaurant so she'll manage ____ (look) in the phone book if necessary.
4 We both work so hard – we deserve ____ (have) a break.	4 We both work so hard – I hate ____ (have) so little time to spend with the children.
5 I can imagine ____ (spend) a romantic weekend in Paris, just the two of us. My mother will have the children.	5 From now on, I intend ____ (spend) more time with the children. I'm going to stop working. Chris will understand.
6 Yes – Paris. I'll enjoy ____ (pick up) a few new phrases in French. I can't remember anything I learnt at school.	6 We must stop ____ (pick up) some milk on the way home – I haven't got anything for Jack's breakfast.
7 I want the waitress ____ (look) over here so I can order a nice bottle of French wine.	7 He'd better stop ____ (look) at that waitress. Otherwise I'm going home!
8 Mm, this wine's lovely. I regret ____ (drive) here now – we should have got a taxi.	8 I hope he doesn't expect me ____ (drive) the babysitter home.
9 I fancy ____ (go) to a club later – we haven't been dancing together for ages.	9 I'm tired and I want ____ (go) home.
10 I can't stand ____ (be) at home all the time – we must do this more often.	10 I'd just like ____ (be) at home with a good video.

A man and his car

1 26 You're going to listen to Laura talking about her father and his car. Listen once and link the phrases in A with the phrases in B. Compare your answers with a partner.

	A		B
a)	a cosy blanket	1	protection for the seats from school shoes
b)	'the precious one'	2	part of the ritual of starting the car and setting off
c)	paper bags	3	used to be a pilot
d)	lighting his pipe	4	the car in the garage
e)	choking passengers	5	protection for the car at night
f)	the Royal Air Force	6	pipe smoke inside the car

2 Are the following statements true or false?

a) Laura's father is very fond of his car.
b) When Laura was a child, her father often took the family out in the car.
c) Laura's sisters damaged the car by banging the door too hard.
d) He reverses out of the drive at high speed.
e) Laura thinks he probably used to go through a similar ritual before taking off in a plane.

Compare your answers with a partner. Listen again and check.

3 Laura uses all the expressions in the box. Use these expressions to complete the sentences. Then look at the tapescript on page 150 and check your answers.

> hair-raising speed   several goes   as close as you'll get   tucked up   got away
> sudden urge

a) A glass of champagne at Christmas is ____ to a millionaire lifestyle in our house! (line 6)
b) I love listening to stormy weather provided I'm safely ____ in bed. (line 11)
c) Every so often, I get a ____ to leave my job and do something completely different. (line 25)
d) I had ____ at taking my driving test before I passed. (line 53)
e) I hate people who drive at ____ down country roads. (line 60)
f) I was quite lazy at school, but I usually ____ with it. (line 71)

Are any of these sentences true for you?

Close up

Language reference p49

1 Look at the verb structures in the following extracts from the listening text in 1 in the previous section. Discuss the questions (*a–f*) with a partner.

… he'**ll get out** his box of matches …
… The pipe **won't light** first go – he'**ll have** several goes at it, and finally …
… he'**ll puff** and puff until the car is full of smoke.

a) Are the extracts about present, future or past habits?
b) Which modal verb is used?
c) Does the main verb describe an action or a state?
d) Do the actions take place just once or many times?
e) Are the actions typical of Laura's father or unusual for him?
f) What difference does it make if you change the modal verb to '*d* (*would*)?

2 Read the following description of morning routines. Change the verbs in **bold** from the present simple to *will/'ll* + verb, but only where you can do so without changing the meaning of the text.

> Ever since I can remember, we've gone through exactly the same routine each morning. My dad (1) **gets up** around seven o'clock – even on Sundays. He (2) **hates** wasting time in bed. He (3) **has** two cups of very strong coffee and a slice of toast before driving off to work. Dad (4) **'s** never late. My mum (5) **doesn't usually get ready** for work till after breakfast. She (6) **likes** to take her time in the morning. Mum (7) **'s got** a part-time job at a nearby bank and she (8) **always leaves** it till the last minute before running out of the house. As for me, my morning routine (9) **varies** from day to day. It (10) **usually depends** on what I've been up to the night before!

Work with a partner. Describe the morning routines of members of your own family to each other.

3 Work with a partner. Take it in turns to make sentences about past situations or experiences by combining phrases from box A and verb structures from boxes B and C.

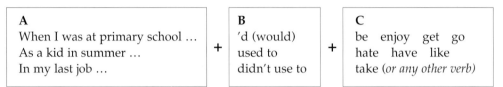

A		B		C
When I was at primary school … As a kid in summer … In my last job …	**+**	'd (would) used to didn't use to	**+**	be enjoy get go hate have like take (*or any other verb*)

Annoying habits

1 🔊 27 In the sentences below a woman is talking about her annoying work-mate. Complete the sentences using the verb phrases in the box. Listen and check your answers.

> will keep using   's always telling   will insist on opening   's forever talking
> 's always leaving   will go on about

a) I share an office with a woman who ____ to her boyfriend on the phone, blowing kisses and saying intimate things that I don't want to listen to. It really gets on my nerves!

b) She ____ all the windows when she arrives in the morning, and then she complains it's freezing and puts the heating on full blast. The office is either freezing or boiling!

c) She ____ half-finished cups of coffee around the desk – then I knock them over, and it's my fault!

d) She ____ her personal problems. Honestly, you'd think I was her therapist or something – I should charge her for my time!

e) She ____ me what to do, which I resent. I mean, I was working here when she was still at school!

f) I've told her hundreds of times to get her own pencil sharpener and scissors, but she ____ mine and not putting them back in their place. So when I need them I can never find them!

(Language reference p49)

2 How does the woman express her annoyance? What verb structures does she use?

3 Work with a partner. Which of the habits in 1 would most annoy you? Put them in order of most to least annoying.

Sounding annoyed

1 🔊 28 Listen to the following extracts from the recording in 1 in the previous section. Mark the stressed words and note the intonation used. Practise saying the sentences with a partner, trying to sound as annoyed as you can

a) She's forever talking to her boyfriend on the phone.
b) She will insist on opening all the windows.
c) She's always leaving half-finished cups of coffee around the desk.
d) She will go on about her personal problems.
e) She's always telling me what to do.
f) She will keep using my pencil sharpener and scissors.

2 Think about people you know. Tell your partner about their most annoying habits.

Language reference: present & past habits

The most common way of speaking about habit is by using a simple tense with an adverb of frequency or adverb phrase.

As a student, she **got up** late **every morning.**
She **hardly ever did** any work.
Now, she **always gets up at seven o'clock.**

Will & would

If you want to emphasize that you are talking about actions (not states) which are characteristic and predictable, you can use *will* or *won't* for the present and *would* (*'d*) for the past.

He**'ll get up** at seven o'clock every morning.
He **won't talk** to anyone until he's finished his breakfast.
I**'d walk** to school every day unless it was raining, when my mum**'d take** me.

Will and *would* are almost always contracted (*'ll, 'd*). If you use the full forms, it can make you sound angry. (See *Annoying habits*.)

Used to

You can use this structure to talk about past habits or past states or situations.
I **used to come** home every day at five o'clock.
I **didn't use to enjoy** sports lessons.

Annoying habits

You can use *will* to show annoyance about the way somebody behaves, especially with *insist on + -ing* form and *keep + -ing* form. In this case, *will* is almost never contracted.
She **will insist on opening** all the windows.

You can also use *always/forever* + continuous to produce the same effect.
She**'s always telling** me what to do.
He **was always asking** people embarrassing questions.

Note: This structure is not always negative.
I loved Sara. She **was always making** jokes.

The big day

Listening   **1**   Read about the following wedding rituals. Are any of them common in your country? What do you think each ritual means?

     a)   The bride and groom cut the wedding cake together.
     b)   The groom gives the bride gold coins during the church ceremony.
     c)   Guests pin money on the bridegroom's suit during the reception.
     d)   Guests throw rice over the bride and groom as they leave the church.
     e)   An older person holds a black umbrella over the bride's head as she leaves her home to go to the groom's home.
     f)   The bride throws her bouquet of flowers over her shoulder into the crowd of guests.

2   🔲   **29** Listen to explanations of three of the rituals and answer the following questions.

     a)   Which rituals do they talk about?
     b)   Which country is each ritual from?
     c)   Did you guess correctly the significance of each ritual?

Anecdote   Think of a wedding you've been to. You are going to tell your partner about it. Choose from the list the things you want to talk about. Think about what you will say and what language you will use.

- ☐ Who was getting married?
- ☐ Where, when and what time of year did the ceremony take place?
- ☐ What was the weather like?
- ☐ What were you wearing?
- ☐ What did the bride and groom wear?
- ☐ Did you know many people at the wedding?
- ☐ Where did you go for the reception?
- ☐ What did you have to eat and drink?
- ☐ Did anybody give any speeches? Who?
- ☐ Did the guests give the bride and groom presents?
- ☐ How did the day end?
- ☐ Did you enjoy the wedding?

Marriage is ...

1 Work with a partner. Choose the best way to complete the following quotations about marriage.

  a) Marriage is a long journey of **disappointments** / **discovery**.
  b) Marriage is for **ever** / **other people**.
  c) Marriage is not a word. It's a **novel** / **sentence**.
  d) Marriage is the **beginning of the end** / **end of the beginning**.
  e) Marriage is the most advanced form of **love** / **warfare** in the modern world.
  f) Marriage is the sole cause of **happiness** / **divorce**.

2 Use words and expressions of your own to replace the words in **bold** in 1.

3 Work in groups. Make up six 'quotations' that begin with the words 'Marriage is ...'. Use the tiles below. You can use each tile as many times as you like.

  a) One quotation that contains a total of five words.
  b) One quotation that contains a total of six words.
  c) One quotation that contains a total of seven words.
  d) One quotation that is as long as you can make it.
  e) One quotation that is as negative as you can make it.
  f) One quotation that is as positive as you can make it.

4 Compare your quotations with other groups. How many do you agree with / disagree with?

Small talk

1 ▭ 30 Work with a partner. You are each going to complete four short conversations. Student A follow the instructions on page 136. Student B follow the instructions on page 138. Then listen and check your answers

2 Choose three of the exchanges from 1. Invent a context for each one. Think of the following questions.

- Where does the exchange take place?
- What has happened just before?
- What will happen straight after?
- What time of day is it?
- Who are the speakers?
- Do they know each other?
- How old are they?

3 Explain the contexts you have invented to other students and discuss your ideas.

4 ▭ 31 Ann is saying goodbye to Bob after an evening at his house. Read the conversation and complete the 'goodbye' expressions using the words in the box. Then listen and check your answers.

| you | better | after | having | be | regards | been | already | must | for |
| Give | Take | Bye | journey | See | will | | | | |

The long goodbye

Ann: I'd (1) _____ be going.

Bob: It's (2) _____ lovely to see you.

Ann: Thank you for (3) _____ me.

Bob: Thanks (4) _____ coming.

Ann: I'll (5) _____ off then.

Bob: Give my (6) _____ to your family.

Ann: I (7) _____ .

Bob: (8) _____ me a ring.

Ann: Okay. I really (9) _____ be off now.

Bob: (10) _____ it easy.

Ann: (11) _____ you.

Bob: Look (12) _____ yourself.

Ann: (13) _____ for now.

Bob: Safe (14) _____ .

Ann: Love (15) _____ .

Bob: Missing you (16) _____ .

5 Work with a partner. Note down ways of saying hello and goodbye in as many different languages as you can.

6

Digital

1 Complete the following facts which appeared in a British newspaper article about text messaging. Use the phrases in the box.

> they'd like to know better   too loud to talk   less than the price of a call
> to write and phone more   nobody need know   to your phone bill
> are work-related

Text messaging

The facts

- It's cheap. You can send messages of up to 160 characters for (1) _____ .
- It's discreet and personal. You can send or receive messages on a bus, in a meeting or in class, and (2) _____ .
- Only 10% of messages sent (3) ____ .
- In a survey of mobile-phone users 44% said that text messaging meant that they told their partner they loved them more often, 53% used it to apologise after rows, and 64% said that text messages are a good way to flirt with people (4) _____ .
- Text messaging appears to have encouraged men (5) _____ .
- People use it to communicate in night-clubs where the music is (6) _____ .
- In some places you can even send a message to a vending machine which will deliver a drink and charge it (7) _____ !

(Information from The Guardian)

2 Would you (or do you) use text messaging for any of the purposes described in the newspaper article?

3 Work with a partner. Using standard English, rewrite the text messages two people sent to one another. The conversation contains all the words in the key. The first line has been done for you.

Man:	DO U WAN2 C ME L8R 4 A DRINK?
	= Do you want to see me later for a drink?
Woman:	WOT RU TRYNG 2 SAY?
Man:	I LUV U ;-)
Woman:	OIC :-0
Man:	PCM
Woman:	IM W/ SOME1 :-(
Man:	WOT ABOUT YR FRIEND? I LUV HER 2. IS SHE W/ NE1?
Woman:	I H8 U

Standard English	Text messaging	Standard English	Text messaging
anyone	NE1	to, too	_____
are you	RU	want to	_____
for	_____	what	_____
hate	_____	with	_____
later	_____	you	_____
love	_____	your	_____
oh I see	_____	**Emotion**	**Sign**
please call me	_____	happiness	_____
see	_____	sadness	_____
someone	_____	surprise	_____

4 Complete the key to the text messaging language.

5 Write a short text message conversation with a partner. Exchange conversations with other students and then write their conversations out in full.

Reading

1 Note down all the words and expressions you associate with the word *computer*. Then read the interview below with a best-selling author about her experiences with computers and add any new words or expressions to your list.

(Based on an article in *The Guardian*)

ONLINE • ONLINE • ONLINE

This week we interview Jessica Adams, best-selling author of *Single White E-mail* and *Astrology for Women*, about her thoughts on computers, the Internet and everything!

Jessica Adams

1 ?

I've had a computer of one sort or another since I bought my first Mac in 1987. I remember it was a little box with a black and white screen, and I think I used to go off and make a cup of tea when it was time to print anything.

2 ?

I have two laptops, and at home I have a huge IBM Aptiva, which is jet black and looks like the sort of thing Darth Vader might use.

3 ?

Very important, but like most of the world, I have a love-hate relationship with computers. As a novelist I love the cut and paste function, which has changed the way I write fiction. As a traveller, I'm hooked on hotmail and Internet cafés. But as a true technobimbo, I really hate the way computers can get stuck, go wrong and generally fail to explain themselves in plain English.

4 ?

For e-mail and writing fiction.

5 ?

I'm afraid the only website I look at regularly is my own. I like to see what readers of *Single White E-mail* are saying about the book. It's never what I expect or imagine!

6 ?

Yes. I once had a very flirtatious online conversation with someone who, embarrassingly enough, turned out to be fifteen. I was thirty at the time.

7 ?

About eight hours. The longest I've ever spent was actually twenty-four hours, when I was writing a story for an Australian magazine entitled *24 Hours on the Net*. It nearly killed me.

8 ?

Yes, I bought a juicer. It's fantastic, and I've become addicted to banana milk shakes!

9 ?

Yes, I really want one of those mobile phones with e-mail and Internet access on them.

10 ?

No, I don't think so. I'm not a geek at all. I don't understand computers – they're just glorified hairdryers or electric kettles to me.

11 ?

Yes, it annoys me to think how much I depend on them. I've been spending far too long on my computer. I must remember to get a life!

12 ?

A computer – sorry about that, humans!

bimbo: an insulting term for a young woman who is attractive but not very intelligent.

geek: an insulting term for someone who spends too much time with computers and not enough time with human beings.

2 Complete the interview by matching the questions (*a–l*) below with the appropriate gaps in the article (*1–12*) in 1.

a) How long have you spent on the Internet in the last week?
b) What do you use your computer for?
c) Have you bought any new gadgets recently?
d) How important do you think computers are?
e) Have you ever chatted with strangers on the Internet?
f) Are there any new gadgets on the market that you want?
g) Do you see yourself as a computer geek?
h) Do you know any good websites?
i) Which would you take to a desert island for company – a computer or a human?
j) How long have you been using computers?
k) Is there anything that irritates you about computers or electronic technology?
l) What kind of computer do you have now?

3 Work with a partner. Choose five of the questions from the interview to ask your partner. Find out as much as you can.

Close up

**Verbs: dynamic
& stative
meanings**

1 Look at the following extracts from the interview in the previous
section. Which verbs describe an action? Which verbs describe a state?

a) I**'ve had** a computer of one sort or another since … 1987.
b) Yes. I once **had** a very flirtatious online conversation …
c) I **bought** a juicer. It**'s** fantastic!
d) I **like** to see what readers of *Single White E-mail* **are saying** about the book.
e) I **don't understand** computers …

Verbs which describe an action have *dynamic* meanings. Verbs which describe a state
have *stative* meanings. Which of the verbs in the sentences above is used both for an
action and for a state?

2 ⬛ **32** Listen to and read the following conversations. Match the conversations with
the pictures (*1–6*).

Conversation A

Man: Sorry, I didn't **hear** what you were …
Woman: Of course you didn't hear. You weren't **listening**, were you? Sometimes I **hate** you.
Man: Stop it. People are **looking**.

Conversation B

Man 1: I'm **thinking** of asking her to marry me.
Man 2: But you only met her last night!
Man 1: It **seems** like I've **known** her all my life.
Man 2: Yeah, right!

Conversation C

Woman: **Look**, over there. Is it a bird? Is it a plane?
Man: No idea. I'm afraid I can't **see** a thing without my glasses.

Conversation D

Woman: You've only got one appointment this afternoon: you're **seeing** Mrs Lloyd at three.
Man: Oh, not again. I **hate** talking to her.
Woman: Yes, but she **likes** listening to you.

Conversation E

Man: Hey, what are you doing?
Woman: I'm **tasting** your soup. It **smells** great and it **tastes** delicious!
Man: But it's not for you. So hands off!

Conversation F

Woman: We **like** each other.
Man: And we **want** to be together.
Woman: That's true. But I don't **think** we **love** each other.
Man: No, no. 'Course not.

3 Work with a partner. Focus on the verbs in bold in the six conversations in 2 and complete the following tasks.

    a) Write a *D* next to the dynamic verbs (describing an action). Write an *S* next to the stative verbs (describing a state).
    b) Circle the three verbs which show both dynamic and stative meanings.
    c) Decide whether verbs with stative meanings can be used with the continuous form.

4 In some of the following statements the continuous form is not possible because the verbs have stative rather than dynamic meanings. Where necessary, correct the verb structure by replacing the continuous form with the simple form.

    a) I'm **having** a brother who loves computer games.
    b) I'm **thinking** of getting a new computer.
    c) I'm **having** problems getting to sleep at the moment.
    d) I've **been knowing** my best friend for more than ten years.
    e) I'm **not seeing** why men should get paid more than women.
    f) I'm **wanting** to go to the USA for my next holiday.
    g) I'll **be seeing** my girlfriend/boyfriend later on today.
    h) I **was remembering** to give my teacher a card for his last birthday.

Transform any five of the statements into questions and ask your partner.

Language reference: dynamic & stative meanings

Dynamic meanings

Most verbs have dynamic meanings. They describe either single acts (*hit, knock, throw*) or activities and processes (*change, eat, walk, work*). Something 'happens'.
*Someone's **knocking** at the door.* (repeated acts)
*I've **been working** here all my life.* (continuous activity)
*The world's climate **has become** warmer.* (process)

Stative meanings

Verbs with stative meanings usually describe a state of mind (verbs connected with knowledge, emotion or perception) or a state of affairs (verbs connected with being or having). Nothing 'happens'.
*I've **known** my best friend for more than ten years.*
*She **has** two laptops and a huge desktop machine.*
*I can't **see** a thing without my glasses.*

Note: The continuous form has a dynamic meaning, and so you cannot normally use verbs with stative meanings in the continuous form.
~~I've been knowing my best friend for more than ten years.~~
Verbs with stative meanings are also normally not used in the imperative form.

You will find a list of verbs that are normally used with stative meanings on page 141.

Dynamic & stative meanings

Some verbs can have both dynamic and stative meanings.

Dynamic	Stative
I've **been having** driving lessons recently. (= taking)	I **have** an old yellow bicycle. (= possess)
I'm **seeing** the dentist this afternoon. (= visiting)	Do you **see** what I mean? (= understand)

Lara Croft

1 If you like computer games, find somebody who isn't very interested in them and tell them about your favourite game. If you don't particularly like computer games, find somebody who is a computer games fan and ask them why they find these games interesting.

Tomb Raider

Tomb Raider is one of the biggest-selling series in video game history. The star of the game, Lara Croft, is famous all over the world.

2 🔊 **33** Read through this magazine quiz on Lara Croft of *Tomb Raider*. Then listen to her talking about her life, and tick (✓) the correct answers.

1 She spends all her money on ...
- ☐ a expensive sunglasses.
- ☐ b weapons.
- ☐ c travel.

2 She lives in ...
- ☐ a a Manhattan attic conversion.
- ☐ b a mansion in the English countryside.
- ☐ c a cave in Egypt.

3 Her favourite pastimes are ...
- ☐ a extreme sports.
- ☐ b needlework.
- ☐ c hunting.
- ☐ d cleaning her guns.
- ☐ e taking care of her pets.
- ☐ f working out.

4 Her favourite film is ...
- ☐ a *The Mummy.*
- ☐ b *Austin Powers.*
- ☐ c *Aguirre, the Wrath of God.*

5 She drives ...
- ☐ a an old Land Rover and a Norton Streetfighter.
- ☐ b a pink Lambretta Scooter and a silver Porsche.
- ☐ c a Rolls Royce and a Harley Davidson.

6 Her ideal man is ...
- ☐ a Pierce Brosnan (James Bond actor).
- ☐ b Jean-Claude Van Damme (action film hero).
- ☐ c Brian Blessed (Shakespearean actor).

7 Her dream is to ...
- ☐ a be as famous as James Bond.
- ☐ b ski down Everest with Brian Blessed strapped to her back.
- ☐ c meet 'Mr Right' and settle down in the country.

(Based on an article in *The Sunday Times*)

3 Work with a partner and do the following task.

a) Write a quiz about yourself using the same questions and multiple choice format as the Lara Croft quiz in 2. Adapt the questions as appropriate.

b) Exchange papers and do your partner's quiz.

c) Check your answers and find out how well you know one another.

Close up

Language reference p58

Present perfect simple & continuous

1 Look at the verbs in these pairs of sentences from the Lara Croft interview. Answer the questions below.

Pair A
They**'ve been** a bit frosty since I started the job.
I**'ve had** my trusty old Land Rover for years.

Pair B
He**'s tried** to climb Everest three times.
He**'s just written** a book.

Pair C
I**'ve been doing** this job since I was 21.
I **haven't been seeing** anyone recently.

Verb structure?
a) What is the name of the verb structure used in each pair of sentences?

Dynamic or stative?
b) Which two pairs of sentences have verbs with dynamic meanings?
c) Which pair of sentences has verbs with stative meanings?

Complete or incomplete?
d) Which pair of sentences shows actions that are complete?
e) Which pair of sentences shows situations that are incomplete or ongoing?
f) Which pair of sentences shows actions that are incomplete or ongoing?

2 Match the beginnings (*a–d*) with the endings (*1–4*) to make four important rules about the use of the present perfect simple and continuous.

a) Verb with dynamic meaning + the present perfect simple:
b) Verb with stative meaning + the present perfect simple:
c) Verb with dynamic meaning + the present perfect continuous:
d) Verb with stative meaning + the present perfect continuous:

1   the action is incomplete or ongoing.   3   not usually used.
2   the action is complete.   4   the situation is incomplete or ongoing.

3 Work with a partner. Choose the most appropriate form of the present perfect, and then ask each other the questions.

a) How long **have you saved / have you been saving** with the same bank?
b) **Have you ever broken / Have you ever been breaking** your arm or your leg?
c) How long **have you had / have you been having** your current e-mail address?
d) **Have you ever been / Have you ever been going** to Berlin?
e) How long **have you driven / have you been driving** the same car?
f) **Have you ever missed / Have you ever been missing** a plane?
g) **Have you ever eaten / Have you ever been eating** oysters?
h) How many times **have you taken / have you been taking** English exams?
i) How long **have you known / have you been knowing** your English teacher?
j) How many times **have you done / have you been doing** exercises on the present perfect?

'Have you forgotten your key again, George?'

4 Complete these jokes by putting the verbs in brackets into the present perfect simple or the present perfect continuous.

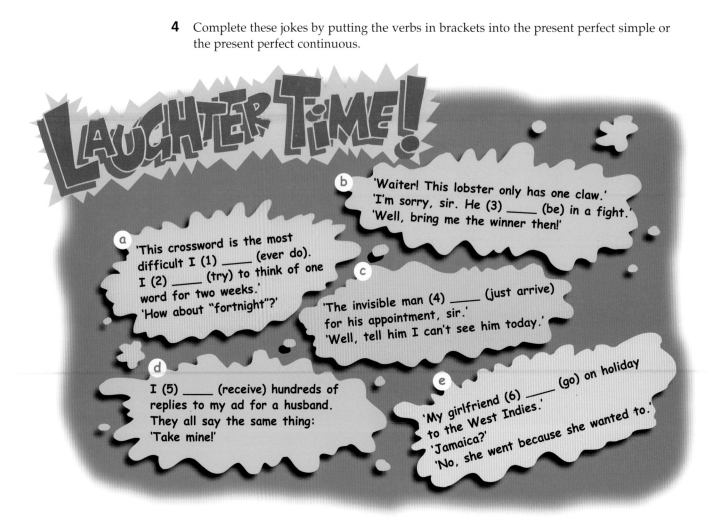

LAUGHTER TIME!

a 'This crossword is the most difficult I (1) _____ (ever do). I (2) _____ (try) to think of one word for two weeks.'
'How about "fortnight"?'

b 'Waiter! This lobster only has one claw.'
'I'm sorry, sir. He (3) _____ (be) in a fight.'
'Well, bring me the winner then!'

c 'The invisible man (4) _____ (just arrive) for his appointment, sir.'
'Well, tell him I can't see him today.'

d I (5) _____ (receive) hundreds of replies to my ad for a husband. They all say the same thing: 'Take mine!'

e 'My girlfriend (6) _____ (go) on holiday to the West Indies.'
'Jamaica?'
'No, she went because she wanted to.'

5 🔊 **34** Listen and check your answers. Which do you think is the funniest joke?

Language reference: present perfect simple & continuous

The present perfect shows a connection between the past and the present. Whether you use the simple or continuous forms will often depend on whether the verb has a dynamic meaning or a stative meaning.

Verb with dynamic meaning + present perfect continuous

This combination can express actions, activities or processes which are incomplete or ongoing. They started in the past and continue now.
I've been doing this job since I was 21.
How long have you been saving with the same bank?

Note: Although generally the present perfect continuous is preferred for incomplete actions, activities or processes, occasionally you may want to emphasise the permanence of the action, activity or process. In these circumstances you can use the present perfect simple. Compare:

I've lived / worked in the same town all my life. (permanent, state-like situation)
I've been living / working in Paris for the last few months. (temporary, dynamic)

Verb with dynamic meaning + present perfect simple

This combination can express actions, activities or processes which are completed. They have 'happened' in a period of time up to and including the present.
He's tried to climb Everest three times.
I've only missed a plane once in my life.

Verb with stative meaning + present perfect simple

This combination can express a situation which is incomplete or ongoing. It started in the past and continues now.
I've had my trusty old Land Rover for years.
How long have you known your English teacher?

Note: You cannot normally use verbs with stative meanings in the present perfect continuous.

Child's play

1 Work with a partner. Say whether you agree or disagree with the following statements.

    a) Children should read more books.
    b) These days it's unsafe for children to play outside on their own.
    c) Given the chance, children would rather watch TV than do things outside.
    d) It's important for children to have a computer and/or a television in their bedroom.

2 Read the article. What do the numbers in the box refer to?

| 1 in 7 | 9 | 72% | 1% | 5 | 1 in 100 | 57% | 1 in 5 |

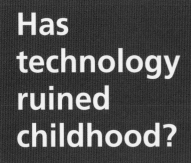

Has technology ruined childhood?

(Based on articles in The Independent and interactions)

Today, parents are increasingly worried about the safety of their children, and because of this, they are not letting their children out to play. As a result, children are no longer playing outside
5 but shutting themselves away in their rooms and losing themselves in individualistic activities such as television viewing and computer games.

Yet, if they had the chance, they would
10 rather get out of the house and go to the cinema, see friends or play sport. In fact, when asked what their idea of a good day was, only 1 in 7 said that they would turn on the television.
15 British teenagers have always retreated to their bedrooms, leaving the younger children to play in communal spaces such as the sitting room, garden or kitchen. However, children from the age of 9 are now turning to their
20 bedrooms as a place to socialise.

Bedroom culture is a phenomenon of the past 20 years with families getting smaller and homes getting more spacious. Increasing prosperity has also contributed to the rise of
25 the bedroom culture.

Of British children aged 6 to 17, 72% have a room they do not have to share with a sibling, 68% have their own music installation, 34% have an electronic games controller
30 hooked up to the television, 21% have a video and 12% have a PC. Only 1%, on the other hand, have an Internet connection in their bedroom.

On average children devote 5 hours a day to
35 screen media. Even so, only 1 child in 100 can be classed as a real screen addict, a child who spends a worrying 7 hours or more watching TV or playing computer games.

Although children generally have a few
40 favourite programmes, they mostly use television to kill time when they are bored and have nothing special to do. Moreover, the distinction between individualistic media use and social activities such as chatting with
45 friends is less extreme than is commonly assumed. Children gossip about television soap characters, make contact with other children on the Internet, and visit friends to admire their new computer games.
50 As the use of PCs proliferates, reading skills are expected to suffer. Nevertheless, 57% of children say they still enjoy reading, and 1 in 5 teenagers can be classed as a book-lover.

As a result of the bedroom culture, it is
55 becoming rarer for children over the age of 10 to watch television with their parents.
Once in their rooms, children tend to stay up watching television for as long as they wish. Consequently it is getting harder to control
60 children's viewing.

One father told researchers that he drew the line at 9 pm. His son, on the other hand, said, 'They tell us to go up at about 9.30 or 10 or something, and then we just watch until
65 they come up and tell us to switch it off at 11 or 11.30.'

3 Complete the sentences using the words in the box.

> losing   kill   devote   classed   draw   shut

a) Children should ____ less time to television and more time to doing sport.
b) One of life's greatest pleasures is ____ yourself in a really good book.
c) Most teenagers nowadays can be ____ as computer-literate.
d) It's okay for children to have mobile phones, but parents should ____ the line at letting them take them to school.
e) Children who ____ themselves away in their bedrooms to play computer games miss out on developing important social skills.
f) A lot of children ____ time playing game-boys while they're waiting for school to start. It would be much better if they interacted with other children.

Do you agree with the statements? Discuss with a partner.

Linkers

1 Sentences *a–g* summarise the article in 2 in the previous section. Add another sentence to each summary point. Use the sentences *1–7*.

a) Parents are worried about children's safety on the streets.
b) Children are spending more time in their rooms watching television and playing computer games.
c) Families are getting smaller and homes are getting bigger.
d) The majority of children have a television, a stereo or a PC in their rooms.
e) On average, children spend five hours a day using screen media.
f) As more children use PCs, experts expect reading skills to suffer.
g) Children watch television in their rooms after bedtime.

1 **Even so**, only a low percentage of children can be classed as screen addicts.
2 **As a result**, they aren't allowing their children to play outside.
3 **On the other hand**, few children have Internet access in their rooms.
4 **Yet** they would prefer to stay out.
5 **Consequently**, it is getting more difficult for parents to control their children's television viewing.
6 Increasing prosperity has **also** contributed to the rise of bedroom culture.
7 **Nevertheless**, many children say that they still enjoy reading.

2 In the extra sentences (1–7) in 1, the word or phrase which links these sentences to the main sentences (*a–g*) is highlighted in bold. Classify each linker in the following table.

adding more information	connecting contrasting ideas	showing cause and effect
also	*even so*	*as a result*

3 Find more linkers in the article in the previous section and add them to the categories.

4 Add linkers to improve the following short newspaper articles.

a A businessman in Swansea thought a bug had struck when his computer exploded. He discovered that a mouse had been inside and left droppings on the circuit board.

b An 80-year-old woman bought a Beatles single in the early sixties. She's never owned a record player. She hasn't heard it yet.

c Air traffic control at Manchester Airport are worried that Furby toys may interfere with navigation equipment. The toys have been banned from flights in and out of Manchester.

d Thieves stole a stereo system and some tapes from a car in Rochester, Kent. They left behind a tape by Julio Iglesias.

e Mobile phones have been interfering with music played on the jukebox in a pub in Oxford. The offending gadgets have been banned.

Discussion & listening

1 Work in groups. Compare the following, discussing the advantages and disadvantages in each case.

  a) e-mail versus 'snail mail' (writing letters)
  b) surfing the Internet versus going to the library
  c) playing computer games versus watching television
  d) shopping online versus going out shopping
  e) watching television versus reading a book

2 [cassette icon] **35** Listen to five people (1–5) talking about the same topics. Did any of them express the same opinions as you?

Writing

1 You are going to present a written argument about the advantages and disadvantages of mobile phones.

Make two lists:

1 Arguments in favour of mobile phones   2 Arguments against mobile phones

2 Work with a partner.

Combine your lists and choose the three most important points in favour of mobile phones and the three most important points against mobile phones. Think about what happens as a consequence of the points you have made.

For example:
Point in favour: *You can use mobile phones anywhere.*
Consequence: *People use mobile phones in inappropriate places (eg cinemas, restaurants).*

Point against: *People tend to have their mobile phones on all the time.*
Consequence: *The phones can cause a disturbance when they ring.*

3 Start your written argument with this opening line:
People often focus on the negative aspects of mobile phones and forget about the positives, of which there are many.

Use the plan and think about the linking words you are going to use to connect the points you have made.

Paragraph 1   Introduction: present the topic
Paragraph 2   Points in favour
Paragraph 3   Points against
Paragraph 4   Conclusion and/or your opinion

'Jane, darling, I'm just on my way home. I shouldn't be too late …'

7

Review 1

In the dog house

Present & past tenses

Put the verbs in the newspaper article into the most appropriate present or past tense.

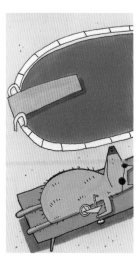

(Based on an article in *The Week*)

A good nose for a bargain

An Alsatian dog called Gunther (1) ___ (recently buy) Madonna's former home in Miami for $8 million. Gunther, who last year (2) ___ (inherit) $150 million from a German countess, (3) ___ (sign) on the dotted line with a paw print.

'Gunther (4) ___ (never be) stupid with his money, at least not since I (5) ___ (work) for him,' (6) ___ (say) an aide, as he (7) ___ (explain) how the dog (8) ___ (earlier reject) Sylvester Stallone's $25 million estate. 'He certainly (9) ___ (have) a good nose for a bargain.'

Gunther, who also (10) ___ (own) property in Germany, (11) ___ (already make) himself very much at home in Miami. He regularly (12) ___ (tour) the countryside in his chauffeur-driven BMW and (13) ___ (take) occasional dips in his swimming pool. 'Gunther (14) ___ (currently think) about his next purchase,' (15) ___ (say) the aide. 'Perhaps he'll follow Madonna to London. I (16) ___ (hear) Barking is a nice area!'

Interview with Madonna

Indirect questions

1 When you are asking about people's personal lives, indirect questions are often more polite than direct questions. Write the indirect questions that Madonna was asked in a recent interview.

a) 'How have your children changed your life?' *'I'd like to know …'*
b) 'Will you have any more children?' *'Do you think …'*
c) 'Do you enjoy scheming up new images all the time?' *'Could you tell me …'*
d) 'Will you ever have plastic surgery?' *'Do you think …'*
e) 'Have you traded love for fame?' *'Would you say that …'*
f) 'What is your star sign?' *'Do you mind telling me …'*
g) 'Why did you stop going to the gym?' *'I was wondering …'*

2 Match the interviewer's questions (*a–g*) in 1 with Madonna's answers (*1–7*).

1 'My sun sign is Leo. My rising sign is Aquarius, and my moon is in Virgo.'
2 'I don't know. Ask me in ten years.'
3 'They've changed my life in a million ways.'
4 'I hope so. I'd like to have another.'
5 'It's a huge waste of time.'
6 'I don't. For me it's really impulsive.'
7 'Well, when you become famous, you do trade one kind of love for another kind of love.'

3 Work with a partner. Think of three personal questions you would like to ask your partner. Make the questions indirect to make them as polite as possible.

Four in a row

Verbs & adjectives + prepositions

Play the game in groups of three: Students A, B, and C. Student A and Student B play against each other. Student C is the referee.

1 Student A chooses a square and makes a sentence using the word in the square plus the preposition which normally goes with it. If the word is used with the correct preposition, Student C marks the square with an A. If the word is used with an incorrect preposition, Student C marks the square with a B. Student C can check the answers on page 137.

2 Repeat the first stage, but with Student B choosing a square and making a sentence using the word with the correct preposition.

3 The game continues until either Student A or Student B has won four squares in a row, horizontally, vertically or diagonally. This student is the winner and gets one point.

4 Change roles. Play again. After three games the winner is the player with the most points.

1 proud	2 fed up	3 dream	4 approve	5 insist	6 prevent	7 worry
8 certain	9 famous	10 interested	11 succeed	12 specialise	13 useless	14 not bad
15 lacking	16 allergic	17 realistic	18 forgive	19 depend	20 afraid	21 well-known
22 keen	23 reliant	24 look forward	25 accustomed	26 fond	27 compatible	28 optimistic
29 accuse	30 apologise	31 good	32 believe	33 rely	34 concentrate	35 consist

Salad surprise!

Articles Complete the newspaper article using *a/an* and *the* where necessary.

Patricia Henderson, (1) _____ teacher from (2) _____ Newcastle, got (3) _____ biggest shock of her life yesterday while preparing (4) _____ dinner for her husband and two children. On putting her hand into (5) _____ bag of ready-prepared salad, she felt something 'large, slimy and moving'. (6) _____ second later, there was (7) _____ rather relieved snake slithering across (8) _____ kitchen table. 'I have always been afraid of (9) _____ snakes and I just screamed and screamed and screamed,' she said. '(10) _____ snake just stared at me. I couldn't move.'

(11) _____ spokesperson for (12) _____ supermarket where she bought (13) _____ salad told (14) _____ reporters they had no idea at all how (15) _____ creature had got into (16) _____ bag. (17) _____ snake, which is almost half (18) _____ metre long, has yet to be identified. Mrs Henderson, who is still recovering from (19) _____ ordeal, said 'I don't think I'll ever be able to eat (20) _____ salad again.'

(Based on an article in *The Daily Mail*)

Five years in space

Unreal
conditionals

1 The astronauts in the rocket are going on a five
year space mission. Imagine you are travelling
with them. If you could take one of each of the
following personal items with you to remind you
of home, what would you take? Say why.

For example:
*I'd take 'Bitter Sweet Symphony' by The Verve. I like
the lyrics, and the music is great.*

a) a piece of music
b) a book
c) a colour
d) a smell
e) a kind of food
f) a drink
g) a sound (not music)
h) a photograph

2 Go around the class and find out what other
people would take. Which are the most popular
items?

Agony aunt

Advice &
recommendations

1 Here are the beginnings of some letters written to a magazine agony aunt. Choose one
of the beginnings, decide what the problem might be, and complete the letter.

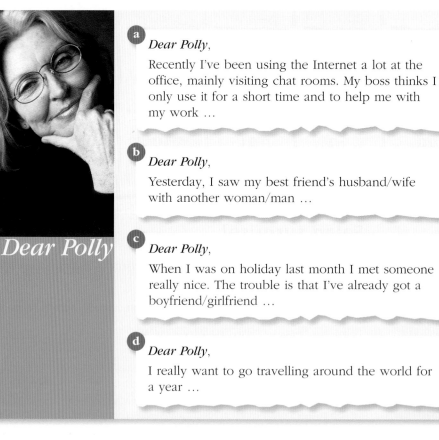

a *Dear Polly*,

Recently I've been using the Internet a lot at the
office, mainly visiting chat rooms. My boss thinks I
only use it for a short time and to help me with
my work …

b *Dear Polly*,

Yesterday, I saw my best friend's husband/wife
with another woman/man …

c *Dear Polly*,

When I was on holiday last month I met someone
really nice. The trouble is that I've already got a
boyfriend/girlfriend …

d *Dear Polly*,

I really want to go travelling around the world for
a year …

LANGUAGE TOOLBOX

If I were you, I'd …

You should …

You need to …

Whatever you do,
don't …

You could try …ing …

Have you thought of
…ing?

It's best (not) to …

It's important (not)
to …

It would be a good
idea to …

2 Work with a partner. Exchange letters and give each other advice. Use the phrases in the
Language toolbox to help you.

3 Exchange letters with some more students. Decide who has given you the best advice.

Wise words

Phrasal verbs   **1**   Match the halves to make some well-known quotes. Use a dictionary if necessary.

a)   The trouble with children is

b)   Never **postpone** until tomorrow

c)   I **disappointed** my friends,

d)   I haven't asked you to make me young again.

e)   To make a mistake is human,

f)   America is the only country where you buy a lifetime's supply of aspirin for $1

g)   If you **stop** smoking, drinking and loving, you don't actually live any longer,

h)   The only way to **remove** temptation

1   I **disappointed** my country.
(*Richard Nixon, American president*)

2   it just seems longer.
(*Clement Freud, British writer*)

3   you can't **return** them.
(*Quentin Crisp, British model and writer*)

4   but to really **do things wrong** you need a computer. (*Paul Ehrlich, American scientist*)

5   what you can do the day after.
(*Mark Twain, American writer*)

6   All I want is to **continue** getting older.
(*Konrad Adenhauer, German politician*)

7   is to **submit** to it.
(*Oscar Wilde, Irish writer*)

8   and **use it completely** in a week. (*Anonymous*)

2   Originally all the quotes in 1 contained phrasal verbs instead of the words in **bold**. Use the phrasal verbs in the box to restore the quotes to their original form.

> get rid of   let down   put off   give back   mess up   give up   go on
> give in   use up

Mad millionaires

Past habits   **1**   Complete the sentences about a selection of mad millionaires and their crazy personal habits. Use *used to* or *would* with the verbs in the box. In some cases both constructions can be used.

> walk   love   be   steal   be   ask   be   not allow   be   stay   race

a)   Towards the end of his life, pioneering aviator, industrialist and Hollywood producer, Howard Hughes _____ terrified of dust and so _____ inside all the time, watching the same film, *Ice Station Zebra*, again and again and again and …

b)   Newspaper publishing magnate, Joseph Pulitzer _____ so acutely nervous of the outside world that he spent his later years in double-insulated, sound-proofed rooms.

c)   John Paul Getty, the oil billionaire, _____ famous for his meanness. He _____ his house guests to use his telephone. Instead he _____ them to use a pay phone in the hall.

d)   Haroldson Lafayette Hunt, who also made an enormous fortune from oil, _____ his secretary's lunch when he was feeling short of money.

e)   Another oil tycoon, James West _____ known as 'Silver Dollar Jim' because he _____ along the Texas highways in one of his thirty cars, throwing handfuls of silver dollars to startled onlookers as he sped by.

f)   Brian Hughes, the 1920s box-manufacturing tycoon, _____ up and down outside his favourite restaurant and scatter fake jewels all over the pavement. He _____ to watch people fighting over the 'gems'.

2   Work with a partner. Discuss which of the millionaires in 1 had the craziest personal habit.

Maze

Verbs + infinitive and/or -ing form

1 Work with a partner. Go through the maze following the instructions below. The first three steps have been done for you. Which is the correct FINISH: *A*, *B*, or *C*?

Instructions

- If the answer is the infinitive without *to* (eg *do*), go straight on (→).
- If the answer is the infinitive with *to* (eg *to do*), turn right (⤵).
- If the answer is the -*ing* form (eg *doing*), turn left (⤴).

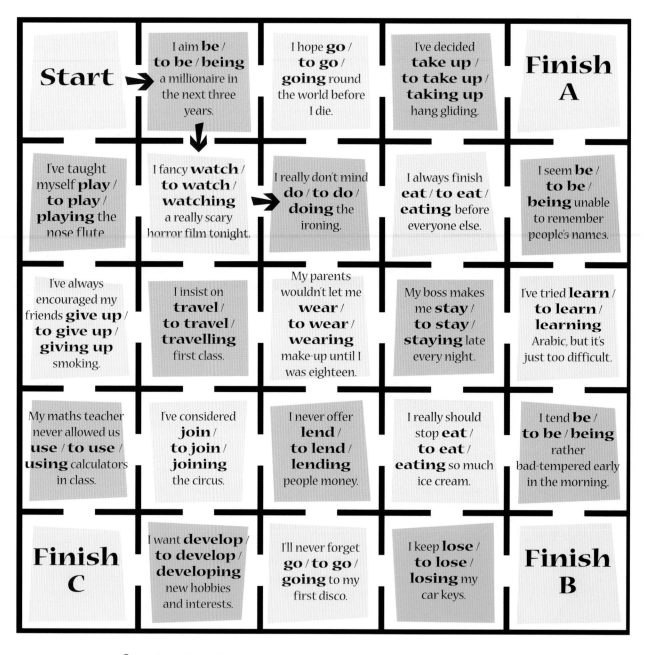

2 Adapt three of the sentences in the maze to make true statements about you.

Cryptic conversations

Verbs:
dynamic &
stative
meanings

1 Complete the first part of each conversation (a–j). Use the present simple or continuous according to whether the verbs are being used dynamically or statively. Then find the second part of each conversation (1–10).

a) 'I ____ (think) the government is doing an excellent job.'
b) 'What ____ (you think) about?'
c) 'I ____ (see) Julie tonight.'
d) '____ (you see) my point?'
e) 'How much ____ (you weigh)?'
f) 'What ____ (you weigh) this flour for?'
g) 'Why ____ (you smell) the milk?'
h) 'Mm. You ____ (smell) gorgeous!'
i) 'We ____ (have) a terrible holiday!'
j) 'I'm sorry, I ____ (not have) time to talk just now.'

1 'Oh, I am sorry. What's the problem?'
2 'That's the third time this week. Is something going on?'
3 'Ugh! It's gone off.'
4 'Oh, OK. What about later?'
5 'Not really. Explain it to me again, will you?'
6 'Oh really, you're so naïve!'
7 'That's not a very polite question!'
8 'Oh, you know – this and that.'
9 'I'm making you a birthday cake.'
10 'Oh, thank you. It's jasmine.'

2 Work with a partner and write the next two lines of at least three of the conversations. Act out your conversations.

Thumb trouble

Present
perfect
simple &
continuous

1 Read this conversation and answer the following questions.

a) What's the problem with Debbie's friend?
b) Has she succeeded in giving up?
c) What methods has she tried?
d) What does Chris suspect?

2 Put the verbs in brackets into the present perfect simple or continuous. In some cases both forms are possible.

Chris: I'm a bit worried about Ellie. She's nearly six and she still sucks her thumb!

Debbie: Oh, I shouldn't worry too much about Ellie. I've got a friend who (1) ____ (suck) her thumb for twenty-nine years!

Chris: You're kidding!

Debbie: No, honestly. She only does it when she's really tired, but you can imagine how strange it looks on a grown woman.

Chris: Very strange. (2) ____ (she ever try) to give up?

Debbie: Of course. She (3) ____ (try) to give up since somebody called her a baby when she was twelve. But she (4) ____ (not succeed) yet.

Chris: What methods (5) ____ (she use)?

Debbie: Well, for example, she (6) ____ (have) therapy for several years.

Chris: (7) ____ (it help)?

Debbie: Not really. Well, I think it (8) ____ (improve) some aspects of her life, but she (9) ____ (not stop) sucking her thumb.

Chris: There must be something she can do.

Debbie: I know, but she (10) ____ (try) everything. She (11) ____ (try) putting mustard on her thumb, but she just got used to the taste, and actually started liking it. Now she has mustard on everything! And apart from that, I (12) ____ (have) hypnosis, I (13) ____ (take up) smoking a pipe, I (14) ____ (wear) gloves, even in bed …

Chris: So do you suck your thumb too?

Debbie: No!

Chris: You said 'I'.

Debbie: Ah – no – I meant my friend … has … um …

3 🔲 36 Listen to the conversation and check your answers.

4 Have you (or anybody you know) tried to give up a bad habit? What methods have they used? Have they been successful?

5 Work with a partner. Write a conversation between two friends. One of them is trying to give up chocolate.

8 *Escape*

Work in small groups. Discuss the following questions.

a) What words and images do you associate with the word *beach*?
b) Have you been to a beach like the one in the photo below? Where was it?
c) When was the last time you spent a day on a beach?

Reading

1 Work with a partner. List all the things that might spoil a typical day at the seaside.

2 Read the article by Bill Bryson on the opposite page. Does he mention any of the things you listed in 1?

3 Look at the text again and decide which of the following statements are true and which are false. Compare your answers with a partner.

a) The author …
   1 enjoys the prospect of a day on the beach.
   2 isn't very proud of his body.
   3 doesn't get bad sunburn.

b) The author's wife …
   1 is looking forward to a day on the beach.
   2 doesn't usually get her own way.
   3 says that Irish setters are very clean.

c) The author's youngest child …
   1 is very demanding.
   2 is called Jimmy.
   3 needed to go to the toilet.

(Adapted from *Notes From A Big Country*, by Bill Bryson)

A day at the seaside

Every year, about this time, my
wife wakes me up with a playful
slap and says, 'I've got an idea.
Let's drive for three hours to the ocean,
5 take off most of our clothes and sit on
some sand for a whole day.'
    'What for?' I will say warily.
    'It will be fun,' she will insist.
    'I don't think so,' I will reply. 'People
10 find it disturbing when I take my shirt
off in public. I find it disturbing.'
    'No, it will be great. We'll get sand in
our hair. We'll get sand in our shoes.
We'll get sand in our sandwiches and
15 then in our mouths. We'll get
sunburned and windburned. And when
we get tired of sitting, we can have a
paddle in water so cold it actually hurts.
At the end of the day, we'll set off at
20 the same time as 37,000 other people
and get in such a traffic jam that we
won't get home till midnight. I can
make interesting observations about
your driving skills, and the children can
25 pass the time sticking each other with
sharp objects. It will be such fun.'
    The tragic thing is that because my
wife is English, and therefore beyond
the reach of reason where saltwater is
30 concerned, she really will think it's fun.
Frankly, I have never understood the
British attachment to the seaside.
    So when, last weekend, my wife
suggested that we take a drive to the
35 sea, I put my foot down and said,
'Never – absolutely not,' which is of
course why we ended up, three hours
later, at Kennebunk Beach in Maine.
    On arrival, our youngest – I'll call him
40 Jimmy in case he should one day
become a lawyer – surveyed the scene
and said, 'OK, Dad, here's the situation.
I need an ice cream, a Li-Lo, a deluxe
bucket and spade set, a hot dog, some
45 candy floss, an inflatable dinghy, scuba
equipment, my own water slide,

a cheese pizza with extra cheese and a
toilet.'
    'They don't have those things here,
50 Jimmy,' I chuckled.
    'I really need the toilet.'
    I reported this to my wife.
    'Then you'll have to take him to
Kennebunkport,' she said serenely from
55 beneath a preposterous sun hat.
    By the time we found a toilet, little
Jimmy didn't need to go any more, so
we returned to the beach. By the time
we got there, some hours later, I
60 discovered that everyone had gone off
for a swim, and there was only one half-
eaten sandwich left. I sat on a towel and
nibbled at the sandwich.
    'Oh look, Mummy,' said number two
65 daughter gaily when they emerged from
the surf a few minutes later. 'Daddy's
eating the sandwich the dog had.'
    'Tell me this isn't happening,' I began
to whimper.
70   'Don't worry, dear,' my wife said
soothingly, 'It was an Irish setter. They're
very clean.'
    I don't remember much after that. I
just had a little nap and woke to find
75 that Jimmy was burying me up to my
chest in sand – which was fine, except
that he had started at my head – and I
managed to get so sunburned that a
dermatologist invited me to a
80 convention in Cleveland the following
week as an exhibit.
    We lost the car keys for two hours,
the Irish setter came back and stole one
of the beach towels, then nipped me on
85 the hand for eating his sandwich and
number two daughter got tar in her
hair. It was a typical day at the seaside,
in other words.
    'Lovely,' said my wife. 'We must do
90 that again soon.'
    And the heartbreaking thing is she
really meant it.

Bill Bryson

Bill Bryson was born
in America but lived
for many years in
England. He's the
best-selling author of
many humorous
travel books.

Lexis   Work with a partner. The words and expressions in the box all come from the text in the previous section. Use them to complete the questions. You may need to change the grammar. Then ask and answer the questions with your partner.

> slap (line 3)   have a paddle (line 17)   put my foot down (line 35)
> inflatable dinghy (line 45)   had a nap (line 74)   dermatologist (line 79)
> nipped (line 84)   tar (line 86)

a) What would you use to remove ____ from the bottom of your feet?
b) What qualifications do you think are necessary to become a ____ ?
c) When was the last time you ____ in the sea?
d) Have you ever had to pump up a Li-Lo or an ____ ?
e) Has a dog ever ____ you on the leg?
f) When you were a kid, in what sort of situations would your teacher ____ and not allow you to do something?
g) Under what circumstances would you give somebody a ____ on the back?
h) Do you know anyone who always ____ after lunch?

Anecdote   Think of a family holiday you went on when you were a child. You are going to tell your partner about it. Choose from the list below the things you want to talk about. Think about what you are going to say and how you are going to say it.

☐ Where did you go?
☐ Who chose the holiday destination?
☐ Was it the first time you'd been there or had you been there before?
☐ Who went on this holiday with you?
☐ How did you get there?
☐ Was it a good place for a holiday?

☐ Where did you stay?
☐ How did you spend your time there?
☐ Did everybody have a good time or was there somebody who didn't enjoy the holiday very much?
☐ Have you been back to the same place since you were a child?

Close up

Reporting verbs   **1**   The following is a brief summary of the text on page 69. Put the lines of the summary in the correct order.

(   ) a)   me that I'd have to take him to Kennebunkport, miles away. On return I was hungry but lost my appetite when my daughter casually **mentioned**
(*1*) b)   Every year, about the same time, my wife would wake up and **announce**
(   ) c)   that I couldn't imagine anything worse, she always **reassured**
(   ) d)   me to go, and three hours later we arrived at the beach. Almost immediately, my son **insisted**
(   ) e)   driving all the way to the ocean. When I **explained**
(*2*) f)   that she had an idea. She'd **suggest**
(   ) g)   on going to the toilet. Too busy sunbathing, my wife calmly **informed**
(   ) h)   that, as we'd all had such a good time, we should do it again soon!
(   ) i)   that I was eating the sandwich the dog had had. The dog then bit me, we lost the car keys and I ended up with severe sunburn. So imagine the shock when my wife **suggested**
(   ) j)   me that we'd have a great time. This particular year, it didn't take her long to **persuade**

(Language reference p72)   **2**   All of the verbs highlighted in 1 are used to report messages. Divide them into list A and list B according to the headings. The first ones have been done for you.

A 'tell' verbs': where the hearer is usually the direct object	**B** 'say' verbs': where the hearer is not usually the direct object
… reassured me that …	… mentioned that …

3 Look at the eight dictionary entries and study the constructions that come after each verb. Add the verbs to list A or list B in 2 as appropriate.

(Collins Cobuild English Language Dictionary)

admit /əd'mɪt/ **admits, admitting, admitted** If you **admit** to someone that something bad, unpleasant or embarrassing is true, you agree, often reluctantly, that it is true. *I am willing to admit that I do make mistakes …*

advise /əd'vaɪz/ **advises, advising, advised** If you **advise** someone to do something, you tell them what you think they should do. *The minister advised him to leave as soon as possible …*

assure /ə'ʃʊə/ **assures, assuring, assured** If you **assure** someone that something is true or will happen, you tell them that it is definitely true or will definitely happen, often in order to make them less worried. *He hastened to assure me that there was nothing traumatic to report …*

claim /kleɪm/ **claims, claiming, claimed** If you say that someone **claims** to you that something is true, you mean they say that it is true but you are not sure whether or not they are telling the truth. *He claimed that it was all a conspiracy against him …*

complain /kəm'pleɪn/ **complains, complaining, complained** If you **complain** to someone about a situation, you say that you are not satisfied with it. *Miners have complained bitterly that the government did not fulfil their promises …*

confirm /kən'fɜːm/ **confirms, confirming, confirmed** If you **confirm** to someone something that has been stated or suggested, you say that it is true because you know about it. *The spokesman confirmed that the area was now in rebel hands …*

convince /kən'vɪns/ **convinces, convincing, convinced** If someone or something **convinces** you of something, they make you believe that it is true or that it exists. *The waste disposal industry is finding it difficult to convince the public that its operations are safe …*

declare /dɪ'kleə/ **declares, declaring, declared** If you **declare** to someone that something is true, you say that it is true in a firm deliberate way. *Speaking outside 10 Downing Street, she declared that she would fight on …*

4 You are going to read a newspaper report about a nineteen-year-old man called Christopher Townsend. Read the text and find out why he had to pay his mother £68.70.

WHERE'S MY CAR?

Son steals mum's car!

UNEMPLOYED TEENAGER, Christopher Townsend, had a strange way of showing concern when his mother went into hospital. He sold her car without her knowledge and used the money to splash out on an extravagant champagne holiday for himself and his girlfriend at a five-star hotel in Paris.

Townsend, 19, received £6,000 for the car when he took it to a garage near his home in Little Dibden, Wiltshire. Although the car was registered in his mother's name, he (1) **convinced / explained** people in the garage that she had gone abroad and had advised him to sell the car.

With the £6,000 in his pocket, he then phoned his girlfriend and (2) **told / announced** her that he had arranged a surprise for her birthday. When he (3) **informed / explained** to her that they were going to Paris the following weekend and that he'd booked a luxury suite in a five-star hotel, she asked him how he could afford it. He (4) **claimed / reassured** to her that he had inherited a sum of money from his grandfather who had died a few months previously.

This was not the only lie Townsend had told his girlfriend: in fact, he had told her a string of lies since they first met. He (5) **assured / declared** her that he was 21 and was working for his father.

The teenager appeared in court yesterday, charged with theft. His mother, Mrs Hawkin, (6) **admitted / told** to reporters that prosecuting him had been the hardest thing she'd ever done. She (7) **confirmed / assured** to them that her son had apologised, but that she still had no idea why he had done it.

The young con-man is now serving six months' community service and has been ordered to pay his mother £68.70, the total amount she has spent on public transport since she has been without her car.

(Based on an article in The Daily Mail)

5 Read the report again and choose the correct reporting verb in each case.

6 Work with a partner and change the grammar so that you can use the reporting verbs you didn't choose in 5.

For example: (1) *… he <u>explained to</u> people in the garage …*

7 Do you think Christopher was punished appropriately? Discuss with a partner.

Language reference: reporting verbs

When you use reporting verbs such as *advise* and *explain*, it's important to know if the hearer is the direct object.

1   With verbs like *tell* the hearer is the direct object.

Mrs Pattinson advised **him** / invited **them** / reminded **us**	to vote for her.
She convinced **us** / persuaded **me** / reassured **everyone**	that she was telling the truth.
He accused **me** of / informed **them** about / congratulated **her** on	giving up.

2   With verbs like *say* where the hearer is NOT the direct object.

Mrs Pattinson explained / announced / suggested	that we should vote for her.
She agreed / refused / proposed	to tell the truth.
He admitted / insisted on / denied	giving up.

If you want to mention the hearer with the following common reporting verbs,
admit, announce, complain, explain, mention, propose, say, suggest, you can use
to + hearer and then a *that* clause.
She complained **to the engineer** that her computer kept crashing.
He explained **to the class** that he would be away for a few days.
I suggested **to Don and Liz** that we all went on holiday together.

You will find a comprehensive listing of different reporting verb patterns on page 142.

I'll never forget you

Listening

'I couldn't stand him,' says
Angela Kenny.

1   Have you ever met anybody on holiday and then stayed in touch with them? Have you or anybody else you know ever had a holiday romance which has developed into a serious relationship?

2   [cassette] **37** Listen to Angela talking about her holiday romance and answer the following questions.

   a)   What was Angela doing when she met Brad?
   b)   Why did immigration officers hold Brad when he arrived in London?
   c)   What did Angela realise when she finally got to see Brad?
   d)   Who do you sympathise with most: Angela, Brad, or neither of them?

3   Listen again and complete the gaps.

   a)   I have **actually**. When I was twenty-six I went travelling to ____ .
   b)   **Come to think of it**, he did look a bit like Brad ____ .
   c)   **Anyway**, we met through a mutual ____ .
   d)   **In fact**, I really thought I'd met my ____ .
   e)   **Do you know what I mean?** Anything ordinary we did felt ____ .
   f)   Well, **eventually** I returned to ____ , and we spent six months on the phone.
   g)   Well, **basically**, it wasn't the best of ____ .
   h)   And **to be honest**, I don't think our relationship was ____ enough.
   i)   Well, **in the end** he was ____ back to Australia.

4   Match each of the words or expressions in **bold** in 3 with its meaning below.

   1   the final result was
   2   Are you following me?
   3   although this may surprise you
   4   I've just remembered this
   5   to be more precise
   6   Let's get back to the subject
   7   after a long time
   8   I really am telling the truth
   9   to put it simply

5 Gill's holiday romance was more successful. Read her story and put the appropriate expressions from 3 in the blanks.

Tony: You're not the type to have a holiday romance, are you, Gill?

Gill: (1) _____ , I am. In fact, I met my husband on holiday.

Tony: No!

Gill: Yes, it's true. I went on a camping holiday in Scandinavia with some university friends, and Ash came along at the last minute.

Tony: Camping in Scandinavia? Not exactly tropical …

Gill: No, (2) _____ , it was a bit cold at times.
(3) _____ , as soon as I saw him I thought, 'Yes, this one's for me.' (4) _____ .

Tony: Oh yes, I know what you mean.

Gill: But then I found out he had a girlfriend back home.

Tony: Oh no!

Gill: (5) _____ I had two weeks to impress him – so I used my best weapon: I put on my little black dress …

Tony: I thought you said it was cold …

Gill: Yes, it was, but, (6) _____ , I didn't notice the temperature. And anyway, it was worth it because it worked – he resisted for a few days, which felt like years! But (7) _____ he surrendered, and we spent the rest of the holiday together. (8) _____ , we were inseparable.

'We're happily married,' says Gill May.

Tony: What happened when you got home?

Gill: It was a horrible time because we knew we wanted to be together, but we both had other relationships to sort out.

Tony: That must have been difficult.

Gill: It was, but it all worked out well (9) _____ . I mean, it's our fifth wedding anniversary in June.

6 [cassette] **38** Listen to Gill's account and compare your version.

7 Work with a partner. Take it in turns to be Gill and practise the conversation, concentrating on getting the correct stress and intonation.

Weather lovely, …

a) Do you usually send postcards when you're on holiday?
b) Look at the five postcards below. Are they the kinds of postcard you would send?
c) Who would you send postcards to?

1 Read the article below and match the character types (*A–E*) to the postcards (*1–5*) on page 73. (The answers are at the end of the exercise.)

Every postcard tells a story

Did you know that the type of postcard you choose, together with the message you write, reveals more about you than the place you're describing? Flowery, long-winded
5   descriptions often come from the indecisive person who loves the sound of their own voice and is incapable of summarising. On the other hand, short, sharp phrases – often illegible – are probably the work of the
10 impatient, time-conscious no-nonsense-taker.
    But within these categories there are millions of variations. Not many people now would dare just to write, 'Weather lovely, wish you were here!'
15 Then there's the choice of card itself. Do you choose a saucy seaside ribtickler, or a tasteful panorama? Look at the examples on the previous page and see which categories fit you best.

20 **A** The culture vulture Sight-seeing is a way of life for the sender of this card. This traveller takes life – at home and away – rather seriously. A bookish sort of person who likes to be well-informed about the
25 places they visit. Can be a little humourless at times

B The joker This sort of card is bound to raise a smile, but it gives no idea at all of what the holiday is really like. The sender is
30 a happy-go-lucky sort of person, more interested in making the most of the short time they have than soaking up the local lifestyle and culture.

35 **C** The indecisive type This card combines lots of different postcards in one, with a view to pleasing everyone. The sender is thoughtful and caring, but through their desire to please everyone, they run the risk of
40 being unadventurous or even uninteresting.

D The arty type The sender of this tasteful scene is a style guru, even on holiday. Image-conscious and stylish (some may say snobbish), they will go out of their way to
45 find unusual postcards. This traveller does not want to be mistaken for one of the crowd.

E The totally tasteless type The irresistible tacky postcard is a genuine, unselfconscious choice. This holiday-maker
50 has a sunny, positive outlook and is happy to share it with friends back home.

Answers: A3, B4, C2, D5, E1

2 The words in **bold** in the sentences below are from the article in 1. Are the statements true or false?

a) A **long-winded** speech is long and interesting. (line 4)
b) A **time-conscious** person is concerned about how quickly time passes. (line 10)
c) A film described as a **ribtickler** is likely to be a comedy. (line 16)
d) A **bookish** person is somebody who reads a lot. (line 23)
e) Somebody who is **well-informed** is likely to have read a lot about the subject they're interested in. (line 24)
f) If you describe somebody as **humourless**, you think they're very funny. (line 25)
g) A **happy-go-lucky** person is somebody who worries about the future. (line 30)
h) A **thoughtful** person is caring and kind. (line 38)
i) Somebody who is **image-conscious** in not interested in the way they appear. (line 43)

3 Do you know anybody who fits any of the five character types described in 1? Tell your partner about them.

Journey from hell

Adjective building

1 The magazine article in the previous section spoke about people being *time-conscious* and *well-informed*. Match each of the words in the box with *well-____* or *____-conscious*.

read	safety	self	known	meaning	dressed	health

Write sentences to illustrate the meanings. Use your dictionary if necessary.

2 Match the prefixes in box A with the adjectives in box B to make the adjectives negative. Check your answers by finding the same negative adjectives in the article in the previous section.

A
un   in   ir   im   il

B
capable   legible   patient   decisive
adventurous   interesting   usual   resistible

3 Which prefixes from box A in 2 form negative versions of these three sets of adjectives?

Set 1	Set 2	Set 3
mature	legal	replaceable
polite	literate	relevant
probable	logical	responsible

4 Read the following story carefully. Complete the text by using prefixes or suffixes from the box to rewrite the adjectives in brackets. The first two have been done for you.

Prefixes: un ir dis	**Suffixes:** less ful ish

Never again!

I hate travelling. It's not that I'm **unwilling** (willing), it's just that I've got a problem. Three problems actually, and they're called Charlie, Ella and Jack. Ranging in age from eleven down
5 to three, they're **irresistible** (resistible) when they're asleep. But when they're awake they're (1) ____ (relent). Individually they're hard work; in twos they're a handful; all together, they're a nightmare. More often than not they're
10 (2) ____ (obedient) and seem to have endless competitions to see who can behave in the most (3) _____ (devil) way. On top of that, they all want my (4) ____ (divided) attention at the same time.
    Under these (5) ____ (stress) circumstances, you
15 may think that it would be foolish of me to even consider travelling alone with my children. Well, I know now that it wasn't just foolish, but downright (6) ____ (responsible).
    I wanted to visit my parents. My husband
20 couldn't come, so I set off on the five-hour train journey with a bagful of toys, a pocketful of sweets and a headful of songs, stories and games.

    But (7) ____ (regard) of my careful preparations, the journey was (8) ____ (hell): it
25 was one of the worst experiences of my life. The final straw was when I arrived, exhausted and (9) ____ (tear), at my parents' house. Instead of being sympathetic, they took great delight in telling me how awful I had been as a child.
30 Thanks, Mum and Dad, that was really (10) ____ (help)!

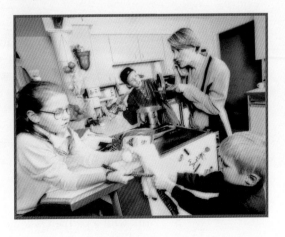

Insider's guide

1 Work with a partner and answer these questions.

a) Have you ever been to any of these cities?
   Buenos Aires, Dublin, Madrid, Sydney, Amsterdam, Prague

b) What do you know about them?

c) What are they known for?

2 In the questionnaire below, each answer is about a different city. Match the questions and answers with the correct city.

BUENOS AIRES   DUBLIN

SYDNEY   MADRID

AMSTERDAM

PRAGUE

1 *What's the weather like?*
There's a local saying: 'Nine months of winter and three months of hell.' But don't be fooled: this exhilarating city offers dazzling skies and more sun than anywhere else in Europe.

2 *What are the locals complaining about?*
Parking restrictions – it takes up to four years to get a parking permit if you live by one of the famous canals.

3 *What's the most popular drink to order?*
You can never go wrong with a well-poured pint of Guinness in one of the hundreds of welcoming pubs.

4 *What are people eating?*
In a city where the scrawny look is in, desserts are surprisingly popular – in particular, a strange substance called *dulce de leche*, a sickly sweet brown goo that is like some sort of caramel-cum-butterscotch-cum-coffee-cum-toffee spread. And don't forget, this city serves the best steaks in South America!

5 *What's the most outrageous stuff on television?*
The weather forecast. Yes, the late-night bulletin on TV Nova has an interesting new presentation angle. The weather girls or boys appear through a window stark-naked. Then the next day's temperature appears on the screen and the weather girl or boy dresses accordingly. And remember, it's often very hot in eastern Europe!

6 *What's the trendy thing to do at the weekend?*
Well, if you haven't got tickets for the opera ... in summer, go to the south coast where dazzling white beaches back on to state forest and national park, and ... in winter, go to the Blue Mountains for some excellent walks and crisp mountain air.

3 Work with a partner. Ask the questions in 2 about your partner's favourite town or city and discuss the answers.

The Travel Talk Game

Play the game in small groups. You will need a dice and counters.

1 Place your counters on the square marked DEPARTURES and throw the dice.
2 The first player to throw a six starts the game.
3 The first player throws the dice and moves their counter along the board according to the number on the dice.
4 Players then play in turns, moving around the board. When a player lands on a square they have to talk about the subject for thirty seconds. (For example: a player who lands on 9 has to talk for thirty seconds about a sea-side resort they know.)
5 If a player has nothing to say or can't talk for thirty seconds, they are allowed to pass and miss a turn.
6 If a player lands on a FREE SQUARE they don't have to do anything.
7 The game continues until the first player reaches the square marked ARRIVALS.

The board squares:

1 DEPARTURES
2 ... the qualities of an ideal travelling companion
3 ... the last time you went on a sightseeing tour
4 ... the worst holiday you've ever been on
5 ... the longest flight you've ever been on
6 ... the biggest tourist attraction in your country
7 ... the last postcard you sent - who to; where from
8 FREE SQUARE
9 ... a sea-side resort you know
10 ... the longest traffic jam you've ever been in
11 ... what you think about package holidays
12 ... where you would go for a romantic holiday
13 ... what you do to pass the time when you're travelling
14 ... the last souvenir you bought on holiday
15 FREE SQUARE
16 ... what you think about cruises
17 ... the furthest point north you've ever travelled to
18 ... something you never travel without
19 ... the thing you miss most about home when you travel
20 ... why your country is a good place for foreigners to visit
21 FREE SQUARE
22 ... what you think about hitchhiking
23 ... a place you've always wanted to go
24 ... your favourite means of transport
25 ... what you think about flying
26 ... what you think about activity holidays
27 ... the most important reasons for having a holiday
28 ... the furthest point south you've ever travelled to
29 ... the worst journey you've ever had
30 ... the most beautiful place you've ever seen
31 FREE SQUARE
32 ... your favourite city
33 ... a holiday romance
34 ... the most exciting holiday you've ever had
35 ARRIVALS

9 Attraction

The perfect face

Work in small groups and discuss these questions.

a) Who do you think is the most handsome man in the world?
b) Who do you think is the most beautiful woman in the world?
c) What makes them more attractive than other men and women?

In a survey, ten thousand British men and women were asked about what they thought represented perfect male and female faces. When the data was processed by computer, these were the results.

Lexis 1 Do these images represent your idea of the perfect male/female face?

2 Match the words in list A with the words in list B. (Sometimes more than one answer is possible.) Then choose one of the images, and use the phrases to describe the perfect male/female face to somebody who hadn't seen the pictures. What is it that makes the faces attractive?

A		B
a)	smooth	teeth
b)	perfect	eyes
c)	sparkling	bone structure
d)	full	in the cheeks
e)	a big	jaw
f)	a turned-up	lips
g)	good	nose
h)	high	skin
i)	a square	cheekbones
j)	dimples	smile

3 39 Five people were asked the question, 'What do you think makes a face attractive?' Listen to their answers and see if their opinions are the same as yours.

4 Use phrases from 2 to describe people that you know.

Reading **1** Read this article which describes research into the nature of beauty. Find out whether, according to the research, the following statements are true or false.

a) Beauty is 'in the eye of the beholder'.
b) Most film stars and supermodels don't have ideal features.
c) Most women prefer men with gentle features.
d) There is more pressure on men to be perfect than there is on women.
e) There are only subtle differences in what is considered to be beautiful by people from different cultures.

2 Work with a partner. Do you agree with the statements in 1?

Is there such a thing as the perfect face? Is beauty something you can measure?

Recent scientific evidence
5 suggests that the answer is 'yes'. A new science, the science of attraction, has come to the conclusion that beauty is objective and quantifiable and
10 not, as the romantics believe, in the eye of the beholder.

Julia Roberts

Is **beauty** in the eye of the beholder?

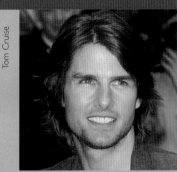
Tom Cruise

For more than a century it was thought that a beautiful face was appealing because it
15 was a collection of average features. Using his computer system, Dr David Perrett of the University of St Andrews has challenged the theory. In a key
20 experiment, photographs of women were ranked for their attractiveness by a number of volunteers. Two composite pictures were then created:
25 one, the average of all the pictures; the other made from those rated most attractive. Although the faces looked very similar at first glance, a
30 significant number said they preferred the composite of most attractive faces.

'The conclusion I reached,' said Dr Perrett, 'was that the
35 most attractive shape was not average. If you look at famous film stars and supermodels, most of them have ideal features – larger than normal
40 eyes, higher arched eyebrows, slightly smaller noses, cheekbones are a little more prominent. Even popular cartoon characters such as
45 Betty Boop, Yasmin from *Aladdin* and Bambi have big eyes, small turned-up noses, big mouths and small chins. And if these features are exaggerated,
50 the attractiveness rating goes up even more. Julia Roberts is a good example of this.'

But what do scientists make of men's faces? Do men with
55 large eyes, high cheekbones and a small chin have the same irresistible appeal? Researchers were a bit shocked at the top-ranking male face. They
60 expected it to have the classic square jaw and strong cheekbones, but instead, women seem to prefer men

with gentle faces. Although
65 there is more pressure on females to be perfect, research suggests that men and women look for many of the same things: for example, expressive
70 features such as arched eyebrows and a big smile were associated with attractiveness in men.

Dr David Perrett puts
75 forward an evolutionary reason to explain why so many women now swoon over baby-faced stars such as Leonardo DiCaprio and Tom
80 Cruise. Women like a man with a feminine face because he is more likely to have higher levels of the female hormone oestrogen and therefore to
85 make a kinder and more trustworthy husband and father.

But do these ideals of beauty manage to cross cultural
90 boundaries? For instance, in some cultures, lips discs, scars and tattoos are considered to be attractive. Professor Cunningham of the University
95 of Louisville, Kentucky, found that there were only very subtle differences between ethnic groups. For example, Asians tended to prefer faces
100 that were slightly less mature and slightly less expressive, whereas blacks preferred faces that were a little more plump. In other words, although there
105 might be a little truth in the old adage that beauty is in the eye of the beholder, by and large, we all seem to be attracted to the same things.

Jean Oldham, beauty editor
Rita Taylor, cosmetic surgeon
Michael Hirst, Christian journalist

Listening

1 Cosmetic surgery is becoming more and more commonplace. Do you think this is a good or a bad thing?

2 [40] You are going to hear a discussion about cosmetic surgery. Do you think these three people are likely to be for or against cosmetic surgery? Listen and find out.

3 Below are some of the points made in the discussion. Work with a partner. Try to remember who made each point. Then listen again and check.

   a) True beauty comes from being intelligent and interesting, not from being physically perfect.
   b) Cosmetic surgery can give people more confidence.
   c) There's nothing wrong with trying to improve on what nature has given us.
   d) People should be grateful for what God has given them.
   e) It is selfish and indulgent to spend money on superficial improvements when there is so much poverty and sickness in the world.
   f) Cosmetic surgery can be more beneficial than a holiday, because the effects last longer.
   g) We should accept ourselves as we are.
   h) Having cosmetic surgery is similar to having your hair dyed or your teeth straightened.
   i) It is good to see life experience showing on people's faces.
   j) People who feel good about the way they look are more likely to do well in their career.

4 Work with a partner. Which points in 3 do you agree with?

Close up

Passive report structures

1 Look at the following extracts from the article on page 79.

   For more than a century it was thought that a beautiful face was appealing …
   … in some cultures, lip discs, scars and tattoos are considered to be attractive.

   a) Who *thought* and who *considers* in the extracts above: *the writer of the article; Dr Perrett; people in general*?
   b) Write a rule about when it is usually good to use the passive.

2 Rearrange the words below to make the beginnings of eight sentences.

   a) reckoned   capital   city   Our   is
   b) said   English   is   food
   c) all   blondes   is   It   believed   wrongly   that
   d) that   It   eating   claimed   been   has   carrots
   e) thought   Diana   was   Princess
   f) men   is   often   It   that   suggested
   g) Politicians   regarded   not   are
   h) assumed   sometimes   that   women   is   It   unmarried

3 Match the beginnings of the sentences (*a–h*) in 2 with the endings of the sentences (*1–8*).

   1 as being very honest.
   2 are looking for a husband.
   3 to be almost a saint.
   4 to have the highest crime rate in the country.
   5 improves eyesight.
   6 to be boring.
   7 only think about one thing.
   8 are stupid.

   Do you agree with the completed statements? Discuss with a partner.

Have/Get something done

1 Read the following sentences and answer the questions about the woman in the cartoon.

1 Helen put her make-up on before her friend's birthday party.
2 Helen had her hair done before her friend's birthday party.

a) Who put Helen's make-up on?
b) Who did Helen's hair?
c) In which sentence can you replace the main verb with *got*?

What do you mean, the party's tomorrow?

Language reference p82

2 Complete the rule by choosing the correct ending.

You can use the structure *have something done* ...
a) when you do something for someone else.
b) when someone does something for you.
c) when you do something yourself.

3 Cindy Jackson talks about why she had several years of cosmetic surgery in her attempt to create the perfect face and body. Complete her account using *had, have* or *having*.

Surgery changed my life!

The features I wanted were the kind of feminine ideal that's embodied in plastic dolls like Barbie and Sindy. I wanted the wide eyes so I (1) _____ my eyes widened as much as I could. (2) _____ my eyes done made me see that I really could change my face, so I decided to (3) _____ everything done that I possibly could.

I wanted the pert, turned-up nose, so I (4) _____ my nose turned up. I wasn't happy with the first nose job – it only made it slightly smaller. So I (5) _____ it done again, and they took more bone out and made the nostrils smaller. Now my nose is as Barbie as it can get for my face and the rest of my features.

My chin bothered me a lot too, so I (6) _____ that moved back, so that it was in line with the upper lip. Then there were my lips – I thought they were too thin, so I tried (7) _____ collagen put in. But that wasn't good enough, so I (8) _____ fat taken from my thighs and injected into my lips. Then I (9) _____ implants put into my cheeks to give me high cheekbones.

Before I had surgery, I was invisible. I have a genius IQ, and it never got me anywhere. Now I get lots of attention. Pretty girls just do.

Cindy Jackson, cosmetic surgery adviser

(Based on an article in *The Sunday Times* and *Without Walls*, a Channel 4 documentary)

4 Do you think it's more important to be beautiful or intelligent?

5 Put the words in the following sentences in the correct order.

a) have my letters by I my secretary typed
b) on Sundays wash I my car
c) my hair get I cut every six weeks
d) at the weekend clean my house I
e) have my nails regularly I manicured

Rewrite the sentences so that they are true for you.
For example: *I type my own letters.* *I get my car washed at the local garage.*

6 How well do you know your town? Work in groups and discuss the following. Where is the best place to ...

a) have your hair cut?
b) get your hair dyed?
c) have your eyes tested?
d) get a tattoo done?
e) have your shoes repaired?
f) get your dry-cleaning done?
g) have a passport photo taken?
h) get your films developed?
i) have some photocopies done?
j) get a duplicate key made?

Language reference: passive structures

Passive report structures

These structures can be used to say what people in general feel or believe. You can find them in formal contexts such as scientific writing or in news reports.

| It | is
has been
was | said
believed that ...
thought |

It used to be said that beauty was in the eye of the beholder.

| He/She/It
They | is/was
are/were | said
believed to (+ infinitive) ...
thought |

But now beauty *is thought to be* objective and quantifiable.

Other verbs that can be used in this way include: *alleged, assumed, claimed, considered, expected, felt, reckoned, regarded, reported, rumoured, suggested.*

Have/Get something done

You can use this structure when someone does something for you – often because you have paid them to do it.

have/get + something (object) + past participle

I'll probably *have/get my car repaired* next week.
How many times has she *had/got her fortune told*?
You really should *have/get your eyes tested*.

Note: *Get* is a little less formal than *have*.

Speed dating

Reading

1 Work in small groups. Discuss the following questions.

  a) What is the minimum length of time you need to spend with somebody to know whether you are attracted to them?
  b) What can you say about somebody from the clothes they wear and the way they talk?
  c) What would turn you off somebody immediately?
  d) If you could ask just three questions to find out whether somebody is your type of person, what would your questions be?
  e) Have you ever spent a whole evening on a date with somebody you didn't like?
  f) What do you think speed dating is?

2 Read the article about a speed dating session and complete the tables. Then answer the questions below.

	Best date	Worst date		Best date	Worst date
Craig			Karen		
Kevin			Lara		
Adam			Sindy		
Jim			Erica		
Tony			Claire		

  a) Who were the most and least popular men?
  b) Who were the most and least popular women?
  c) Which two men had the same taste in women?
  d) Which couple fell for each other?

3 Would you ever try speed dating? Discuss with a partner.

(Adapted from an article in *The Mirror*)

Your dream partner ... in five minutes!

The idea is simple – why devote a whole evening
to one blind date when you can meet five
potential mates in less than half an hour? Five
men and five women are introduced by a master
5   of ceremonies or chaperone. Each 'couple' is
given five minutes to get to know each other
before moving on to the next candidate. At the
end of the session, if the attraction is mutual,
they can walk off together into the sunset (or at
10 least swap telephone numbers).

We went along to a Speed dating night where
these five women and five men had signed up for
the event, all hoping to meet their dream-partner,
safe in the knowledge that if they hate each other
15 on sight, the suffering will last only five minutes
or three hundred excruciating seconds.

Craig, 21: a student

IDEAL DATE: I'm looking for someone
who makes me laugh and someone I
20 can learn something from. She has to
be a brunette though.
BEST DATE: Claire – she's a brunette with a great
personality. She made me laugh, and I'd like to see
her again.
25 **WORST DATE**: Erica – ugh! Awful manners and jokes.
She is very absorbed with herself: totally self-centred.

Kevin, 31: a telecom salesman

IDEAL DATE: I've had a few serious
relationships, but at the end of the
30 day, nothing materialised. My ideal
date is a lively, pretty girl who is amusing and good
to talk to.
BEST DATE: Sindy – bubbly and lively. I'd definitely like
to see her again.
35 **WORST DATE**: Lara – didn't seem to be on the same
planet as the rest of us. Too spaced out for me.

Adam, 21: a party planner

IDEAL DATE: I broke up with my
girlfriend of a year three months ago
40 so now I'm after someone who is a
good laugh but who you can get on a deeper level
with.
BEST DATE: Karen – stayed very enigmatic, which I
liked. Very attractive. I'd like to see her again.
45 **WORST DATE**: Erica – a bit dizzy. I prefer somebody a
bit more down-to-earth.

Jim, 25: a computer consultant

IDEAL DATE: I didn't come into this
thinking I was going to meet the ideal
50 girl. I just wanted a bit of a laugh. I
wouldn't use this technique to find my future
girlfriend.

BEST DATE: Sindy – sensible and fun. The sort of
woman I'd take home to meet my parents
55 **WORST DATE**: Claire rather stand-offish and just not
interested. She didn't ask any questions about me,
and the five minutes went by very slowly.

Tony, 23: a journalist

IDEAL DATE: I rarely pull when I'm out
60 and about unless I know the girl first,
as I'm quite shy. I'd like to meet
someone who's good fun and easy to chat to.
BEST DATE: Sindy – lovely girl, a superb laugh. I felt
really comfortable with her. I'd definitely like to see
65 her again. Name the date.
WORST DATE: Lara – rambled on too much about her
home town in Ireland. A relief when the five minutes
were up.

Karen, 26: a student
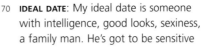

70 **IDEAL DATE**: My ideal date is someone
with intelligence, good looks, sexiness,
a family man. He's got to be sensitive
and trustworthy. In other words, I'm looking for the
ideal man!!
75 **BEST DATE**: Craig – really cute, young, friendly and
good-looking.
WORST DATE: Tony – harmless, but slightly boring and
much too quiet.

Lara, 23: a piano tutor

80 **IDEAL DATE**: I like people who are
open-minded and different.
BEST DATE: Adam – I found him
charming, young and really sexy.
WORST DATE: Jim – he was polite, but a bit too straight
85 for me.

Sindy, 23: a florist

IDEAL DATE: My ideal man is someone
interesting, amusing and full of life. I
love being outgoing and friendly, so
90 this was the perfect dating game for me.
BEST DATE: Tony – wonderful, interesting and fun.
WORST DATE: Adam – a very cool bloke but not
someone I'd date. Too young.

Erica, 22: an actress and singer

95 **IDEAL DATE**: I like tall mature men who
are quite a lot older than me.
BEST DATE: Adam – a bit young, but by
far the coolest and most laid-back.
WORST DATE: Kevin – laddish and unambitious.

100 ### Claire, 25: an editorial assistant

IDEAL DATE: I always manage to go out
with very intense men who get very
obsessive even though I'm just looking
for fun.
105 **BEST DATE**: Adam – sexy, exotic: a really pretty boy. Yes!
WORST DATE: Tony – sweet but not very inspiring. A bit
drippy.

Lexis

1 Decide if these words usually have positive or negative meanings. Check your answers in the article.

a) self-centred (line 26)
b) enigmatic (line 43)
c) down-to-earth (line 46)
d) sensible (line 53)
e) stand-offish (line 55)
f) sensitive (line 72)
g) trustworthy (line 73)
h) open-minded (line 81)
i) straight (line 84)
j) mature (line 95)
k) laid-back (line 98)

2 Choose words from the list in 1 which best replace the words in **bold** in these sentences.

a) My ideal partner would have to be someone **caring**, good-looking and **dependable**.
b) I think I'm quite a **level-headed** sort of person. I haven't done anything crazy yet …!
c) I'd say I feel **relaxed** about work – I never let things worry me.
d) People think I'm **unfriendly**, but actually, I'm just really shy.
e) My parents are extremely **conventional**. I wish they were more **tolerant**.
f) I prefer to go out with people older than me. You can have more interesting conversations with somebody who's **experienced and grown-up**.
g) I know somebody who likes to think she's **mysterious**. In fact, she's very boring.
h) My friend's very wealthy, but you'd never know it because he's so **unpretentious**.
i) I've got a friend who's rather **selfish** – probably because her parents spoilt her when she was a child.

3 Can you identify with any of the sentences in 2? Discuss with a partner.

Word building

1 You can turn certain adjectives into nouns by adding the suffixes: *ity* and *ness*. Add suffixes and make any necessary changes to turn the adjectives in the box into nouns.

For example: *sensitive* ➔ *sensitivity*   *happy* ➔ *happiness*

| flexible   lively   friendly   compatible   sad   generous   weak   mature   sexy |

2 Compound adjectives are made of two parts and are usually joined by a hyphen. Join words from box A to words from box B to make synonyms for the adjectives in box C. The first one has been done for you.

| **A**   absent-   big-   easy-   quick-   self-   stuck-   two-   warm- |
| **B**   assured   faced   going   headed   hearted   minded   up   witted |
| **C**   a) forgetful *absent-minded*   b) hypocritical   c) confident   d) arrogant   e) kind   f) snobbish   g) intelligent   h) relaxed |

3 Work with a partner. Describe members of your family or close friends using words from 1 and 2. See if your partner would like to meet them!

Word stress

1 🔊 41 Mark the stress on each of the adjectives in the box. Then listen and check.

| sensitive   happy   flexible   lively   friendly   compatible   sad
generous   weak   mature   sexy |

2 🔊 42 Mark the stress on each of the nouns in the box. Then listen and check.

| sensitivity   happiness   flexibility   liveliness   friendliness   compatibility
sadness   generosity   weakness   maturity   sexiness |

3 What is the effect on the word stress when you change an adjective into a noun by adding the suffix *ity*? What is the effect on the word stress when you change an adjective into a noun by adding the suffix *ness*?

Blind Date

Listening

1 Read about *Blind Date*. Have you ever seen or heard of a television programme like this? Do you have a programme like this in your country? What do you think of it?

James

2 You're going to listen to James choosing his date on *Blind Date*. Look at the photo. What sort of person do you think he is? What sort of person do you think his ideal date would be?

Blind Date

Blind Date, hosted by Cilla Black, has been running on British TV since 1985. In the programme, a man and a woman take it in turns to choose their date from three members of the opposite sex who are hidden behind a screen. Each player asks three questions to the three hidden contestants and then has to choose one of the contestants on the basis of their answers. The following week the players and the successful contestants are invited back to the programme to talk about their dates together.

3 Here are the three questions James asked the three contestants. (Note that the three contestants are not the three women in the picture at the top of the page.) Before you listen to the three women answering the questions, decide what answers you would give. Discuss your answers with a partner.

a) They say that the way to a man's heart is through his stomach, and I must say, I do like my food. If you were to cook me a meal, how would you impress me?

b) I've got two pet frogs which my friends say are like me – a good set of legs, like a drink and come alive in the evening. Imagine you had a pet that reflected your personality, what would it be?

c) I'm a very superstitious sort of person and I believe that wishes can come true. If one of your wishes were to come true, what would it be?

4 🔲 43 Listen to the answers. Try to visualise what the three women look like as you listen to them answering the questions. Compare your ideas with a partner.

5 Work with a partner. Discuss these questions.

a) Who do you think gave the best answers? (Number 1, Number 2, or Number 3?)
b) Which one do you think he'll pick? Why?

Turn to page 137 to see which one he chose.

6 🔲 44 A week later, James and the woman he chose were invited back to the programme to talk about their date together. Listen and find out how they got on.

a) Does he want to go out with her again?
b) Does she want to go out with him again?

7 Listen again and tick the information that is correct about James and Melanie.

Melanie thought that James …
a) was tall, dark and handsome.
b) had eyebrows like caterpillars.
c) wasn't interested in getting to know her.
d) was a nice person to kiss.

James thought that Melanie …
a) was a total flirt.
b) fancied him a lot.
c) was ugly.
d) was very slim.

8 Work in groups of three. Make up answers to the following *Blind Date* questions. Compare your answers with other members of the class. Choose the best answers for each question.

a) Imagine you were shipwrecked on a desert island. What one thing would you want to have with you apart from me?
b) I like to think I can learn something from the person I have a relationship with. Supposing we went out together, what could you teach me?
c) If you were to have a film made of your life, which actor would you choose to play the part of you and why?

Close up

Unreal conditional clauses

1 Complete the questions with *be, were* and *would*.

a) If you ____ going out on your first date this evening, how would you ____ feeling now?
b) Just imagine somebody turned up for a first date with their best friend, what ____ you say?
c) Supposing you could go out with anyone in the world, who ____ it be?
d) Assuming money ____ no object, what would be your ideal evening out?
e) What ____ you think of somebody if they ____ to introduce you to their family on your second date?
f) Assuming your first date went well, how long ____ you wait before phoning somebody again?
g) Supposing somebody ____ late for your date, how long ____ you wait?
h) Suppose you ____ to discover that you had nothing in common with your first date, what ____ you say at the end of the evening?

2 Look again at the questions in 1 and underline the different expressions we can use instead of *if*.

3 Work with a partner. Ask each other the questions in 1. How similar are your attitudes towards dating?

Language reference: unreal conditional clauses – alternatives to *if*

You usually begin an unreal conditional clause with *if*, but when you are making questions, there are various other alternatives.

Conditional clause			Main clause				
If		past simple					
Imagine (that)		past continuous			*would*		infinitive
Supposing (that)	subject	*were to* + infinitive	(question word)	*could*	subject	*be* + present participle	?
Suppose (that)		*might*			*might*		*have* + past participle
Assuming (that)		past perfect					

Imagine you **were meeting** someone for the first time, how **would** you **introduce** yourself?
Suppose you **didn't enjoy** the first date, **would** you still **go** on a second date?
Assuming that you **were to go** on another date, where **might** you **be planning** to meet?
Supposing that neither of the dates **had been** successful, what **might** you **tell** the person?

Never Ever

Song **1** ▭ 45 Complete the first part of *Never Ever* by All Saints. Then listen and check your answers.

A (1) ____ questions that I need to know.
How you could ever (2) ____me so?
I need to know what I've (3) ____ wrong,
And how (4) ____ it's been going on.

Was it that I never (5) ____ enough attention?
Or did I not (6) ____ enough affection?
Not only will your answers (7) ____ me sane,
But I'll know never to (8) ____ the same mistake again.

You can tell me (9) ____ my face,
Or even (10) ____ the phone.
You can write it (11) ____ a letter.
Either way I (12) ____ to know.

Did I never treat you (13) ____?
Did I always (14) ____ the fight?
Either way I'm going (15) ____ of my mind.
All the (16) ____ to my questions I have to find.

All Saints

*Never Ever was
Melanie Blatt,
Shaznay Lewis and
Natalie and Nicole
Appleton's first
number one single.*

2 Discuss these questions with a partner.

a) How does the person in the song feel?
b) Who is she talking to?
c) What has happened?
d) What does she want to happen?

3 ▭ 46 Here are lines taken from the rest of the song. Choose words from the box to complete the sentences. Compare with a partner. Then listen and check your answers. The tapescript is on page 154.

right	hole	feeling	wrong	pain	know	daze	mind

a) Boy, I'm in a ____ .
b) Find peace of ____ .
c) I'm sure I ain't done nothing ____ .
d) When you gonna take me out of this black ____ ?
e) The way I'm feeling, yeah, it just don't feel ____ .
f) Need to be free from ____ .
h) I really need to ____ .
g) I heard that this ____ won't last that long.

4 Work with a partner. Imagine the man's side of the story. Think about the following questions.

a) What happened last time they were together?
b) What does he think she did wrong?
c) How is he feeling now?
d) Does he want the relationship to continue?

Write the conversation between the man and the woman the next time they meet. Act out your conversation in front of the class.

10 *Genius*

The genius of the Guggenheim

Reading

1 Look at the pictures of the Guggenheim Museum in Bilbao. Which of the words in the box could you use to describe the museum?

> metallic   19th century   post-modern   hideous
> space-age   shiny   tough   sprawling   semi-derelict
> eccentric   important   run-down   contemporary

2 Read the article opposite. Which of the words in the box in 1 are used to describe the following places.

a) The Guggenheim Museum (*mark the words with a tick:* ✓)
b) The city of Bilbao (*mark the words with a cross:* ✗)
c) The area around the museum (*underline the words*)

3 Read the article again and explain the connections between:

a) Thomas Krens + jogging
b) The Guggenheim Museum + urban sprawl
c) Bilbao + the Bay of Biscay
d) The Basque government + Bilbao's global reputation
e) The city council + a wine-bottling warehouse
f) Thomas Krens + the Pompidou Centre and the Sydney Opera House
g) Frank Gehry + the waterfront site

Where to go to see a *masterpiece*

(Based on an article in *Observer Life*)

If Thomas Krens, the newly appointed director of the Solomon R. Guggenheim Foundation, had not gone jogging one April evening in 1991, his brainchild, the Bilbao Guggenheim – a metallic, post-modern, space-age museum – would almost certainly never have been built.

From the moment you leave the airport and wind through the green hills of northern Spain towards the ochre-brown 19th century city of Bilbao, the Guggenheim Museum can be glimpsed in the distance, like a shiny, modern toy surrounded by hideous urban sprawl.

What on earth possessed the Guggenheim Museum to come to a place like Bilbao? The story goes something like this.

Bilbao is Spain's fourth largest city: a tough, sprawling, former shipbuilding community that faces out onto the Bay of Biscay. In the 1980s, the Basque regional government began a redevelopment programme for the city. They commissioned the best and the brightest in the international architectural world to design a new subway system, a new airport terminal, a new congress and music hall, and a new railway station. But, in order to cement the city's growing global reputation, they wanted an art museum.

In 1991 Basque officials approached the Guggenheim Foundation and met Thomas Krens, the fourth director in the museum's 60-year history. Krens was eager to establish a European base for the Guggenheim and with this ambition in mind, he came to Bilbao.

But there was a problem. Krens could see at once that the site chosen by the city council for its new art museum, a former wine-bottling warehouse in the centre of town, was a non-starter. Krens had two models in his head – the Pompidou Centre and the Sydney Opera House. Both buildings had demanded an extraordinary amount of space, and Bilbao, an over-crowded riverside city did not seem to have the space.

Then, by chance, Krens found the ideal site. An athletic man, he went out running one evening. His route took him past the Jesuit University overlooking the river Nervion, and it was here that he noticed, at one of the many curves of the river, a semi-derelict waterfront zone which was perfect for what he wanted to achieve.

The site was approved in a week, and Californian architect Frank Gehry was chosen to realise the project.

Gehry immediately fell in love with the eccentric Basque city and the place Krens had found for him on which to build the most important building of the century.

He says now, with affectionate laughter, 'What is it? A dirty river and a bunch of run-down buildings.' Yet he revelled in the chaos and dirt of the post-industrial environment, and was determined not to change anything about the waterfront site.

The Bilbao Guggenheim dominates the city at every turn. It is a contemporary art museum like no other, and a building that must rank as one of the eight wonders of the modern world. It's well worth the visit – and there are some interesting works of art inside too.

---

4 Complete these sentences from the text using words and phrases in the box.

> dominates   green hills   overcrowded   redevelopment programme
> overlooking   well worth   run-down   subway

a) The city of Bilbao is set in the ____ of Northern Spain.
b) The image of the city has improved recently, because the local government is investing in a ____ .
c) A recent addition to the public transport of the city is a new ____ system.
d) The city centre is noisy and ____ .
e) There are some beautiful buildings ____ the river.
f) On the outskirts of the city there are a lot of ____ areas.
g) The Guggenheim Museum ____ the city.
h) It's a fascinating city and ____ the visit.

Anecdote

Think about the most impressive building or monument you've ever seen. You are going to tell your partner about it. Choose from the list below the things you want to talk about. Think about what you will say and what language you will need.

☐ Which city and which country is it in?
☐ When did you first see it?
☐ What is it called?
☐ Why was it built originally?
☐ What is used for?

☐ Is it modern or old?
☐ Do you know who designed it?
☐ What do you most like about it?
☐ How does it affect the environment?
☐ Is it a popular tourist attraction?

LANGUAGE TOOLBOX

on the south coast of …

on the River Danube / on Lake Como

in the Ruhr valley

set in / surrounded by rolling hills / farmland / forest / mountains

a 19th century / medieval / modern building

a stone / brick / glass building

Genius UNIT 10 **89**

I know what I like!

1 Work in small groups. Discuss your answers to the following questions. Use words from the box if necessary.

a) What's your favourite style of art?
b) What styles of art don't you like?
c) When was the last time you went to an art gallery?
d) What have you got on your walls at home?
e) If you could afford it, what kind of art would you have in your home?
f) Which is your favourite famous work of art?

LANGUAGE TOOLBOX

look + adjective: She doesn't look very happy.

look like + noun: She looks like a man.

look as if / as though + verb phrase: It looks as if they've just got married. / They look as if they've just got married.

2 How would you describe these three paintings by the Mexican artist, Frida Kahlo? Work with a partner and discuss what you think might be the story behind each picture.

Frida and Diego Rivera, 1931 (left)

Self-portrait with cropped hair, 1940 (right)

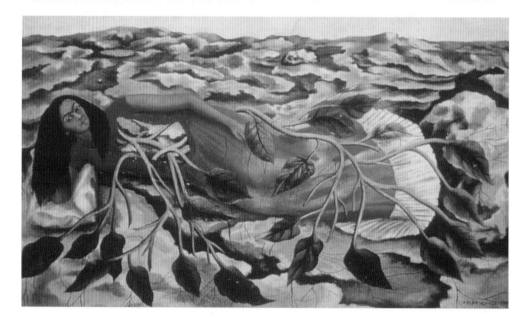

Roots, 1943

3 Test your memory! Work with a partner. Look at the three paintings for thirty seconds and try to memorise as many details as possible. Then turn to page 137 and answer as many questions as you can.

4 Read the following summary of Frida Kahlo's life story and discuss any aspects of her life that you can see depicted in the three paintings in 2.

Frida KAHLO

FRIDA KAHLO was born in Coyoacán, Mexico in 1907. However, she claimed her birthdate as 1910, the year of the Mexican Revolution, saying that she and modern Mexico had been born together.

5   When she was six years old she contracted polio and spent nine months confined to her room. As a result, her right leg was very thin and made her walk in a strange way. When she returned to school, the children teased her. From then on, she 10 always concealed her right leg.

    When she was eighteen, she was seriously injured in an accident between a streetcar and a bus: a metal handrail pierced her body. Over the years she underwent thirty-two major operations 15 and suffered enormous pain for the rest of her life.

    She was her father's favourite daughter, and he called her his dove.

    She married a famous muralist, Diego Rivera, when she was twenty. He was forty-two and had 20 been married twice before.

    She told a journalist, 'When I was seventeen (subtracting three years from her age) Diego began to fall in love with me. My father didn't like him because he was a communist and because they 25 said it was like an elephant marrying a dove.'

    They had a stormy relationship. Her husband was often unfaithful and even had an affair with Cristina, Frida's younger sister. Frida also had extramarital affairs, including 30 one with Leon Trotsky when the Russian leader was exiled from the Soviet Union.

    In January 1939 she travelled to Paris where she met Picasso. The Louvre purchased one of her self-portraits.

35   In April, on her return to Mexico, Frida and Diego began divorce proceedings. Frida was devastated and for a while stopped wearing the traditional Mexican dresses that Diego loved so much. Ironically, she painted some of her most 40 powerful works during her separation from Diego. The couple remarried in December 1940.

    In 1946 she had surgery on her spine, and in 1953 her right leg was amputated below the knee.

    Frida was never able to have children.

45   She said, 'My painting carries within it the message of pain.' And when asked why she painted herself so often, 50 she replied 'Because I am all alone.'

    She died in July 1954, 55 barely two weeks after taking part in a communist demonstration.

5   📼 47 Listen to three people discussing the paintings. How did their interpretations of the paintings compare with yours?

Collocation

1 Complete these sentences about Frida Kahlo's tragic history of ill-health.

a) When she was six years old she contracted **polio / an accident**.
b) She spent nine months confined to **travelling / her room**.
c) When she was eighteen she was **heavily / seriously** injured in an accident.
d) Over the years she **underwent / tolerated** thirty-two major operations.
e) In 1946 she had **illness / surgery** on her spine.

2 Replace the words in **bold** with words from the box to make five new sentences.

badly   an unknown virus   survived   laser treatment   a wheelchair

a) He/She contracted **a tropical disease**.   d) He/She **had** a major operation.
b) He/She was confined to **his/her bed**.   e) He/She had **an operation** on his/her spine.
c) He/She was **slightly** injured.

3 Work with a partner. Can you name any other famous people who have suffered from serious health problems?

For example: *Christopher Reeve (the actor who played Superman)* **was seriously injured** *in a horse riding accident several years ago and* **has been confined to a wheelchair** *ever since.*

Close up

Modals of deduction

1 📼 48 Listen to the conversation. Which of the pictures on the left are the people talking about?

2 Listen again and complete the phrases below.

a) It ____ be a fairly modern picture.
b) It ____ be a Picasso.
c) He ____ be in a prison.
d) I think he ____ be crying.
e) He ____ be much of a painter.
f) He ____ have been in a bit of a hurry.

3 In which of the sentences above is the speaker …

a) sure about what he is saying?
b) not sure about what he is saying?
c) talking about the past?

4 Work with a partner. Student A use the ideas below to make sentences about one of the pictures. Student B guess which picture is being described. Then change roles.

He She It	can't could may might must	be a man / woman. be a religious picture. be from the 17th/18th/19th/20th century. be thinking about the past. be feeling lonely. have drunk too much. have seen something frightening. have been running away from someone.

5 Turn to page 137 and look at the paintings from which these details were taken. Tell a partner which one you like best.

6 Using *must* and *can't* to say you're sure about something is very common in spoken English. Work with a partner. Complete these comments with either *must* or *can't*. Speculate on a possible context for each comment.

a) What? On my salary? You ____ be joking!
b) With four young children to look after, I realise that it ____ be easy for you.
c) Hi, you ____ be Jane. Please follow me.
d) Cheer up! It ____ be as bad as all that!
e) They ____ have seen me. Otherwise they'd have stopped and said hello.
f) Sorry. What was that? I ____ have been day-dreaming.
g) Fabulous concert. There ____ have been over a thousand people there!

Word linking

1 📼 49 Listen to the conversation and mark the stresses in the verb phrases which are in **bold**. Complete the last line of the conversation.

Ann: Well, I **must have had** them when I came in.
Bill: That's right. So they **can't have gone** very far.
Ann: Oh, Bill, I **can't have lost** them, can I?
Bill: No, they **must have fallen** on the floor near where we were sitting.
Ann: Oh, I can't see them anywhere.
Bill: Well, someone **must have picked** them up.

Ann: They **can't have been stolen**, can they?
Bill: No, they **must have been handed in** at the lost property office.
Ann: Oh, … look … here they are! Under the seat.
Bill: Huh, you **can't have been looking** very carefully!
Ann: Sorry. I can't ____ a thing without my ____ !

2 Work with a partner and practise the conversation, concentrating on linking together *can't + have (+ been)* and *must + have (+ been)*.

3 Imagine you've lost something important. With your partner make up and perform a short conversation in which you speculate about what has happened.

Language reference: modals of deduction

When we want to speculate or make deductions about a particular situation, we can use the following modal verbs:

- *must, can't* when we are 99% sure about something.
- *may (not), might (not), could* when we think something is possible.

These modal verbs can be followed by present and past infinitives.

Present: *It can't **be** as bad as all that!*

*I think he might **be working** late today.*

Past: *Diego may **have found out** about Frida's affair.*

*Sorry, I must **have been daydreaming**.*

Eureka

1 Work in small groups. The pictures show products that have been invented over the last five hundred years. Discuss in what order you think they were invented, and guess a date for each one.

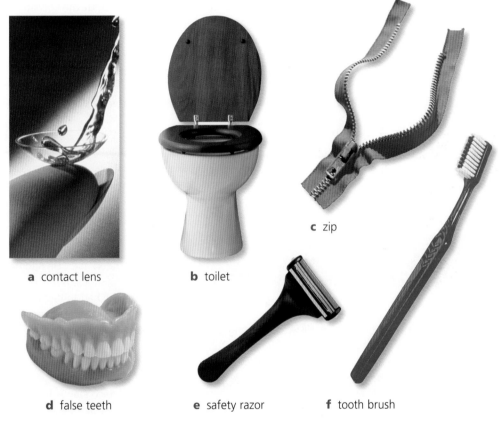

a contact lens **b** toilet **c** zip

d false teeth **e** safety razor **f** tooth brush

Turn to page 139 to check your answers.

2 Decide how you would order the inventions in 1 according to the following criteria.

- The most/least important for society
- The most/least important for you personally
- The most/least likely to be changed or replaced by future technology

3 Look at the following suggestions for new inventions. Which ones do you think would make your life easier?

- A vacuum cleaner that can be programmed to talk about any sport.
- Flowers and chocolates that automatically deliver themselves on any occasion with a suitable personalised message.
- A pill that you can take which makes chocolate and ice cream non-fattening.
- Cars with an automatic self-parking device.

Listening **1** ▶ 50 Listen to an interview with Trevor Baylis about his invention, the clockwork radio. Put these questions in the order in which they are asked.

a) How many radios are produced each month?
b) How easy was it to find a backer and set up production?
c) What advice would you give to somebody who had a good idea?
d) What gave you the idea for the clockwork radio?
e) In what ways has the clockwork radio changed your life?
f) How long did it take you to design a prototype?
g) How long was it then before the production of them started?

Trevor Baylis

Trevor Baylis' passion is inventing – especially products that might help the physically handicapped. In 1993 he invented the clockwork radio.

2 Match Trevor Baylis' responses (1–7) to the questions (a–g) in 1.

1 'Don't go down the pub and tell everyone about it.'
2 '... it would have taken me two or three months, I guess ...'
3 '... I'm sure they must be doing 200,000 a month.'
4 '... I was actually watching a programme about the spread of AIDS in Africa ...'
5 'Well, the important thing was funding.'
6 '... I do get involved with lots more television and radio.'
7 '... I was given a chance through the BBC World Service to meet up with the guys from the BBC *Tomorrow's World* programme ...'

3 Listen to the interview again and check your answers.

4 Complete this summary of Trevor Baylis' story using the words in the box. Compare with a partner.

> dream money backer lifestyle Baygen prototype concept spread
> invention filed

Dream Invention

One evening in 1993, Trevor Baylis was watching a programme on television about the AIDS epidemic in Africa. The programme explained that the only way to stop the (1) ____ of AIDS was to educate people about the disease. However, broadcasting the information was extremely difficult. Most people didn't have a radio as there was no electricity, and batteries were too expensive. At this point Trevor Baylis dozed off and had a (2) ____ . In the dream he imagined that he was Colonel Baylis out in the jungle listening to some music on an old gramophone. When he woke up, he had dreamt up the (3) ____ of the clockwork radio.

It took him just two to three months to get a (4) ____ off the ground and decide that his idea could really work. He (5) ____ a patent, and then the problems began. By April of the following year he was a very frustrated man. He had been trying to find a (6) ____ for his idea, but every British company he had contacted had turned him down. However, his unexpected TV appearance on the BBC programme, *Tomorrow's World*, changed everything. Trevor Baylis was approached by a South African businessman, and soon (7) ____ was found to set up a company with a factory based in Cape Town. The company was called (8) ____ , which stands for Baylis Generators. Today 200,000 radios are made in Africa each month, with demand outstripping supply.

His invention has made Trevor Baylis a wealthy man, but he says his (9) ____ hasn't changed. He gets most satisfaction from the fact that Baygen products are helping the needy.

According to Trevor Baylis, you do not need to be a genius to be an inventor. He believes there is an (10) ____ in all of us, and his main aim now is to establish an Academy of Inventors. His advice to anybody who has a good idea – keep the idea to yourself until you've filed a patent, and never give up.

5 What do you think of the clockwork radio? Had you ever heard of it before? What would you say was the most useful product to have been invented in the past twenty years.

Word families   Trevor Baylis is an *inventor*. His *invention*, the clockwork radio, was an *inventive* solution to a difficult problem of electricity supply in remote African villages.

1   Complete columns one, two and three with the correct word, using a dictionary if necessary.

1 Noun (study)	2 Noun (person)	3 Adjective +	example collocations
a) science			research, advances
b)		technological	advances, research
c)	mathematician		equations, research
d)		chemical	reactions, weapons, engineering
e)	physicist		health
f)		genetic	engineering
g) biology			weapons
h)		economic	growth, research

2   Work with a partner. Underline the stresses in the words in the first three columns in 1.

3   Complete these sentences taken from newspaper reports using collocations from 1.

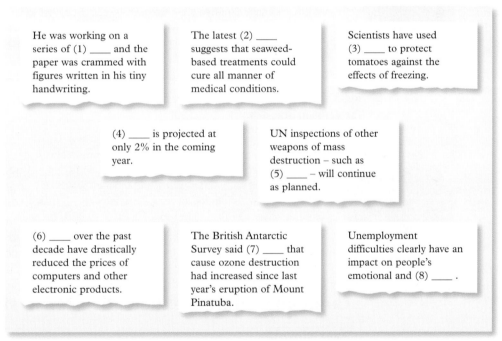

He was working on a series of (1) _____ and the paper was crammed with figures written in his tiny handwriting.

The latest (2) _____ suggests that seaweed-based treatments could cure all manner of medical conditions.

Scientists have used (3) _____ to protect tomatoes against the effects of freezing.

(4) _____ is projected at only 2% in the coming year.

UN inspections of other weapons of mass destruction – such as (5) _____ – will continue as planned.

(6) _____ over the past decade have drastically reduced the prices of computers and other electronic products.

The British Antarctic Survey said (7) _____ that cause ozone destruction had increased since last year's eruption of Mount Pinatuba.

Unemployment difficulties clearly have an impact on people's emotional and (8) _____ .

(Adapted from Cobuild English Collocations)

Close up

Narrative tense structures

1   Look at the following sentences which briefly summarise where the idea for the clockwork radio came from. Name the tenses used.

One evening in 1993, Trevor Baylis (1) **was watching** a programme on television. He (2) **dozed off** and (3) **had** a strange dream. When he (4) **woke up**, he (5) **had dreamt up** the concept of the clockwork radio.

Language reference p96

2   Which tense structures are used …

a)   to show a simple past event?
b)   to show a background activity in progress?
c)   to show clearly that one past event happened before another past event?

3 Read about the invention of the Post-it note. Complete the text with time expressions from the box.

> a few months previously   One Sunday   In 1977   The following day
> Each Sunday

(1) _____ , Art Fry was a product designer with the huge 3M Corporation in the USA. (2) _____ , as a member of his local church choir, he used to check which hymns he was to sing during the service, and mark them with bits of paper in his hymnbook. Inevitably, just as a hymn was about to start, the paper used to drop out, and Fry used to have a frantic search for the right page. (3) _____ he was listening to the sermon when his mind began to wander. He remembered that (4) _____ , a research colleague had made a glue which had been discarded when it proved to have poor sticking power. (5) _____ he managed to obtain some of this failed glue and started making his bookmarks with it. Post-its are now a billion dollar business.

4 Read about the invention of the microwave oven. Choose the correct verb structures.

In 1946, Dr Percy LeBaron Spencer (1) **worked / was working** on a radar-based research project when he (2) **felt / was feeling** something sticky in his pocket. It turned out to be a melted peanut bar. Spencer guessed that it (3) **had been affected / was affected** by high frequency radio emissions from the magnetron – a key component in radar. He (4) **heard / had heard** stories of partially cooked birds being found at the base of early radar installations but had, until now, dismissed them. Intrigued, he sent a boy out to buy a packet of popcorn. When he placed it close to the magnetron, the popcorn exploded. By the end of that year, the first prototype microwave oven (5) **was installed / had been installed** in a Boston restaurant.

5 Read about the invention of the ice lolly. Complete the text with the correct structure for the verbs in brackets.

In 1923 Frank Epperson was a lemonade-mix salesman. He (1) _____ (demonstrate) his product one afternoon to prospective customers and (2) _____ (leave) a glass of lemonade with a spoon in it on a windowsill. The night that followed was cold, and the temperature plunged to below zero. In the morning, Epperson (3) _____ (discover) his glass of lemonade still sitting where he (4) _____ (leave) it. He (5) _____ (pull) the spoon out of the glass, and found that he had a prototype ice lolly in his hand.

Language reference: narrative tense structures

Past simple

The past simple is usually used to fix events in the past. You can use it to describe the main events of a story.
*Trevor Baylis **dozed off** and **had** a dream.*

Past continuous

The past continuous is often used in contrast with the past simple. You can use it to describe an activity which was in progress when the main events of the story happened.
*Art Fry **was listening** to the sermon one Sunday when his mind began to wander.*

Past perfect simple & continuous

The past perfect can be used to refer to an event (simple) or activity in progress (continuous) which clearly took place before the time of the main events of the story.
*Epperson discovered his glass of lemonade still sitting where he **had left** it.*

Trivia pursuit – Genius edition

Play the game with two to six players divided into two teams: Team A and Team B. You will need a dice and two counters.

1 Before you start the game, write four general knowledge questions to ask the other team when they land on a white *Free* square.
2 Place your counters on the square marked START and toss a coin to see which team starts.
3 The first team throws the dice and moves their counter along the board according to the number.
4 Teams then play in turns, moving along the board. The other team asks you a question on a topic according to the colour of the square you land on. If you get it right, you can play again. If you get it wrong, it's the other team's turn to play.

The first team to reach FINISH are the class geniuses!
Team A turns to page 139 for their questions. Team B turns to page 140 for their questions.

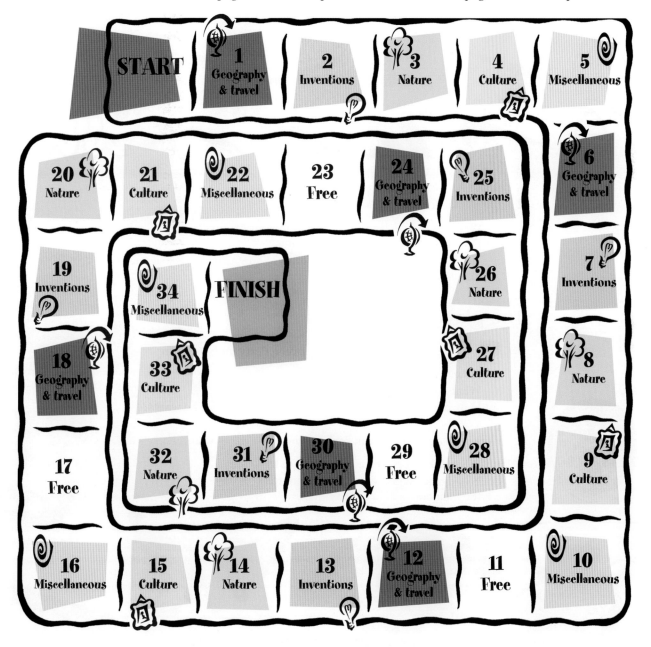

11 Sell

1 Work in small groups. Look at 'Know your logos!' Identify the brand in each case. Choose the correct version of each of the logos. Check your answers on page 136.

Know your logos!

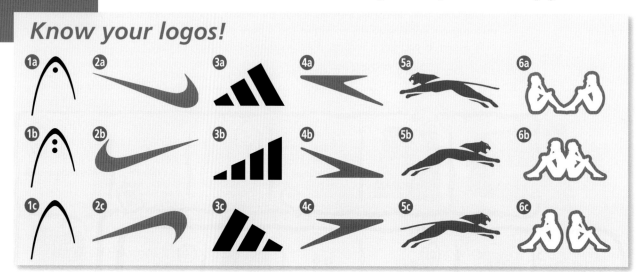

2 Discuss the following questions.

a) Which of these brands are popular in your country?
b) Do you own anything of these brands?
c) How many more logos can you draw? Show your logos to a partner and see how many brands they can identify.

The playground pound

Listening **1** 📼 51 Listen to a conversation between Perry and his mum.

a) How old do you think Perry is?
b) What does he want and why?
c) How does he try to persuade his mum to buy what he wants?

2 Work with a partner. Think back to when you were around Perry's age.

a) What did you pester your parents to buy you?
b) What's the biggest craze among pre-teens in your country at the moment?

Yo-yo

Tamagotchi

Furby

Poo-Chi

Pokémon

Game Boy

Joe Smedley, marketing executive and Sally McIlveen, headteacher

3 You are going to listen to these two people talking about children and advertising. Read some of the things they say and guess which person is likely to have made each statement.

a) 'Basically, children nowadays are being constantly brainwashed by all the advertising that goes on around them.'

b) 'Brands give children a sense of identity and help them fit in with a peer group.'

c) 'I really believe that the government should put a stop to this aggressive television advertising.'

d) 'Companies donate free computers and other school equipment in exchange for advertising their brands on exercise book covers, posters and that sort of thing. I think it's fantastic – the kids benefit and the companies get brand loyalty from a very early age.'

e) 'I'd love to be a child today. They really know what they want and they have so many more choices.'

f) 'I don't think all this choice is liberating for children – it just means that they're getting older younger, and I think that's a shame.'

4 🔲 **52** Listen and check your answers. Work with a partner. Do you agree or disagree with the statements in 3?

Lexis In the statements in 3 in the previous section *peer group*, *television advertising* and *brand loyalty* are all examples of noun + noun collocations.

1 Test your collocations! Complete each panel with a word from the box to form fifteen typical noun + noun collocations.

brand	consumer	advertising	market	sales

(a) ____ force
figures
pitch

(b) ____ awareness
loyalty
name

(c) ____ forces
leader
share
research

(d) ____ goods
spending

(e) ____ agency
campaign
executive

2 Work with a partner. Which of the collocations in 1 fits these dictionary definitions?

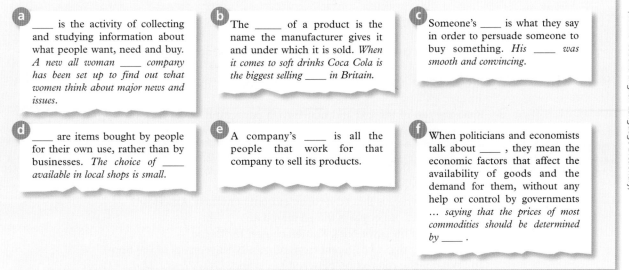

a ____ is the activity of collecting and studying information about what people want, need and buy. *A new all woman ____ company has been set up to find out what women think about major news and issues.*

b The ____ of a product is the name the manufacturer gives it and under which it is sold. *When it comes to soft drinks Coca Cola is the biggest selling ____ in Britain.*

c Someone's ____ is what they say in order to persuade someone to buy something. *His ____ was smooth and convincing.*

d ____ are items bought by people for their own use, rather than by businesses. *The choice of ____ available in local shops is small.*

e A company's ____ is all the people that work for that company to sell its products.

f When politicians and economists talk about ____ , they mean the economic factors that affect the availability of goods and the demand for them, without any help or control by governments *… saying that the prices of most commodities should be determined by ____ .*

(Collins Cobuild English Language Dictionary)

3 Write sentences using three more of the collocations in 1.

Commercials

1 ⏹ 53 You are going to listen to four people (Alison, Ben, Celia and Dan) talking about television commercials they have seen. They do not directly mention the product that was being advertised. Match the commercials they describe with four of the pictures (a–f).

2 Work with a partner. Take it in turns to be Student A and Student B. Student A describe an advertisement you have seen at the cinema or on television. Do not say what the advertisement was for. Student B listen to your partner describing their advertisement and try to guess what the advertisement is for. Ask questions if you need more information.

3 Discuss which advertisements you like most and which you like least. Explain why. Which advertisements do you think are the most effective at selling the product?

Reading **1** Work with a partner. Look at the picture on the opposite page which is taken from a well-known TV advert. Discuss possible answers to the following questions.

a) What was the commercial advertising?

| hairspray | jeans | life insurance | underwear | washing powder |

b) In which country and in what decade did the action take place?

2 Read the first paragraph of *Commercial breakdown* and check your answers to 1.

3 Read the rest of the text and match each paragraph (A–E) with the appropriate part of the picture (1–5).

4 Answer these questions about the text.

a) How successful was this ad?
b) In what ways is this advertisement not genuinely American?
c) What kind of people is the ad aimed at?
d) Why was the actor Nick Kamen chosen for the ad?
e) How was this ad different from other advertisements of the time?
f) What is the connection between Levis and: *Elvis Presley; Marvin Gaye*?

(Bartle Bogle Hegarty, London)

Commercial breakdown

A good-looking young man walks into a small-town American launderette. He strips off and waits for his
5 jeans to wash. Not much of a storyline, but this remains one of the most popular TV adverts that has ever been made. Made to promote Levis
10 501s, the ad was a massive success the minute it hit British TV screens in 1985. It epitomises everything that was, and perhaps still is, cool.
15 Set in 1950s America, with its associations with Marlon Brando and Elvis Presley (both of whom had been photographed wearing Levis),
20 the advert was making a clear statement: this is genuine, original, authentic. It represented youthful rebellion, radical chic and sex
25 appeal, which was perfect for Levis' intended positioning of their brand in the market.

Interestingly, although the commercial conjures up an
30 authentic American scene, it was in fact made by a British creative director for a British advertising agency with British actors.

35 **A** Even though we can't see her face, it's clear that the woman with the washing basket is more than a little interested in the scene that is
40 taking place in front of her. But what is she looking at? Her eyes are directed at the jeans that are hanging out of the machine. She wants them,
45 not him. And she's fussy – it's not any old pair of jeans, but a pair of 501s.

B The old washing machines are the biggest clue
50 to 1950s America. Every period in history likes to look back nostalgically to a mythical past when life was

simpler and less complicated.
55 And the 1950s, with the birth of rock and roll, have always had a special place in the history of what is cool. But for cool music, turn to the 1960s.
60 The soundtrack, Marvin Gaye's *I Heard It Through The Grapevine*, was released in 1968. A haunting soul classic, it's the story of a man
65 who learns that his girlfriend is seeing someone else. A man, perhaps, who goes to the launderette now that his girlfriend has left him?

70 **C** Unlike the majority of adverts, this ad was co-created by a woman, Barbara Nokes, who was creative director of the London-based agency,
75 Bartle Bogle Hegarty. In the fiercely male-dominated world of advertising, this advert established new ground by making a man into an object
80 of sexual desire. It was perhaps the first time that we had seen a man take his clothes off on screen. However, this 'revolution'
85 seems to have had little lasting effect.

D Do you recognise the face? Is it James Dean? A young Elvis? Actually, the actor
90 was Nick Kamen, who went on to become a successful pop star with a hit that was written by Madonna. He had a 1950s face and was
95 considered such a heart-throb that even now there are websites devoted to him.

E Completely uninterested in the scene taking place in
100 front of his eyes, the old man is the antithesis of everything the ad stands for. This is all about the young rebel – the rugged individual who
105 couldn't care less about conventions. The presence of an old guy in a straw hat lets us know exactly who the commercial is aimed at.

1 Find the following words or phrases in the text on page 101 and choose the best definition for each word or phrase.

a) epitomises (line 13): **is a bad example of / is a typical example of**
b) conjures up (line 29): **makes something disappear / creates a picture of**
c) fussy (line 45): **very concerned about details / not concerned about details**
d) a heart-throb (line 95): **a very attractive man / a very unattractive man**
e) couldn't care less about (line 105): **is very interested in / is not at all interested in**

2 Complete these questions with one of the words or phrases from 1. You may have to change the grammar.

a) What sort of images does rock and roll music ____ for you?
b) Who, in your opinion, is the most popular ____ in your country?
c) Name something that you ____ .
d) What do you think best ____ the decade in which you were born?
e) Are you ____ about the brands of clothes you buy?

3 Work with a partner. Ask and answer the questions in 2.

Discussion

1 Work in groups and discuss the following questions.

a) What other advertisements (TV, cinema, magazines) for jeans have you seen?
b) If you were making a TV advertisement for jeans, how would you do it?
  • Who would the advertisement be aimed at?   • Where and when would the
  • What storyline would you use?   advert be set?
  • Which actors would you want to use?   • What music would you use?

2 Compare your ideas with other groups.

Close up

Relative clauses

1 Underline the relative clauses in these lines from the text on page 101.

a) It represented youthful rebellion, radical chic and sex appeal, which was perfect for Levis' intended positioning of their brand in the market.
b) Unlike the majority of adverts, this ad was co-created by a woman, Barbara Nokes, who was creative director of the London-based agency, Bartle Bogle Hegarty.
c) Her eyes are directed at the jeans that are hanging out of the machine.

2 Choose the description which best defines the function of each relative clause in 1.

Type 1 It gives extra information about something in the main clause. (*non-defining*)
Type 2 It identifies something in the main clause. (*defining*)
Type 3 It comments on the whole of the main clause. (*non-defining*)

3 What punctuation is used to show that a relative clause is non-defining?

4 Work with a partner. Look at each of the following sentence pairs and decide which is the most suitable follow-up sentence (1 or 2).

Main sentence		Follow-up sentence	
a)	She offered me some cigarettes that were very strange.	1	They were red and blue.
b)	She offered me some cigarettes, which was very strange.	2	She knows I don't smoke.
c)	He's going out with Julie, who I can't stand.	1	He should be going out with me!
d)	He's going out with Julie, which I can't stand.	2	She's such a gossip.
e)	She bought me an expensive tie which I didn't like.	1	Why waste money on ties?
f)	She bought me an expensive tie, which I didn't like.	2	It was a horrible orange colour.
g)	My brother who lives in Rome is a model.	1	My other brother is an accountant.
h)	My brother, who lives in Rome, is a model.	2	He absolutely loves his job.

5 Look again at the main sentences in 4 and answer the questions.

  a) What kind of relative clause does each main sentence contain? (Refer to the three types in 2.)
  b) Which of the four relative pronouns *who, which, whose* and *that* cannot be used with non-defining relative clauses?

6 Rearrange the words to make defining relative clauses. In each case there is one word too many. The first one has been done for you.

  a) **a job** in that it interested are you   *a job* that you are interested in ~~it~~
  b) **a bank account** it out never that runs
  c) **a boss** get him/her with who you on
  d) **a car** it that down never breaks
  e) **a government** voted that them you for
  f) **a friend** who you he/she down lets never
  g) **a home** in there happy you that are
  h) **a partner** love you him/her who in are with

7 In the first item in 6 you can omit the relative pronoun, *that*. In the second item you can't. Why not? In which other defining clauses in 6 can you omit the relative pronoun?

8 Work with a partner. Put the items in 6 in order of importance for you in your life.

Language reference: relative clauses

Relative clauses are usually found after a noun or a noun phrase. Like adjectives, they describe or give information about the person or thing being talked or written about.

Non-defining relative clauses

You use non-defining relative clauses to give extra, non-essential information about the person or thing you are talking about. You can also comment on the whole of the main clause. You always begin a non-defining relative clause with a relative pronoun, and you separate it from the main clause with commas.

*He's going out with Julie, **who** I can't stand.*
(extra information about Julie)
*He's going out with Julie, **which** I can't stand.*
(comment on the whole of the main clause)
*He's going out with Julie, **whose** brother is my boss.*
(extra information about Julie)

Pronouns for non-defining relative clauses:

	Person	Thing
Subject	... , who ...	... , which ...
Object	... , who (whom) ...	... , which ...
Possessive	... , whose ...	... , whose ...

Defining relative clauses

You use defining relative clauses to state exactly which person or thing you are talking about.
When the relative pronoun is the subject of the relative clause you must use *who, that* or *which.*
*I like friends **who** never let me down.*
*I want a bank account **that** never runs out.*

When the relative pronoun is the object of the relative clause you can omit *who, that* or *which.*
*He's got a job (**that/which**) he's really interested in.*
*She's got a boyfriend (**who**) she's really in love with.*

You can never omit *whose.*
*That's the man **whose** dog bit my son.*
*John's the boy **whose** mum I met last week.*

When the relative pronoun is the object of the relative clause, you don't need another object pronoun.
She got a new car that she's very proud of.
(NOT ... proud of ~~it~~.)
He's the man whose case I took by mistake.
(NOT ... whose case I took ~~it~~.)

Pronouns for defining relative clauses:

	Person	Thing
Subject	... who / that ...	... that / which ...
Object	... (that / who) ...	... (that / which) ...
Possessive	... whose ...	... whose ...

Truth or tabloid?

1 Work with a partner and discuss the following questions.

a) Do you think celebrity scandals help sell magazines and newspapers?

b) Which magazines and newspapers print celebrity scandals in your country?

c) What scandals are in the news at the moment? Do you think they are true?

d) How do you think it feels for celebrities to read false stories about themselves?

e) How do you think it feels to live with a famous person?

2 Read this extract from an article by Phil Bronstein, husband of Hollywood film star, Sharon Stone. Do you feel sorry for him?

The truth about life with **Sharon Stone**

(Adapted from an article in *The Observer Review*)

When I married a movie star I knew the papers would make up stories – I'm an editor too.

Yes, it's true. I'm the one, the guy they call El Macho. The only thing is, I don't know who
5 'they' are. I know who I am, more or less, but I don't know the man these people claim to know. Of course, what they write is not really about me. Is it?

I'd love it if people at supermarket checkouts
10 were interested in me because I'm the executive editor of *The San Francisco Examiner*. But what they're interested in is the fact that I married a movie star. That's it. On the world stage, I'm Mr Sharon Stone.

15 On one level, I understand the obsession. We run celebrity stories, even gossip, in *The Examiner*. But what I don't understand is where they get this stuff from.

They say people were at my wedding whom I
20 have yet to meet; they insist my wife was pregnant when we got married; they claim I'm running for mayor of San Francisco; the day we got back from a lovely Mexican vacation, my wife and I saw on the news-stands that we had broken up. But the one I liked
25 best was the story in a mainstream newspaper (*The Irish Independent*) describing my wife's purchase of an Irish home. Great, but not a single piece of it true.

3 If you were Phil Bronstein, which piece of 'news' would you find most upsetting?

Listening

Shelley Russell and Jim Falmer

1 ▭ 54 Listen to a programme discussing truth and accuracy in the tabloid newspapers. Work with a partner and use the words in the box to explain why the actress is not happy with the tabloid editor. Who do you sympathise with most?

co-star	bath	hotel room	good friend	champagne	divorce

2 Use the words in the box to complete the phrases used by the speakers in the discussion in 1. Then listen again and check your answers.

was	is	but	saying	here	question	but	is	finish	on	is

a) Sorry, _____ ...
b) If you would just let me _____ ...
c) But the thing _____ ...
d) Hang _____ , ...
e) Anyway, to get back to what I was _____ ...

f) The point I'm trying to make here _____ ...
g) What you didn't do _____ ...
h) If I could just come in _____ ...
i) If you would let me answer the _____ ...
j) The problem _____ ...
k) I'm sorry to interrupt you, _____ ...

3 Use the following table to categorise the phrases according to their function.

Interrupting	Returning to the topic	Introducing a new point
Sorry, but ...	*If you would just let me finish ...*	*But the thing is ...*

4 Work in small groups and discuss the following statements. Take it in turns to agree or disagree. Think of as many points as you can.

a) For celebrities, any publicity is good publicity – the more sensational the better.
b) It is a newspaper editor's job to increase circulation, not to worry about the accuracy of every article they print.
c) The public have a right to read articles about the private lives of famous people.

Close up

Emphasis (cleft sentences)

1 Read the two sentences below. Then read how Sharon Stone's husband, Phil Bronstein, expressed the same ideas in his article. Discuss the differences between the two ways of saying the same thing.

They are interested in the fact that I married a movie star.
I don't understand where they get this stuff from.

What Phil Bronstein actually said:
What they're interested in is the fact that I married a movie star. (line 11)
What I don't understand is where they get this stuff from. (line 17)

Language reference p106

2 Change the emphasis of the following sentences using the sentence beginnings provided.

a) I don't understand why I never seem to have any money. *What I don't understand is ...*
b) I like weekends because I can stay in bed late in the morning. *The thing I like about weekends is ...*
c) People who finish my sentences for me really annoy me. *What really annoys me is ...*
d) I feel like going to the cinema tonight. *What I feel like doing tonight is ...*
e) I hate winter because it gets dark so early. *The thing I hate about winter is ...*
f) I'd really like to live abroad in the future. *What I'd really like to do is ...*

3 How many of the sentences in 2 are true for you? Compare with a partner. Make appropriate changes so that all the sentences are true for you.

4 Only one of the following statements about celebrities is true. Which one?

    a) Anna Kournikova was attacked by a mad fan during a match.
    b) Julia Roberts starred in *Notting Hill* with Tom Cruise.
    c) Kate Moss used to go out with Johnny Depp.
    d) Ricky Martin had a big hit with a song called 'Angels'.
    e) Gwyneth Paltrow got married to Brad Pitt in 2000.
    f) Leonardo DiCaprio was Obi-Wan Kenobi in *Star Wars Episode 1: The Phantom Menace*.

5 Work with a partner. Use the information in the box and correct all the false statements in 4, beginning with *It wasn't ...* or *It was ...* . The first one has been done for you.

> Robbie Williams   Jennifer Aniston   Hugh Grant   Monica Seles   Ewan McGregor

For example:
    a) *It wasn't Anna Kournikova who was attacked by a mad fan during a match. It was Monica Seles.*

6 Work in pairs. Write three false statements like in 4 about celebrities from your country. Pass them to other students to discuss and correct.

Stress in cleft sentences

1 🔊 55 Using cleft sentences can allow you to focus attention on how you feel about something. Which are the important words in the sentences below? Listen and see if those words are stressed. Mark where there is a momentary pause in each sentence.

    a) What I love about Peter is his wicked sense of humour.
    b) The thing I can't stand about this country is the weather.
    c) What I really hate about my job is having to work at weekends.
    d) The person I really like in this class is Maria.
    e) What I find annoying about politicians is that they never give a straight answer.
    f) The thing I find difficult about English is the spelling.
    g) What I would really like to do is to take a year off.
    h) The thing that I respect most about my boss is her generosity.

2 Work with a partner. Use the beginnings of at least three of these cleft sentences to express your feelings about things that are important to you. Make sure you stress the important words.

The thing I like about ... is ...   What I find difficult about ... is ...
What I can't stand about ... is ...   The thing I would dearly love to do is ...
The thing that I find annoying about ... is ...   What worries me about ... is ...

Language reference: emphasis (cleft sentences)

What structures (= *The thing(s) that*)

You can use *What ... is/was ...* to emphasise either the subject or the object of a sentence.
***Classical music** often helps me to concentrate.*
= What often helps me to concentrate is
classical music.
*I don't understand **where they get this stuff from**.*
*= What I don't understand is **where they get this stuff from**.*

It is/was ... + relative clause

You can use this structure to emphasise almost any part of a sentence.
Brad Pitt married Jennifer Aniston in Los Angeles in 2000.
***It was Brad Pitt** who married ...*
***It was Jennifer Aniston** who married ...*
***It was Los Angeles** where Brad Pitt married ...*
***It was in 2000** that Brad Pitt married ...*
You often use this structure when you are correcting what other people say.
***It wasn't Gwyneth Paltrow** who married Brad Pitt. It was Jennifer Aniston.*

Hype is the intensive use of publicity and advertising in order to make people aware of something.

(Collins Cobuild English Language Dictionary)

Hype

1 Work with a partner and discuss the following questions.

a) What's the most popular film at the cinema at the moment?

b) Why do you think it's so popular?

c) Have you been to see it?

2 Some of the things that can make a film into a box-office hit are: *special effects, a great plot, famous stars* and *a huge budget*. Work with a partner. Write down any other factors you can think of.

3 Read the article below about *The Blair Witch Project*: one of the big cinema success stories of the last few years. Find out how many of the points you listed in 2 contributed to the success of this film.

4 According to the text, what particular factors were responsible for the success of *The Blair Witch Project*?

5 Work with a partner and discuss the following questions.

a) Would you go and see a film like *The Blair Witch Project*?

b) What was the last horror or suspense film you saw?

c) What's the scariest film you've ever seen?

THE BLAIR WITCH
PROJECT

THE BUDGET
The Blair Witch Project was made in two years on a budget of $25,000.

THE DIRECTORS
For directors Dan Myrick and Ed Sanchez it was their first feature film.

THE IDEA
Myrick and Sanchez agreed that there had never been a film that had really scared them and decided to make one. Together, they came up with the idea of a 200-year old legend about a series of unexplained disappearances.

THE PLOT
The story is set in the woods of Burkittsville, Maryland. Three student filmmakers go into the woods to shoot a documentary about the Blair Witch legend, and disappear. A year later their footage is found. This film is a compilation of the footage they took showing how they were lost and were terrorised by something unseen.

THE ACTORS
Three unknown actors were chosen to play the parts of the three student filmmakers.

THE SHOOT
The film was shot in just eight days. The actors, who used their real names in the film, were sent into the woods for eight days without directors, crew or script. They were given hand-held cameras and told to film everything they saw.

The only contact that they had with the crew was through notes and minimal rations left for them to pick up daily. They knew their 'characters' well, and knew the general set-up of the 'story', but everything that happens as the story unfolds was a surprise to them, which is why the film is so believable.

THE HYPE
Six months before the first screening of the film, the directors set up a website, www.blairwitch.com. They filled it with Blair Witch mythology, updated every Friday with new information. The net went wild and the site scored fifty million hits before the film even opened.

A documentary called *The Curse of the Blair Witch* was shown on American television.

The public were encouraged to believe that the story was real and not a work of fiction. The directors told the press, 'We're not saying it's the truth and we're not saying it's not.'

The film opened in just twenty-seven cinemas across twenty states in America. This was another clever marketing ploy – people were queuing for miles, and the media went mad.

THE OUTCOME
It is one of the most profitable films of all time.

Lexis   **1**    56 Six people (a–f) were interviewed as they went into the cinema to see *The Blair Witch Project*. Listen and choose the option which describes how they were feeling.

a)   **a bit / totally / extremely** nervous
b)   **distinctly / utterly / a little** uneasy
c)   **scared / nervous / frightened** to death
d)   **scared / afraid / bored** stiff
e)   **completely / terribly / quite** apprehensive
f)   **absolutely / quite / very** terrified

2   In 1 there are two other options in each case. Cross out the one which does not form an acceptable collocation and write an example sentence with the other.

For example:
~~totally~~ / **extremely** *nervous*   *My grandfather's driving makes me extremely nervous.*

3   Work with a partner. Look at the adjectives in the box and sentence frames A and B. Discuss the questions below.

| interesting   amazing   brilliant   boring   disappointing   dreadful |
| extraordinary   entertaining   funny   good   spectacular   ridiculous |

Sentence frame A (*gradable adjectives*): The film was quite/very/extremely _____ .
Sentence frame B (*absolute adjectives*): The film was quite/absolutely _____ .

a)   Which adjectives fit sentence frame A, and which fit B?
b)   Does the meaning of *quite* change in frames A and B?

4   Use adverb + adjective expressions from 3 to tell your partner about videos, TV programmes, concerts or sports events that you've seen recently.

5    57 Listen to the six people in 1 being interviewed after the film. What was the general reaction to the film?

6   On the recording, the speakers use similar words to the ones in bold in these comments. Try to remember the exact words used by the speakers. Listen and check your answers.

a)   (1) **Terribly** disappointing … it does not live up to (2) **expectations**
b)   (3) **Utter** rubbish
c)   it was a (4) **huge** letdown
d)   I feel (5) **thoroughly** disillusioned
e)   I don't think I've ever been so bored in my (6) **whole** life
f)   A (7) **complete** waste of time

Anecdote   Think of a film you've seen which has disappointed you. You are going to tell your partner about it. Choose from the list the things you want to talk about. Think about what you will say and what language you will need.

☐ What was the name of the film?
☐ When did you go to see it?
☐ Why did you go to see it?
☐ Had you seen trailers or read reviews?
☐ Was it hyped?
☐ Why didn't it live up to the hype?
☐ What did you particularly dislike about the film?

☐ Who was in it and who directed it?
☐ Were there any characters you could identify with?
☐ Were there any characters who annoyed you?
☐ What did your friends think about it?
☐ Would you go and see another film by the same director?

12 *Student*

Work with a partner and complete the following tasks.

a) Write a list of qualities that make a good teacher.
b) Compare your lists. Then agree on a class list of the three most important qualities.
c) Follow the same procedure to compile a list of qualities that make a good student.

Could do better

Reading   **1**   What kind of student do you think Robbie Williams was? Read his description of his school life below. Were you right?

(Adapted from *Take That: our story*)

MY first day at school I saw all these kids crying as they said goodbye to their mums, but I was more concerned with playing with the lads. I told Mum to go home; she was more upset than I was!

After Millhill Primary School I went on to St Margaret Ward which was the local High School. I was there until sixteen and ended up with eight or nine GCSEs. I was a good lad at school in that I never got caught. I did the normal laddish stuff that you'd expect a fourteen-year-old to get up to. I didn't smoke, but I went to smoker's corner. And you weren't allowed to wear trainers, so I'd always put

them on. I always used to be the one that would make the class laugh. Then as soon as the teacher turned round, I'd sit straight and the rest of the class would be laughing and they'd get told off.

I joined *Take That* in the middle of going from school to college. In fact I'm still registered at the Sixth Form College at St Margaret's now. When I go in next time I'll probably get detention for being a few years late!

Robbie Williams

Name:

Robert Peter Williams

Date of birth:

13th February 1974

Career: Robbie joined the band *Take That* in 1990 when he was only 16. Then in 1996 he left the band and went on to pursue a very successful solo career.

---

2   Using the information in Robbie Williams' description, choose the correct alternative to complete these sentences.

1   Robbie was ...
    a)   the class clown.   b)   the class genius.
    c)   bottom of the class.

2   Primary school is for children ...
    a)   from two to five years old.
    b)   from five to eleven years old.
    c)   from eleven to sixteen years old.

3   A GCSE is ...
    a)   a punishment.   b)   a qualification.
    c)   a school subject.

4   You take your GCSEs at the age of ...
    a)   sixteen   b)   fifteen.   c)   fourteen.

5   A detention is ...
    a)   a punishment
    b)   a qualification.
    c)   a school subject.

6   You go to sixth form college ...
    a)   when you're five.
    b)   when you're eleven.
    c)   when you're sixteen.

Listening   **1**   ▭ 58 Listen to John and Clare talking about teachers that they remember from school. Match the descriptions to the pictures below.

2   Listen again and complete the sentences with *ML* (Madame Lorenzo) or *MT* (Mr Tucker).

a)   ____ taught French.
b)   ____ never changed his/her jacket.
c)   ____ was near to retirement.
d)   ____ was popular with the boys.
e)   ____ shouted a lot.
f)   ____ probably did not go to university.
g)   ____ said cruel things to the students.
h)   ____ was married.

3   The expressions below come from the recording you have just listened to. Complete the sentences with words from the box. You may need to change the form of the verbs.

> amount to much   have the chance   join the army   reduce (someone) to tears
> settle down

a)   Good teachers never ____ their students ____ .
b)   Pupils who don't ____ at school rarely manage to get good jobs later.
c)   Travelling is a waste of time – young people should be encouraged to ____ as soon as possible.
d)   People should be able to ____ if they want, but compulsory military service should be abolished.
e)   Everybody should ____ to go to university if they want to.

Do you agree or disagree with the statements?

Anecdote   Think back to your favourite teacher at school. You are going to tell your partner about them. Choose from the list the things you want to talk about. Think about what you will say and what language you will need.

☐ Was it a man or a woman?
☐ What was their name?
☐ What did they look like?
☐ What sort of clothes did they use to wear?
☐ Were they strict or easy-going?
☐ What subject did they teach?
☐ Were you good at that subject?
☐ Where did you sit in the classroom?
☐ What sort of things did you use to do in class?
☐ What was special about your favourite teacher?
☐ Were they popular with your classmates?
☐ Are you still in touch with them?

Teachers and parents know best

Lexis **1** Match the two halves of these expressions to make some questions about education.

a) In which school subjects did you always use to **get**
b) When was the last time you **failed an**
c) How easy is it to **get a**
d) Have you ever **taken a course**
e) What qualifications do you need if you want to **go**
f) What sort of things do you think it is best to **learn**
g) What time of day did you find it hardest to **pay**
h) How do you **apply for a place at**

1 **in another foreign language**?
2 **low marks**?
3 **attention** in class?
4 **on to further education**?
5 **exam**?
6 **by heart**?
7 **university**?
8 **grant** for further education?

2 Work with a partner. Ask each other the questions in 1.

3 Read and answer questions about the following people who proved their teachers wrong.

a) Who did more than get married and raise a family?
b) Who followed the teacher's advice and didn't go on to university?
c) Who failed an exam in a subject which she later proved to be very good at?

Look at us now!

HENRY WOODS

is an actor. He is at present filming a series to be shown on television in the autumn.

ROMY ADAMS

runs a catering company. She started off in her own kitchen and now runs three catering teams from premises in north London and caters mainly for conferences.

My maths teacher would die if she knew that I run my own company and do all the accounts myself. On my school report, she wrote, 'I see very little point in entering Rosemary for maths GCSE. Judging by the consistently low marks she has been getting this term, she is bound to fail the exam.' She was right of course, but when I wanted to set up my own company, I enrolled at the local college and took an evening course in maths and accounting and I was one of the best in the class! A bit of motivation goes a long way!

ANN WATERMAN

is a judge and has been an active member of parliament for the last ten years.

I was sent to a rather old-fashioned boarding school run by nuns. I obviously didn't make much of an impression there, because their final comment was, 'She has been a mediocre student and is highly unlikely to go on to further education. We think she is best suited to getting married and raising a family.' The first thing I did when I left school was to join the women's liberation movement.

History was the only subject I was any good at, and that's because the history teacher would sit and tell stories and bring it all alive. He never made us learn lists of dates by heart – he didn't need to because his stories made it all so memorable anyway. But other teachers used to say things like, 'Henry lives in a dream world. He needs to pay more attention.' I was hoping to go to university, but then one of my teachers wrote a comment on my report which took away all my confidence. He put, 'Henry is not expected to pass his A-levels with sufficiently high grades to gain a place at university.' So I didn't apply for a place at university. I went to acting school instead, and the rest is history, as they say. I suppose it was fate, but I still feel angry with that teacher.

4 Read the texts again. Two of the expressions in **bold** used in 1 are not used. Which ones?

5 Find expressions from the texts in 3 which mean the same as the structures underlined.

1: It is inevitable that she will fail the exam.
2: We do not think that she will go on to further education.
3: The school predicts that Henry will not pass his exams with sufficiently high grades.

6 Complete these predictions about education in Britain. Do you think these things will happen in your country? When?

a) Classrooms (*expected*) get less crowded as the birth-rate continues to decrease.
b) It (*highly unlikely*) that classroom teachers will ever be replaced by computers.
c) Standards of spelling and grammar (*likely*) get worse because of new technologies.
d) As more families go online, students (*bound*) rely more on the Internet to help them with their homework.

7 Work with a partner. Write down three more predictions about the future of education in your country. Find out if other students agree.

Listening

1 Work in small groups and discuss the following questions.

a) At what age do you think you should ...
– stop listening to parents and teachers and do what you feel is right?
– be financially independent?
– leave the family home?
b) Have you ever taken your parents' advice and regretted it?
c) Do you intend to follow in your parents' footsteps?

2 🔊 59 Listen to Mr and Mrs Barrington talking about their eighteen-year-old daughter, Saffron. Decide which of the following sentences best summarises their feelings about Saffron's plans for the future.

a) They want Saffron to go to university but they're worried about supporting her financially.
b) They think Saffron should get a university degree before she tries to become a pop singer.
c) They think that it would be a waste of time for Saffron to go to university because she really wants to be a pop singer.

3 Listen again to the conversation and complete these extracts, using the phrases in the box.

taste of freedom   up to her   out of her system   behind her   make it

a) Now she reckons she's going to _____ in the pop world.
b) That's true, but once she gets a _____ , she'll find it more difficult to go back to college.
c) At least if it doesn't work out she'll have a qualification _____ .
d) We're just hoping that she'll get it _____ and then come to her senses and go back to her studies.
e) ... we can't afford to pay for her to live in London, so it's _____ to make it work.

4 Work with a partner. Decide whether you agree or disagree with the following statements. Do you think your parents would have the same opinion?

a) If you want to go travelling, it's best to get it out of your system before you start a career. Afterwards it's too late.
b) Once young people have had a taste of freedom, it's difficult for them to go back and live with their parents.
c) The more qualifications you've got behind you, the better your chances are of getting a good job.
d) You don't need musical talent to make it in the pop world these days: just good looks and a good manager.
e) Whether or not you succeed in life is up to you. Nobody else can help.

Close up

Future forms **1** In the previous section Saffron's parents expressed their worries about their daughter's future plans. Here Saffron gives her point of view. Think carefully about the context and choose the most appropriate future form for each case.

Interviewer: You're leaving school soon, aren't you?

Saffron: Yes, (1) **my A-levels start / my A-levels'll start** next week, but I'm not too bothered about the results, because when I leave
5   school (2) **I'm concentrating / I'm going to concentrate** on my music career. I'm lead singer in a band and I don't need any qualifications to be a pop star. I see my future very clearly – (3) **I'm going to**
10   **be / I'm being** incredibly famous and fabulously rich.

Interviewer: So you've already got a contract then?

Saffron: Er, no, not as such. Actually, we haven't got a manager yet, but the minute I've taken
15   my last exam, (4) **I'm finding / I'm going to find** a really good one.

Interviewer: So, do you intend to continue living at home?

Saffron: No way. (5) **I'll have moved / I'm moving**
20   to London just as soon as I've left school. London's where it all happens in the music industry.

Interviewer: Do you think (6) **you'll be able / you're able** to live
25   off your music right from the start?

Saffron: Well, if we don't make it straight
30   away (7) **we're having to / we might have to** get part-time jobs for a few months or something. I know (8) **it's being / it's going to be** hard at first, but I bet you, by this
35   time next year, (9) **we're having / we'll have** had a record in the charts.

Interviewer: And where do you see yourself in five years from now?

Saffron: In five years' time (10) **I'm staying / I'll be**
40   **staying** in posh hotels and won't be able to walk down the street without being recognised. In fact, (11) **I'll give / I'm giving** you my autograph now if you like – (12) **it'll be / it's being** worth a
45   fortune in a few years' time!

2 ☐ **60** Listen and check your answers. Whose ideas do you agree with: Saffron or her parents'?

3 Work with a partner. Copy out and complete this table summarising some of the different future forms. Use an example from the interview in 1 to illustrate each use.

Form	Use	Example
a) *will ('ll)* + infinitive	1 for prediction 2 to make an offer	1 _____ 2 *I'll give you my autograph now if you like.*
b) *might* + infinitive	for possibility	
c)	1 to talk about your intentions 2 to base a prediction on present evidence	1 _____ 2 *I'm going to be incredibly famous.*
d) Present continuous	for plans and arrangements	
e)	for fixed future events	*My A-levels start next week.*
f) Future continuous	to talk about something happening around a certain time in the future	
g)	to talk about something completed by a certain time in the future	*By this time next year, we'll have had a record in the charts.*

4 Work with a partner. Look at these sentences about the future from the interview in 1. Underline the main clause. Put the subordinate clause in brackets ( ). Circle the conjunction.

For example: ... ((when) I leave school), <u>I'm going to concentrate on my music career.</u>

a) ... the minute I've taken my last exam, I'm going to find a really good one. (line 14)
b) ... I'm moving to London just as soon as I've left school. (line 19)
c) ... if we don't make it straight away we might have to get part-time jobs ... (line 28)

1 Which clause tells you that the sentence is about the future?
2 Is it possible to use a future form in both main and subordinate clauses?
3 In which clause do you have to use the present simple, continuous or perfect?

5 Use the verbs in brackets and complete these sentences about the future using an appropriate verb structure.

a) If I ____ (fail) my exams my parents ____ (kill) me.
b) I ____ (grow) a moustache as soon as I ____ (leave) school.
c) I ____ (never read) another poem once I ____ (take) my literature exam.
d) You ____ (like) the new teacher once you ____ (get) used to her.
e) He ____ (not come out) until he ____ (do) his homework.
f) When I ____ (finish) my business course I ____ (set up) my own business.

6 Complete the following sentences in any way that is true for you.

a) Once this lesson has finished ...
b) The moment I get home today ...
c) When I have enough money ...
d) As soon as I have some free time ...
e) When I'm next on holiday ...
f) This time next year ...
g) In five years' time ...
h) By the time I retire ...

Compare your sentences with a partner.

'Well, let's get started – you haven't got all day.'

Language reference: future forms

Will ('ll), (be) going to, present continuous

These are the three most common forms for talking about the future.

1 *Will ('ll)* – predictions/decisions reacting to circumstances such as offers, promises and requests.
   It'll be worth a fortune in a few years' time.
   I'll give you my photograph now if you like.

2 *(be) going to* – intentions/predictions based on present evidence.
   I'm going to concentrate on my musical career.
   Look at those clouds. It's going to pour down.

3 The present continuous – plans/arrangements
   I'm moving to London next month.

Present simple

You can use this form to talk about fixed future events: timetables, routines, schedules.
My A-levels start next week.
The plane leaves at 15:40.

Might & may

If you want to speculate about a future possibility you can use *might* or *may*.
We might have to get a part-time job.

Future continuous

You use this tense to talk about something happening around a certain time in the future.
In five years' time I'll be staying in posh hotels.
This time next week I'll be trekking in Nepal.

Future perfect

You use the future perfect to talk about something completed by a certain time in the future.
By this time next year, we'll have had a record in the charts.
The builder will have finished the kitchen walls by the end of the week.

Verb structures after *if, when, as soon as ...*

When it is clear from the main clause that the sentence is about the future you don't use a future form in the subordinate clause.
When I leave school, I'm going to concentrate on my musical career. (NOT ~~When I will leave school, ...~~)
It'll be a miracle if she's passed the exam.
(NOT ... ~~if she will have passed the exam.~~)

Other conjunctions which introduce subordinate clauses: *after, as soon as, before, once, the moment, the minute, unless, until.*

Backpacking

1 Work in groups and discuss the following questions.

  a) Is it common for students to go backpacking in their summer holidays?
  b) What do you think are the advantages and disadvantages of backpacking?
  c) If you could go backpacking anywhere in the world, where would you go and what would you do?

2 Read the first part of a newspaper article about students who go backpacking. Why should you always take travellers' tales with a pinch of salt?

Why students love a journey to hell

The summer holidays are approaching, and the buzz has already started in university bars across the land. Once again, students are competing with one another to see who can plan the toughest and most dangerous foreign trip this summer.

But travellers' tales should be taken with a pinch of salt. Everyone loves to exaggerate and embellish to make things sound better. If you say you did a bungee jump in Queensland of 44 metres, someone will say they did one of 98 metres at the Victoria Falls. If you got diarrhoea, they had amoebic dysentery or malaria. If you were stopped by police, they were dodging gunfire.

Part of the fun of travelling in your teens and twenties is the telling of tales afterwards. It's part of the rite of passage from child to adult, and there's nothing wrong with that.

(Based on an article in *The Sunday Telegraph*)

3 Find words and expressions in the text that mean:

  a) exciting atmosphere
  b) stories
  c) to make a story more interesting by adding details which may be untrue
  d) avoiding
  e) a normal part of growing up

4 Tom Griffiths is a graduate of Manchester University. He recalls backpacking as a student. Read the two versions of his backpacking story. Which do you prefer and why?

Version 1

'I was staying in this dirty hostel room which was full of big ants. One had already bitten my thigh, which had swollen up. So I was trying to kill them when I spotted one on the ceiling. I climbed onto the top bunk and hit it with my shoe. Then I fainted. The blades of the electric ceiling fan had hit my head and knocked me to the ground. I was taken to hospital where I had five stitches.'

Version 2

'I was staying in this filthy hostel room which was swarming with huge ants that looked like lobsters. One had already bitten my thigh, which had swollen up like a balloon. So there I was, going berserk trying to kill them all, when I spotted an enormous ant on the ceiling. Climbing onto the top bunk, I bashed it with my shoe. Then I blacked out. It turned out that the blades of the electric ceiling fan had dented my skull and knocked me to the ground. I had to be rushed to hospital where I had emergency surgery.'

Lexis

1 Did the ants really look like lobsters? Work with a partner. Find ten more examples of exaggerated language in version 2 in the previous section. Use your dictionary if necessary.

2 Work with a partner. Read two versions of Tom's second story. Combine elements from each version to re-write the story as dramatically as possible.

Version 1

'While I was travelling, I got an incredibly painful tropical ear infection after I fell into a smelly latrine. I felt very ill and stayed in bed with a raging fever for a few days. Wracked with pain, I couldn't eat, and I lost so much weight that I looked like a skeleton. Eventually, I managed to get hold of some antibiotics which made me better.'

Version 2

'While I was travelling, I got an unpleasant ear infection after I fell into a stinking latrine. Feeling like death, I lay in bed with a high temperature for what felt like a lifetime. I was in pain so I couldn't face eating anything, and I lost a lot of weight. Finally, I got some antibiotics which brought me back from death's door.'

3 🔊 **61** Listen and check your story in 2 above.

4 Match each of the informal exaggerated expressions (*a–j*) from column A with its meaning (*1–10*) in column B.

A	B
a) I was at death's door.	1 I thought it was amazing.
b) I burst into tears.	2 I thought it was beautiful.
c) I was scared stiff.	3 I was very happy.
d) It took my breath away.	4 I started crying.
e) I was at the end of my tether.	5 I was very tired.
f) It was mind-blowing.	6 I was going crazy.
g) I was on my last legs.	7 I was desperate.
h) I was dying for a drink.	8 I was very thirsty.
i) I was going out of my mind.	9 I felt very ill.
j) I was over the moon.	10 I was very frightened.

5 Choose five of the expressions from column A above and use them in sentences describing the last time you felt like this.

For example:

The first time I saw Istanbul, it took my breath away. I thought it was the most beautiful place I'd ever seen.

Yesterday I was late for school and in a hurry – and I couldn't find my keys. I looked everywhere. After ten minutes I was going out of my mind – then I found them, in my jacket pocket!

LANGUAGE TOOLBOX

Then ..., Later ...,
Suddenly ..., Eventually ...,
Finally to my horror, ...,
The worst thing was ...,
It turned out that ...

6 Work with a partner. You are going to imagine that you recently came back from an exciting and eventful journey. One of the dramatic things that happened to you was a six-hour boat journey. Prepare a story from the notes below. Make it as dramatic as possible.

It was a small fishing boat.
There were a lot of people on the boat.
The sea was calm when we left the harbour.
The sky turned black.
A storm blew up.
We noticed there were no lifejackets or radio in the fishing boat.
The waves were big.
We thought we were going to die.
I cried and then I fainted.

7 Tell your story to another pair of students in the class.

Job hunting

CVs

1 Arrange the following tips for writing a curriculum vitae (CV) under the headings *DOs* and *DON'Ts*.

a) mention your bad points or failures
b) sound enthusiastic
c) be funny or too informal
d) emphasise your good points and embellish them where possible
e) sound desperate
f) keep it simple
g) use decorative devices or lots of different fonts
h) check your typing, spelling and punctuation
i) use family or friends as referees
j) include dates
k) include irrelevant information

2 Read Ben Arnoldson's CV. Apply the tips in 1 above and identify where he has gone wrong.

Ben Arnoldson

❄ ✳ ❄ ✳ ❄ ✳ ❄ ✳ ❄ ✳ ❄ ✳ ❄ ✳ ❄

Ben Arnoldson
311 Cowley Rd Oxford
TELEPHONE 01865 372 827
mobile 0788 98878977
e-mail beautifulben@hotmail.com

DOB 12.8.81
Education
St Thomas Comprehensive
❖ 8 GCSEs
Oxford College of Further Education
❖ English A-level grade C
❖ Geography A-level grade D
❖ History A-level failed with a relatively high grade

EMPLOYMENT
➤ Worked in a shop
➤ Worked as a waiter
➤ Worked as a DJ
➤ Did some babysitting
➤ Worked as a typist

Other skills
✓ I can tyPe
✓ I can speak supermarket French and holiday Spanish

PERSONAL INTERESTS
❑ Donating blood – 14 litres so far
❑ Music

References
Mrs Beryl Arnoldson, 311 Cowley Rd, Oxford ☎ 01865 372 827

❄ ✳ ❄ ✳ ❄ ✳ ❄ ✳ ❄ ✳ ❄ ✳ ❄ ✳ ❄

3 Match each job (*a–f*) in list A with a way of embellishing it (*1–6*) in list B.

A
a) Worked in a shop
b) Did some babysitting
c) Worked as a DJ
d) Worked as a typist
e) Worked as a waiter
f) I can speak supermarket French and holiday Spanish

B
1 Have a working knowledge of French and Spanish
2 Child-minding. Gained experience in working with children
3 Clerical assistant. Improved my word-processing
4 Acquired interpersonal skills in the catering trade
5 Was involved in the music industry
6 Shop assistant. Gained experience of the retail trade

4 Re-write Ben's CV making the necessary changes and additions. See page 140 for an improved version.

Character reference

1 Ben has applied for a job at a children's holiday camp. Read the character reference that his friend Pete has written for him. What impression of Ben do you get from Pete's description?

2 🔲 62 Listen to a conversation between Pete, who wrote the reference, and Kate, another of Ben's friends. Which gives the most truthful impression of Ben's character, the character reference or the conversation?

3 Work with a partner. Match these extracts from Pete and Kate's conversation with the more positive descriptions used in the reference. The first one has been done for you.

a) ... he needs a bomb under him to get him going in the morning.
... he may not be best suited to early morning tasks.
b) ... He's good in a crisis.
c) ... he's good at causing a crisis ...
d) ... he's still got blue hair ...
e) ... he hates taking orders from anybody.
f) ... he is a bit immature.
g) ... he's a big-headed show-off who goes out every night ...

> **Ben Arnoldson: holiday camp assistant**
>
> I have known Ben Arnoldson for ten years, since we started at secondary school together. He is self-assured, outgoing and extremely sociable.
>
> As regards working with children, I have no hesitation in recommending Ben for the job. Children find him entertaining, and he is very good at relating to them on their own level.
>
> Provided he is interested in what he is doing, he gives total commitment to a job. However, he may not be best suited to early morning tasks.
>
> Ben is a natural leader and shows great initiative under pressure.
>
> While his critics may see him as a bit of a trouble-maker, he is in fact the sort of person who responds well to a challenge.
>
> Although Ben's appearance is unconventional, it is always interesting.

4 If you were applying for a job, who would you ask to write a reference for you? Which aspects of your character would they need to describe in a more positive way?

Angels

1 *Angels* was Robbie Williams' first major chart success. What other songs do you know by him?

2 Work with a partner. Read the lyrics of *Angels* below and try to work out the missing words from the context and the sound of the lines.

3 [cassette] **63** Listen to the song and check your answers. The tapescript is on page 158.

I sit and (1) _____ .
Does an angel contemplate my fate?
And do they (2) _____ ,
The places where we go
When we're grey and (3) _____ ?
'Cos I have been told
That salvation lets their wings unfold.
So when I'm lying in my (4) _____ ,
Thoughts running through my head,
And I feel that love is (5) _____ ,
I'm loving angels instead.

And through it all
She offers me (6) _____ ,
A lot of love and affection,
Whether I'm right or wrong.
And down the waterfall,
Wherever it may (7) _____ me,
I know that life won't break me,
When I come to call, she won't forsake me,
I'm loving angels instead.

When I'm feeling (8) _____ ,
And my pain walks down a one way street,
I look (9) _____ ,
And I know I'll always be blessed with love,
And as the feeling (10) _____ ,
She breathes flesh to my bones.
And when love is (11) _____ ,
I'm loving angels instead.

4 What frame of mind do you think Robbie Williams was in when he wrote this song? Choose words from the box.

| thoughtful | unhappy | broken-hearted | in love | reflective | spiritual |
| depressed | philosophical | angry | grateful | | |

5 How did you feel when you listened to the song? Discuss with a partner.

13 Home

What does *home* mean to you? Read some people's answers. Which three do you relate to most?

a) Home is a roof over my head. (*Gorban, 27, UK*)
b) Home is a warm bed. (*Hye-Yun, 15, South Korea*)
c) Home is warmth, love and safety. (*Andrea, 30, Croatia*)
d) Home is all the effort and sacrifice that I've ever made. (*Vera, 76, Serbia*)
e) Home is where my mother is. (*Guiseppe, 28, Italy*)
f) Home is where I go to change clothes between parties. (*Ivan, 19, Russia*)
g) Home is where most of my memories are. (*Josef, 70, Czech Republic*)
h) Home is where I can scream at the top of my lungs and no one minds. (*Natalie, 14, USA*)
i) Home is where you always want to go back to. (*Jorge, 34, Argentina*)

(Quotes from *COLORS: Home*)

Ideal homes

Lexis **1** Complete the sentences below with words from the box. Use singular or plural forms as necessary. Compare with a partner.

flat/apartment cottage detached house bungalow semi-detached house villa terraced house chalet houseboat hotel suite

a) I live in a/an …
b) Most of my friends live in …
c) I know a few people who live in …
d) I know one person who lives in a/an …
e) I can't think of anybody I know who lives in a/an …

LANGUAGE TOOLBOX

It's a four-bedroomed apartment /
a three-storey house /
on the fifth floor of a
high-rise building /
on an estate in the
centre
on the outskirts /
in the suburbs.

It looks out over the city /
the mountains.

2 Think of three houses you like and describe them to your partner.

For example: *I really like my uncle's house. It's a two-storey house …*

3 Match these objects with a part of the house. See if your partner agrees.

Object		Part of the house
a) empty suitcases	1	the cellar
b) a fireplace, a mantelpiece	2	the staircase
c) wine, coal	3	the porch
d) a desk, bookcases	4	bedroom
e) a doormat	5	the lounge
f) banisters	6	the loft
g) wardrobe, chest of drawers	7	the study

4 How many of these objects are in your own house? What part of your house are they in?

5 Work with a partner. Decide what all the items in each of the following groups have in common.

A	B	C	D
rugs tiles parquet wooden floorboards fitted carpets	blinds shutters double glazing curtains	power points shelves paintings radiators	a letterbox a latch a knocker a bolt a doorbell

6 Complete the sentences so that they are true for you. Discuss with a partner.

a) My ideal home would be a ... with ... and ...
b) It would have a view overlooking ...
c) The rooms would be painted ...
d) On the floor I'd have ...
e) The most beautiful room would be ...
f) I'd share my home with ...

Listening   **1**   Work with a partner. Look at the pictures and discuss these questions.

a) Which room do you like best and why?
b) What kind of people do you think these rooms belong to?
c) What kind of house do you think each person lives in?

2 You're going to listen to a psychologist talking about the rooms in 1 and what each room says about the person who lives there. Before you listen, match his interpretation to the room you think it applies to.

a) This is someone who lives in the world of imagination.
b) A real eccentric lives here.
c) There's plenty of evidence to suggest that this is a successful career person.
d) This person wants to be ready to pack their bags and leave at short notice.
e) I'd say this person is a bit of a party animal.
f) I think this is someone who doesn't actually spend much time at home.

3   🔲 **64** Listen and check your answers to 2.

4 Do you agree with the psychologist's comments? Turn to page 138 for the real people's comments.

Anecdote Think about your favourite room. You are going to tell your partner about it. Choose from the list the things you want to talk about. Think about what you will say and what language you will need.

☐ Which is your favourite room?
☐ What do you use it for?
☐ How is it decorated?
☐ What sort of furniture does it contain?
☐ What kind of floor covering does it have?
☐ What do the windows look out on to?
☐ What's the best thing in the room?
☐ Is it usually tidy?
☐ Who cleans it?
☐ Is there anything you'd like to change about it?
☐ How much time a day do you spend in it?
☐ In what ways do you think your favourite room reflects your personality?

Close up

Quantity

Language reference p123

1 Work with a partner. Look at these eight extracts from the listening in the previous section. What do all the extracts in group A have in common? What do all the extracts in group B have in common?

A
a) there are <u>very few</u> clues
b) there are <u>loads of</u> bright colours
c) there are <u>hardly any</u> personal objects
d) there aren<u>'t any</u> family photos

B
e) there is <u>very little</u> natural light
f) there's <u>far too much</u> stuff
g) there is<u>n't really enough</u> furniture
h) there is <u>plenty of</u> evidence

2 Replace the underlined quantity expressions in 1 with a similar alternative from the list below. You can use some expressions more than once.

1 a lot more … than necessary
2 lots of
3 more than enough
4 not a sufficient amount of
5 not many
6 not much
7 almost no
8 no

3 Add an appropriate quantity expression from the box to make the sentences true for you. Compare your answers with a partner.

| all of   most of   several of   not (very) many of   a few of   hardly any of |
| none of |

a) _____ my friends live in small villages.
b) _____ the people in my neighbourhood go to work by car.
c) _____ the shops near my home are open on Sunday.
d) _____ the houses in my street have big gardens.
e) _____ my neighbours keep pets.
f) _____ the buildings in my area were built in the last ten years.
g) _____ the people I work with smoke.
h) _____ these exercises are easy.

4 Look at the difference between the quantity expressions *a little* and *little* and *a few* and *few* in the sentences (1–4). Then answer the questions below.

1 My father speaks **<u>a little</u>** English so he'll probably understand you okay.
2 My father speaks **<u>little</u>** English so he might not understand you very well.
3 Listen. I've got **<u>a few</u>** things to tell you.
4 **<u>Few</u> women** understand men.

a) Which of the underlined expressions have a positive meaning?
b) Which quantity expressions are similar in meaning to *some*?
c) Which is similar in meaning to *not much*?
d) Which is similar to *not many*?

5 Use an appropriate quantity expression from the box to complete the sentences.

> few   a little   little   a few

a) I don't want much. All I need is ____ money.
b) Excuse me. Could I ask you ____ questions, please?
c) ____ school children learn Latin these days.
d) We did it because we wanted to have ____ fun.
e) Unfortunately, ____ politicians ever tell the truth.
f) The weather has been very bad. We've had ____ sunshine this summer.

6 Choose the correct verb form for these statements.

a) There **isn't** / **aren't** nearly enough night life.
b) There**'s** / **are** loads of traffic.
c) There**'s** / **are** very few tourists.
d) There**'s** / **are** no underground system.
e) There**'s** / **are** plenty of jobs for young people.
f) There**'s** / **are** plenty of parking in the centre.

Change the statements as necessary to describe your home town. Add two more statements and then compare your answers with a partner.

Language reference: quantity

You use determiners (*every, most, no*) and quantifiers (*all of, most of, none of*) to express quantity.

Which quantity expression?

1 The quantity expression you use depends on whether the noun is countable (C) or uncountable (U)
   There's **far too much** stuff (U) in the room.
   Not many of the people (C) I work with smoke.

   Sometimes you can use the same quantity expression for both countable and uncountable nouns.
   He's got **loads of** money (U).
   I've got **loads of** coins (C) in my pocket.

Note: You will find more information on countable and uncountable nouns on page 142.

2 When there is an article (*a, an, the*), a possessive pronoun (*my, your*, etc.) or a demonstrative pronoun (*that, these*, etc.) before the noun, you use a quantity expression with *of*.

   *Several **of my** friends live in small villages.*
   (NOT ~~Several my friends~~ ...)
   *Most **of the** people in my neighbourhood go to work by car.* (NOT ~~Most of people~~ ...)

3 When you want to talk about small numbers or amounts you can use *a few / a little* to stress the positive (*some*) or *few / little* to stress the negative (*not many/much*).
   *We did it because we wanted to have **a little** fun.*
   *Please hurry up! There's very **little** time.*

Which verb form?

You use a singular verb form if the noun after *of* is uncountable or singular. You use a plural if the noun is countable.
There's lots of traffic (U) in the centre.
*There **are** lots of tourists (C) in summer.*

Rise and shine

1 How do people in the class start the day? Ask questions to find someone who …

- slept more than eight hours last night.
- slept with the curtains or blinds open.
- woke up naturally, without an alarm clock.
- can remember what they dreamt about – and is willing to tell you!
- had breakfast in an east-facing room that gets the sunlight in the morning.
- had something cooked for breakfast.
- spent more than twenty minutes eating breakfast.
- got dressed after they'd had breakfast.

2 Work with a partner. The food and drink in the box are a mixture of breakfast items from around the world. Answer the questions.

a) Is there anything in the list that you or your family normally have for breakfast?
b) Is there anything you would find difficult to eat or drink at breakfast?
c) Is there anything you would find difficult to eat or drink at any time?

> jam   eggs sunny side up   green tea   rice   bacon   cereal   pancakes
> miso soup   cold meat   cheese   toast   pickled vegetables   bread rolls
> orange juice   coffee   grilled fish   boiled eggs   omelette

3 🔊 **65** The food and drink in the box in 2 are some breakfast items from the USA, Germany and Japan. Which items do you think belong to a typical breakfast from which country? Listen and check.

4 What's the most unusual breakfast you've ever had? Tell your partner.

Reading   **1** Look at the picture and discuss why this kitchen might not be a good room in which to start your day.

> **Feng Shui** Feng Shui (pronounced 'fung shway') is a Chinese system for deciding the right position for a building and for placing objects inside a building in order to make people feel comfortable and happy.

2 Read about how Feng Shui can help you start your day well. Find eight ways to improve the room in 1 in order to achieve good Feng Shui.

(Based on an article in *The Sunday Mirror*)

START YOUR DAY

THE FENG SHUI WAY

The right breakfast can make or break your day according to Feng Shui consultant, Simon Brown. And it's no good just eating the right food either – you've got to eat it in the right place.

5   Morning is a very important time because it's the transition from sleeping to waking. It's best to wake naturally, by sunlight flooding into the room, or from a rumbling stomach. Parents will find it easier to get children out of bed if they need breakfast. By eating their

10 last meal between six and seven the night before, their food is properly digested by bedtime, and they're hungry in the morning.

When you've made your way, bleary-eyed, to the table, you should find it an inspiring place to start the

15 day. If you get off on the wrong foot, you can usually guarantee the rest of the day will go from bad to worse. 'The worst thing you can do is eat breakfast in a kitchen with last night's washing-up on the work surface,' says Simon. 'It should be clutter-free.' For an uplifting room to

20 send you off full of energy use bright colours, like red and yellow. But for a calmer effect, decorate with pastel greens and blues, and choose the plates and bowls in the same way. If you're planning to re-do your kitchen, let the energy flow through the room by using wooden

25 worktops and tables, and ceramic tiles for the floors. Ideally, your breakfast place should be facing east, so you see the sun rising over your bowl of corn-flakes. You can also create a Feng Shui environment with plants and fresh flowers. Failing that, inspire yourself with a picture

30 on the wall to look at while you eat. Simon explains, 'Look around the room and think about the things that make you feel positive. Have a picture of something that motivates you, like a photo of a holiday destination you're saving up to visit or a car you would love to buy.'

3 Replace the underlined words and expressions in the sentences below with words or expressions from the text in 2.

a) If I stay up after midnight, I look very <u>sleepy</u> in the morning. (line 13)
b) If I miss breakfast, I <u>start the day badly</u>. After that, it usually <u>continues to deteriorate</u>. (lines 15 and 16)
c) At the end of every day, my desk is completely tidy and <u>clear of rubbish</u>. (line 19)
d) A place where I can dance all night and watch the sun <u>coming up</u> in the morning – that's my ideal <u>place for a holiday</u>. (lines 27 and 33)

4 Which of the statements in 3 do you think are true for your partner? Ask and find out.

5 Work with a partner. Answer the questionnaire below. Then turn to page 137 to check your answers.

> **TRUE OR FALSE?**
> a) People who go to work on an empty stomach have better concentration and memory than those who eat breakfast.
> b) People who eat breakfast are slimmer than those who skip it.
> c) If you only eat sugary cereals for breakfast, it's better to miss it out completely.
> d) A breakfast of fruit juice, cereal and toast has 1,000 calories.
> e) One in five teenage girls skip breakfast to lose weight.
> f) According to Feng Shui, if you have difficulty waking up, it's a good idea to try sleeping with your head facing east.
> g) If you eat breakfast, you're more likely to snack on crisps and fizzy drinks during the day.
> h) After breakfast, people's moods improve.

The Freedom Ship

It will be the world's largest ship, home to 65,000 people who will live and work in a tax-free city on the sea

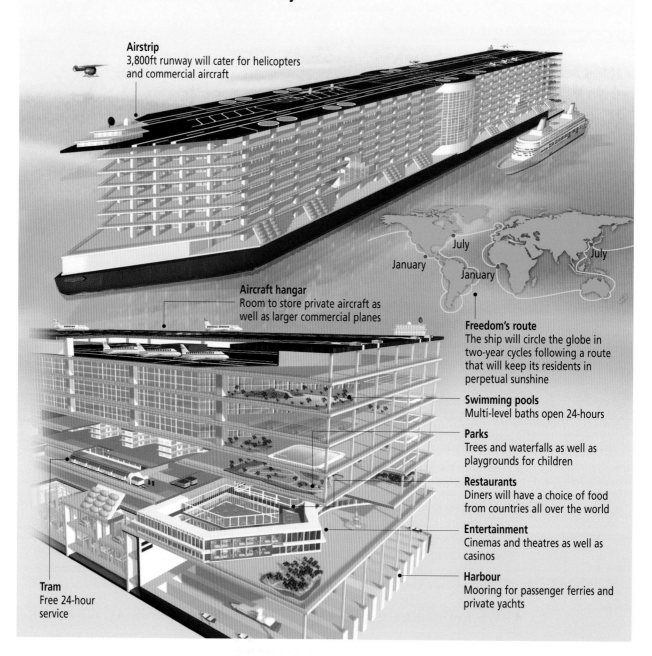

Airstrip
3,800ft runway will cater for helicopters and commercial aircraft

Aircraft hangar
Room to store private aircraft as well as larger commercial planes

Tram
Free 24-hour service

July
January
January
July

Freedom's route
The ship will circle the globe in two-year cycles following a route that will keep its residents in perpetual sunshine

Swimming pools
Multi-level baths open 24-hours

Parks
Trees and waterfalls as well as playgrounds for children

Restaurants
Diners will have a choice of food from countries all over the world

Entertainment
Cinemas and theatres as well as casinos

Harbour
Mooring for passenger ferries and private yachts

Reading

1 The *Freedom Ship* is a project to build a ship more than six times bigger than the biggest ship currently in operation. Work in small groups. Look at the illustration and discuss what might be the advantages and disadvantages of living on such a ship.

2 Work with a partner. Complete this paragraph with what you think are suitable numbers to describe some characteristics of the *Freedom Ship*. Then read the article opposite and see how close your guesses are.

> The *Freedom Ship* will be almost (1) ____ long and (2) ____ high. It will provide a tax haven home for (3) ____ people. Its immense size means that even a (4) ____ metre wave would displace it by less than (5) ____ centimetres. The price of apartments ranges from (6) $____ to (7) $____ , and the total estimated cost of the ship is (8) $____ .

'Floating Monaco' set to cruise the world

(Based on an article in *The Sunday Times*)

Almost 1.3 kilometres long and thirty storeys high, it could cruise the high seas, providing a tax haven home for 65,000 people.
5 Engineers are planning to build the ship, the largest ever, complete with 20,000 apartments, an airport, golf courses, hospitals, a university – and even a free tram
10 service. The idea is for the 2.7 million ton vessel to circumnavigate the globe once every two years, spending a quarter of its time in transit and the
15 rest anchored close to big cities such as New York.

Called the *Freedom Ship*, it is the dream of Engineering Solutions, a company based in
20 Florida which has given up all its other work to concentrate on building the enormous vessel. The proposed ship is so large that it will have to be built at sea.

25 The perks for passengers lie not only in the facilities. They will not have to pay tax or excise duty, although they will have to pay a monthly amount towards the
30 vessel's upkeep.

Passengers will be screened to ensure a crime-free environment. 'It is a chance to create the world's first ideal community,' said
35 Norman Nixon, 58, the project manager. 'The inspiration for the project was to design the best place in the world for living and having fun.'

40 Because of its immense size, the ship will be able to withstand hurricane-force winds, while its width means that even a 25 metre wave would displace it by less than
45 two centimetres. Power will be provided by a hundred engines at the rear.

The *pièce de résistance* will be an airport on the ship's top deck,
50 capable of handling commercial flights, as well as the private planes and helicopters of millionaire residents. Docking space for yachts and hydrofoils will be
55 provided on the bottom deck.

According to the company, reservations and deposits have already been placed for 100 homes by customers from all over the
60 world. The price of apartments ranges from $150,000 for the most basic to $4.2 million for penthouses, which will have three bathrooms and fifty metres of
65 windows with panoramic views. Residents will be able to work on board, and the company says that a number of contracts have already been signed for restaurants, shops
70 and businesses.

The plans have been greeted with a mixture of surprise and scepticism from ship engineers. Dr John Brown, the engineer
75 who designed the *Queen Elizabeth* and the *QE2* said, 'While it will clearly float and is capable of being built, I think we should stop thinking so big. I
80 can't think of anything worse than being thrown together in that space with 65,000 other people.'

The aim is for the sewage to
85 be incinerated in electric toilets to reduce pollution, while waste that cannot be burnt will be stored and sold for scrap when the ship nears a port.

90 The total estimated cost of the ship is $5.4 billion, and buyers of the first two thousand apartments are being offered a 35% discount to arouse interest. Construction is
95 due to start when $180 million has been raised, and the project is intended to be fully self-financing.

The *Freedom Ship* will have a
100 prestige similar to that of the *Titanic*, which was the largest ship in the world when it was launched on May 31, 1911. However, Brown, 98, believes
105 people are starting to miss the point. 'If they really want such a big ship to get away from it all, then perhaps they shouldn't leave dry land in the first place. There
110 is much more space on terra firma.'

---

3 Find answers to these questions in the article.

a) How long will it take the *Freedom Ship* to go round the world?
b) Where is this enormous ship going to be built?
c) Why will passengers be investigated before they can buy a home on the ship?
d) What was the idea behind the project?
e) What will enable the *Freedom Ship* to resist severe weather conditions?
f) What will be the most impressive thing on the ship?
g) Who has expressed doubt about the project?
h) How are they trying to stimulate interest among prospective buyers?

4 Look through the article again and find alternative words and expressions to replace those underlined in 3.

5 With the *Freedom Ship*, Norman Nixon says that he is trying to create 'the world's first ideal community'. Discuss what you think he means by this and whether you think such a concept is possible or desirable.

Close up

1 The passive sentences below are all from the article about the *Freedom Ship* in the previous section. Match the beginnings and the ends of the sentences.

a) The proposed ship is so large that it **will have to be**	1 **launched** on May 31ˢᵗ, 1911.
b) Reservations and deposits **have already been**	2 **built** at sea.
c) Waste that cannot be burnt **will be**	3 **offered** a 35% discount.
d) The buyers of the first two thousand apartments **are being**	4 **stored** and sold for scrap.
e) $180 million **has been**	5 **placed** by customers from all over the world.
f) The *Titanic* **was**	6 **raised**.

2 Work with a partner. Consider the passive sentences in 1 and discuss the questions.

a) Which verb do you combine with a past participle to form the passive?
b) Which sentences refer to the past, which to the present and which to the future?
c) In which case do we know the agent of the verb?
d) Which preposition introduces the agent?

3 Complete these descriptions of two famous structures using appropriate passive forms. Which famous structures are being described? Check your answers on page 136.

> **A**
> On the morning of August 14, 1961, German citizens awoke to find their country (1 **divide**) into two by 166 kilometres of concrete and barbed wire. For the next twenty-eight years, friends and family (2 **separate**) by this symbol of the Cold War. It (3 **finally dismantle**) in 1989, almost as suddenly as it (4 **erect**).

> **B**
> The first stone of this great cathedral (1 **lay**) in 1882, and it (2 **still build**) today. The work (3 **recently speed up**) by the use of new technology, but many believe it (4 **never finish**). Some even feel it (5 **should leave**) exactly as it was when its creator, the architect, Gaudi, died in 1926.

4 Work with a partner. Look at the following questions based on text B in 3.

1 *Who laid the first stone?*
2 *What has recently speeded up the work?*
3 *Who should have left it exactly as it was?*

a) Which question can you answer?
b) Why is it difficult or impossible to answer the other questions?
c) What does this tell you about one of the most important reasons for using the passive?

5 Think about your neighbourhood and/or your home town. Make a list of all the major changes that have been made in the time that you have lived there. Compare your list with a partner. Do you think the changes have been positive or negative. For example:
The street was widened last year.
A new supermarket was opened last week.
Traffic lights were installed a few years ago at the junction at the bottom of our road.

Language reference: the passive

There are several specific cases where you should use the passive.

1 When you don't know who the agent is. *The wheel **was invented** about 3,500 years ago.*
2 When the agent is obvious to everybody. *She **has been arrested** and **charged** with theft.*
3 When you don't want to identify the agent. *I **was told** not to mention it.*

The agent

If it is necessary to mention the agent of the passive (i.e. the 'doer' of the action), you use the preposition *by*. *Power will be provided **by a hundred engines at the rear.***

Home page

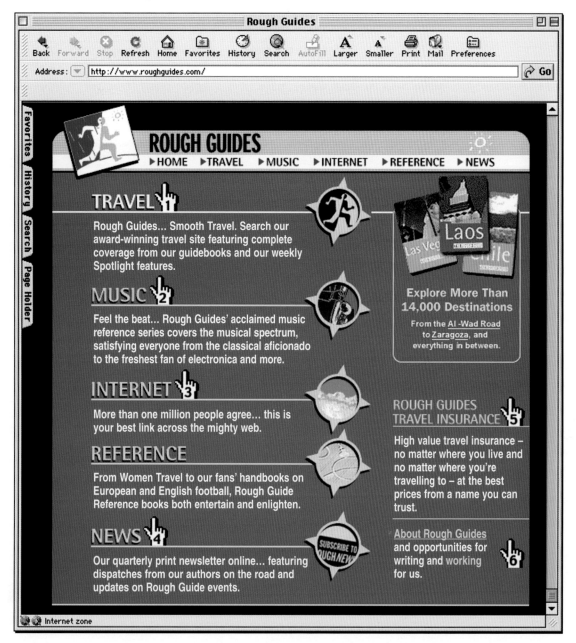

Reading   **1** The extracts below are from web pages that are linked to the home page above. Match the extracts to the numbered symbols (1–6) on the home page.

a) Though we don't have any employment opportunities at this time, we do have the occasional opening and encourage you to send us your resumé (CV) and cover letter for our files.

b) Create a personal web page; how to stay connected when travelling the world; tune into live music broadcasts; go online bargain hunting; play games; and loads more.

c) Don't forget to check out the Rough Guide CDs, which are produced in collaboration with World Music Network (http://www.worldmusic.net). View the catalogue, find out what's hot on the jukebox, or place your orders or join the network.

d) For details of the benefits provided by each kind of policy click here, and for details of the activities considered hazardous click here.

e) As the media would have it, the shantytowns of Cape Town are little more than hotbeds of crime and disease. See what lies behind the popular images of South Africa's displaced communities ...

f) We're also exhibiting at the Trips Worldwide Latin American & Alternative Caribbean Travel Show on Saturday 28th October at Cabot Hall, Canary Wharf, London, in aid of Latin American charities.

2 Imagine you have designed and constructed a class website. Look at the home page below. The words in red are hypertext links to more web pages on the same site. Discuss what sort of information you might find if you clicked on any of these hypertext links.

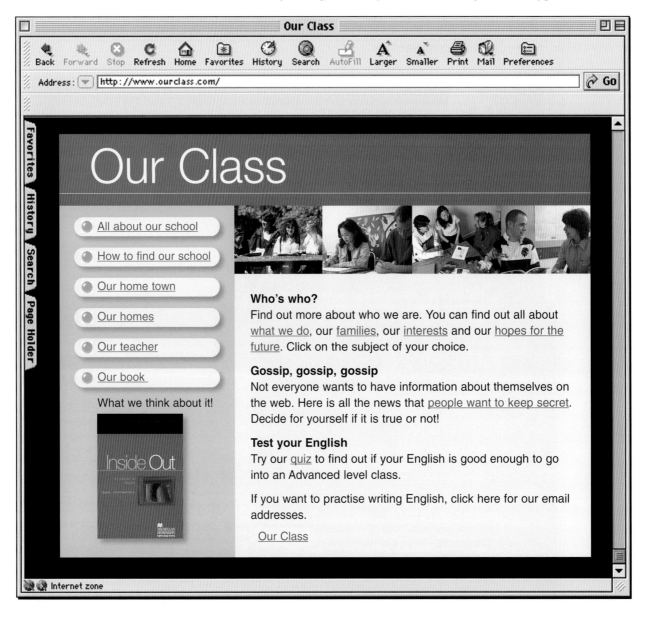

3 Think about *your* class and decide how you would like to redesign the home page in 2. There are some suggestions for replacement hypertext links below, or alternatively use your own ideas. What do you think Internet surfers would be most interested in reading?

Actually, we're famous...	Speak English	Have a laugh
Many of us are famous people in disguise! Click here to find out who we really are and why we are pretending to be English students.	Do you speak English in the classroom? Click here for our guide to the most useful classroom phrases in English (with translations).	This is a short collection of jokes we have enjoyed. Warning: some of these jokes lose a lot in the translation.
Our favourite websites	Our football team	Sing and learn – our suggestions for useful English songs.
Holidays in our area	Our homes	Tips for learning difficult languages

4 Work in small groups. Each group should choose one or more web pages to write based on the hypertext links you have selected for your home page.

14 Review 2

Don't quote me on that!

Reporting verbs

Choose the correct verb structures in the sentence beginnings (a–f). Then match the sentence beginnings to the sentence endings (1–6).

a) In 1977, Ken Olsen, president of Digital Equipment Corporation, **suggested journalists / suggested to journalists** …

b) US writer Wilson Mizner once famously **advised his colleagues / advised to his colleagues** …

c) Decca records, on rejecting the Beatles in 1962 **explained the press / explained to the press** …

d) In 1943 Thomas Watson, Chairman of IBM computers, **told a conference / told to a conference** …

e) Albert Einstein, when once asked about the consequences of his discoveries, **admitted the questioner / admitted to the questioner** …

f) In 1899, Charles Duell, commissioner of the US patents office **announced the American people / announced to the American people** …

1 that he thought there was a world market for maybe five computers.

2 that everything that could be invented had been invented.

3 they didn't like their sound, and guitar music was on the way out.

4 that there was no reason why anyone would want a computer in their home.

5 to be nice to people on the way up, because they would meet them again on the way down.

6 that he never thought about the future.

Dilemma

Unreal conditionals

1 Match the sentence halves (a–f and 1–6) to make six questions.

a) If you could spend a year on a desert island with another person, …	1 what serious crime might you consider committing?
b) Assuming you could have the answer to any one question, …	2 what would you ask?
c) Imagine you could relive any one experience of your life, …	3 who would you most like to spend the time with?
d) Supposing you would never be caught, …	4 what would you spend it on?
e) If you could be any famous person's partner, …	5 whose would you like to be?
f) Imagine you had to spend $1 million before the end of the day, …	6 which experience would you choose?

2 Work in small groups. Discuss the questions in 1.

3 Now, write four similar questions of your own and ask them to your classmates. Decide who has given the most interesting or unusual answers.

> If …   Assuming …   Imagine …   Supposing …

Unsolved mysteries

1 Divide into groups of three. Each person read one of the extracts and then retell the story to the other group members. Use a dictionary if you wish.

Great mysteries of the world

The Bermuda Triangle

The story of the Bermuda Triangle began in 1945 when, in perfect flying conditions, a squadron of five American air force bombers on a training mission suddenly disappeared from radar, never to be seen again. Just before disappearing, they reported that all the planes' compasses had stopped working and that they were lost. Since then, sixteen planes and numerous ships have simply vanished without trace in this same area, including on December 30, 1976 the supertanker, *Grand Zenith*, carrying over thirty million tons of oil. Most reported a failure of their navigational equipment.

Mysterious rain

Over the last few hundred years, there have been numerous reports of strange objects falling from the sky. In 1680, hundreds of live rats fell on a village in Norway. Showers of fish, frogs, lizards and worms have all been documented. In 1977, a couple walking home from church in Bristol in England were rained on by hundreds of hazel nuts falling from a clear blue sky. In 1984, a single house in Lancashire was bombarded with apples, and in 1989, it rained sardines on a small town in Australia. In 1994 a pensioner in France was rained on by enough coins to do her weekly shopping.

The curse of Tutankhamun

On 26 November 1922, the archaeologists Howard Carter and the Earl of Carnarvon finally discovered the remains of the Egyptian pharaoh Tutankhamun, which had not been seen for over 3,000 years. It was said that a curse of death would be on anyone who disturbed Tutankhamun's body. Very shortly after the discovery, a cobra, which was considered by the ancient Egyptians to be a royal snake, bit and killed Howard Carter's pet canary. Shortly after, the Earl of Carnarvon fell ill and died. At the exact moment of his death all the lights in Cairo suddenly and inexplicably went out. At this same moment in England, the Earl's dog began to howl and then died. Three of the archaeologists' assistants died shortly after this, and then a French professor visiting Egypt to see the tomb died on the night of his arrival. An exhibition of the treasures opened in London in 1972. The curator of the museum publicly laughed when questioned about the curse. Four weeks later he was dead. Curse or coincidence?

2 In your groups, discuss the possible causes of these mysterious events. The ideas in the box may help you. Which theories do you think are the most likely?

alien abductions	Earth's magnetic field	violent weather	poison	a whale
magic	tornadoes	a practical joke	a giant sea monster	passing airplanes
murder	a tidal wave			

School daze

1 Complete the following stories by putting each verb into an appropriate tense.

a) A student at Oxford (1) ____ (sit) an exam when he (2) ____ (ask) a supervisor for a glass of red wine and a plate of scones, correctly adding that this tradition (3) ____ (be) the right of Oxford scholars dating back to medieval times. The wine and the scones (4) ____ (bring) to the exam room, and the student (5) ____ (enjoy) the lot before finishing his exam. A few weeks later, the student (6) ____ (be) shocked to find that he (7) ____ (fail) the exam, not because he (8) ____ (perform) badly, but because he (9) ____ (not wear) his sword as he sat the exam.

b) A student who (10) ____ (sit) an exam (11) ____ (continue) to write a full five minutes after the professor (12) ____ (tell) everyone to stop. When the student (13) ____ (try) to hand in his paper, the professor (14) ____ (tell) him not to bother, as he (15) ____ (already fail). 'Do you know who I am?' the student angrily (16) ____ (ask) the professor. When the professor (17) ____ (reply) that he (18) ____ (never see) the student before, the student (19) ____ (push) his paper into the middle of the pile of other papers and quickly (20) ____ (run) out of the room.

2 ▭ **66** Listen and check your answers.

3 Have you ever had an exam experience you'd rather forget?

The *Harry Potter* phenomenon

The *Harry Potter* series of books has become a world-wide phenomenon since the first book was published in 1997. Complete the following facts by adding an appropriate relative pronoun.

a) As it is well documented that young boys tend not to read books by female authors, JK Rowling, ____ real name is Joanne Kathleen, chose to use only her initials, so people wouldn't realise she was a woman.
b) The first story ____ JK Rowling ever wrote was called *Rabbit*. She was just six years old.
c) The name Potter comes from a neighbour ____ lived four doors down from author JK Rowling when she was a youngster.
d) Harry Potter's affection for Kings Cross is inspired by JK Rowling's parents, ____ first met on a train as they were leaving the famous London railway station.
e) The initial sales of *Harry Potter and the Prisoner of Azkaban*, ____ was published in 1999, were delayed until four o'clock as it was feared that thousands of children would play truant from school to get hold of a copy.
f) The fourth book, *Harry Potter and the Goblet of Fire*, sold 372,775 copies in the UK alone on the first day of its release, ____ made it the fastest-selling book in history.

The thing I ...

1 Choose a topic from the box. Rearrange the words in *italic* and then complete the sentences about the topic you have chosen.

> my country   pop music   women   television   fashion   money
> computers   travel   men   sport   English   work   children

a) The *thing most I like* about ... is ...
b) One *I of the things don't like* about ... is ...
c) What *understand I don't* about ... is ...
d) What *annoys really me* about ... is ...
e) The *I amusing find thing really* about ... is ...
f) One *always hated thing I've* about ... is ...

2 Work in groups. Share your sentences with each other. Are your views similar or different and do you agree with each other's statements?

3 Choose another topic from the box and make some more sentences.

Revved up or relaxed?

1 Choose the correct tense or verb form in each question in the questionnaire.

Do you like to know exactly where you are in life, or are you quite happy going with the flow? Answer the following questions to find out.

1 Do you know what you **will do / will be doing** one hour from now?
  a I know exactly.
  b No idea.
  c No, but I can guess.

2 Do you know where you **are going / go** on your next holiday?
  a It's at the planning stage.
  b It's already booked.
  c No, but I know it'll be somewhere hot!

3 Do you know where you **are being / are going to be** in five years' time?
  a Yes, I know exactly.
  b Yes, more or less.
  c Wherever life takes me.

4 By the end of today, do you think you **will be making / will have made** any important decisions?
  a Yes, of course.
  b No, I never make decisions.
  c Maybe.

5 What **are you doing / will you do** this evening?
  a Nothing.
  b The cinema, then dinner with friends.
  c I'm open to offers.

6 By the end of the week, **will you decide / will you have decided** what you **are going to do / do** over the weekend?
  a Yes, of course.
  b No idea.
  c It depends on my friends.

7 When your favourite band or singer releases their next CD, **are you buying / will you buy** it …
  a after you hear what your friends say about it?
  b as soon as it's released?
  c only after you've heard it yourself?

8 Have you thought about what you **are doing / are going to do** when you retire?
  a Not for one second.
  b Yes, but not for long.
  c It's all planned, and I can't wait!

OR?

ANALYSIS

Under 10: You're very relaxed and easygoing, preferring to go with the flow most of the time and trusting that things will work out okay. While this can often be a good thing, you should maybe start being a bit more decisive as you could find life taking control of you, if you're not careful.

10–20: You have probably got a good balance between being quite easygoing and happy to go with the flow and knowing when you must be decisive and get things organised. You should get on in life very well.

Over 20: You certainly like to be on top of things and leave nothing to chance. Perhaps you should relax a little and try going with the flow from time to time. You might then have more time to enjoy life and not organise it!

Score:

1 a3, b1, c2	3 a3, b2, c1	5 a2, b3, c1	7 a2, b1, c3
2 a2, b3, c1	4 a3, b1, c2	6 a3, b1, c2	8 a1, b2, c3

2 Answer *a*, *b* or *c* for each question, then exchange your completed questionnaire with a partner. Read the analysis to find out your partner's score and to see what the score means.

I've got loads of …

Quantity Play the game in small groups.

1 Choose a letter. You each have three minutes to complete the sentences with something that begins with this letter. The sentences must be true for you.

2 Score one point for each correct sentence. Your classmates must judge whether or not the sentences are true for you.

3 If someone else in the group has the same sentence, you each score two points.

4 After everyone in the group has read out their sentences, choose another letter and play again. The winner is the person with the most points after three rounds.

> For example: *For the letter P – I've got a few pens, I've got loads of photographs, I've got very little patience …*
>
> | I've got | a few … |
> | | loads of … |
> | | very little … |
> | | only one … |
> | | too few … |
> | | far too many … |
> | | more than enough … |

Language trivia quiz

Passive structures

1 Complete the sentences by putting the verb into the correct form of the passive.

a) It ____ (think) that English ____ (speak) as a first or second language in about **20 / 50 / 100** countries and that it ____ (currently learn) by about **3 / 30 / 300** million people worldwide.

b) The longest word in any language is in English and is just over **2,000 / 20,000 / 200,000** letters long. It's a scientific term which ____ (use) to describe a complex process in human biology.

c) It ____ (suggest) that before the end of the 21st century **30 / 50 / 75** per cent of all the conversations in the world ____ (hold) in English.

d) The country with the highest number of languages is New Guinea. In fact, more than **1 / 5 / 10** per cent of the world's languages ____ (speak) there.

e) Members of the Mazateco tribe in Mexico can hold conversations just by **whistling / clicking their teeth / flicking their tongues**. Meaning ____ (express) by changes in pitch.

f) The longest name of a city ____ (reckon) to be the full name for Krungthep, the Thai name for Bangkok. It is **75 / 175 / 275** letters long.

g) It ____ (estimate) that the artificial language Esperanto, which ____ (invent) by Russian physician Ludwik Zamenhof in the 1880s, currently has about **40,000 / 400,000 / 4,000,000** speakers worldwide.

2 Try to guess the correct answer for each of the facts. Check your answers below.

> a) 50; 300   b) 200,000   c) 50   d) 10   e) whistling   f) 175   g) 4,000,000

Additional material

1 Images

a) 1989   b) 1969   c) 1990   d) 1977

11 Sell

1a) Head   2b) Nike   3a) Adidas   4c) Speedo   5c) Slazenger   6b) Kappa

1 Images

Close up.
Indirect questions, 4

Student A

Answer Student B's questions. Do not show the information about David Beckham to Student B.

David Beckham

Full name: David Robert Joseph Beckham
Date of birth: May 7, 1975
Place of birth: Leytonstone, London
Zodiac sign: Taurus
Hair: Light brown
Eyes: Dark blue
Height: 1.82 m
Weight: 85 kg
Distinguishing marks: His son's name is tattooed on his back.
Squad number: 7
Position: Midfield (for Manchester United)
Family: Parents Sandra and Ted, sisters Joanne and Lynne, wife Victoria, son Brooklyn Joseph
Married: Victoria Adams ('Posh Spice') in July 1999
Quote: 'I shaved my head because too many people were copying my style and I got fed up with all the lookalikes.'

4 Body

Sounding sympathetic, 3

Student A

Take it in turns to read out your problems. When you hear your partner's problem, react sympathetically or unsympathetically and then give some advice.

a) Whatever time I go to bed, I have trouble getting to sleep.
b) I can't help being late for everything.
c) I can't cook.
d) I can't seem to meet any interesting people.

e) I keep forgetting things.
f) My hair's a mess.
g) I want to give up smoking.
h) I'm trying to lose weight before my holiday.

5 Ritual

Small talk. Lexis, 1

Student A

1 You have the first lines of four two-line conversations. Your partner has the second lines. Read out your line. Then listen and write down your partner's response to complete each exchange.

a) A: What have you been up to lately?
    B: _____
b) A: Long time no see.
    B: _____
c) A: Alice sends her love.
    B: _____
d) A: How do you do.
    B: _____

2 You have the second lines of four two-line conversations. Your partner has the first lines. Listen to your partner read out the first line and then choose and read out the correct response.

> I won't.   I will.   Not so bad, thanks.
> You're welcome. You must come again soon.

13 Home

Close up. The passive, 3

Answers

A *The Berlin Wall* divided communist East Germany from capitalist West Germany from 1961 to 1989.
B *The Sagrada Familia* in Barcelona, Spain is the longest-running construction project under way in the world today.

7 Review 1

Four in a row

Answers

1 proud of	10 interested in	19 depend on	28 optimistic about
2 fed up with	11 succeed in	20 afraid of	29 accuse of
3 dream of / about	12 specialise in	21 well-known for	30 apologise for / to
4 approve of	13 useless at	22 keen on	31 good at / for
5 insist on	14 not bad at / for	23 reliant on	32 believe in
6 prevent from	15 lacking in	24 look forward to	33 rely on
7 worry about	16 allergic to	25 accustomed to	34 concentrate on
8 certain of / about	17 realistic about	26 fond of	35 consist of
9 famous for	18 forgive for	27 compatible with	

9 Attraction

Blind date. Listening, 5

Number 1 (Suzy) Number 2 (Melanie) Number 3 (Ruth)

James chose Number 2 (Melanie).

13 Home

Rise and shine. Reading, 5

Answers

a) False.
b) True. People who skip breakfast eat more fat.
c) False. Anything is better than nothing.
d) False. It has only 400 to 500 calories.
e) True.
f) True.
g) False.
h) True.

10 Genius

I know what I like!, 3

Test your memory! Do the tasks and answer these questions about the three paintings on page 90.
Then look back and check your answers. Which painting did you remember best?

Frida and Diego Rivera, 1931
a) Describe Frida's clothes.
b) What jewellery is she wearing?
c) What is Diego holding in his right hand?
d) There's something above Frida's head – what is it?
e) What colour is Diego's shirt?

Self-portrait with cropped hair, 1940
a) Describe Frida's face.
b) What is she wearing?
c) What is she holding in her right hand?
d) She's sitting on a chair – what's it made of?
e) What's at the top of the painting?

Roots, 1943
a) Describe the landscape.
b) What is Frida leaning on?
c) Is her hair tied up or loose?
d) Which part of her body do the roots seem to be coming from?
e) What colour are the leaves?

10 Genius

Close up. Modals of deduction, 5

Artemisia Gentileschi, *Judith Slaying Holofernes*, c. 1612–21 (Uffizi, Florence/Scala)

Edgar Degas, *Absinthe*, 1876 (Musée d'Orsay, Paris)

Pablo Picasso, *Guernica*, 1937 (Museo del Prado, Madrid)

Francisco de Goya, *The Third of May 1808*, 1814 (Museo del Prado, Madrid)

Jacques-Louis David, *The Death of Marat*, 1793 (Musées Royaux des Beaux Arts de Belgique, Brussels)

1 Images

Close up.
Indirect questions, 4

Student B

Answer Student A's questions. Do not show the information about Victoria Beckham to Student A.

Victoria Beckham ('Posh Spice')

Full name: Victoria Caroline Adams Beckham ('Posh Spice')
Date of birth: April 17, 1974
Place of birth: Hertfordshire, England
Zodiac sign: Aries
Hair: Brown
Eyes: Brown
Height: 1.67 m
Weight: 46 kg
Distinguishing marks: A diamond in her fingernail.
Family: Parents Tony and Jackie, sister Louise, brother Christian, husband David Beckham, and son Brooklyn Joseph
Career: In summer 1996, joined *The Spice Girls* who sold over 50 million albums worldwide.
Favourite designers: Gucci, Armani and Prada
Married: David Beckham in July 1999
Pets: Two Rottweiler dogs
Quote: 'I love Madonna, but I've never felt tempted to change my image as often as she does.'

4 Body

Sounding sympathetic, 3

Student B

Take it in turns to read out your problems. When you hear your partner's problem, react sympathetically or unsympathetically and then give some advice.

a) Whatever time I go to bed, I have trouble getting up in the morning.
b) I keep getting colds.
c) I can't dance.
d) I'm afraid of flying.
e) I hate my tattoo.
f) I've got terrible hiccups.
g) My partner keeps buying me unsuitable presents for birthdays and Christmas.
h) I'm addicted to my mobile phone.

13 Home

Ideal homes. Listening, 4

Room 1: Paula, astrologer
'Most of what he said is true. I'm a night owl and I do live in organised chaos. But I can find anything I want in about thirty seconds flat.'

Room 2: Colin, sales director for publishing company
'He certainly guessed the details of my job right – I do travel a lot and I also entertain a lot, but always in restaurants. I am single, but I think that if I found the right person, commitment wouldn't be a problem.'

5 Ritual

Small talk. Lexis, 1

Student B

1 You have the second lines of four two-line conversations. Your partner has the first lines. Listen to your partner read out the first line and then choose and read out the correct response.

> Yes, it must be over a year.
> How do you do.
> Oh, not much. The usual.
> Thank you. Give her mine.

2 You have the first lines of four two-line conversations. Your partner has the second lines. Read out your line then listen and write down your partner's response to complete each exchange.

a) A: Keep in touch.
   B: _____
b) A: Thank you for a lovely evening.
   B: _____
c) A: Don't forget to phone me.
   B: _____
d) A: How are you?
   B: _____

10 Genius

Eureka, 1

Answers

Listed in order of invention:

f) The toothbrush – The first mention of a toothbrush with bristles at right angles to the handle is in a Chinese encyclopaedia of 1498.

b) The toilet – Queen Elizabeth I was delighted to add this new 'throne' to her collection when her godson Sir John Harrington invented it in 1597.

d) False teeth – Before French pharmacist Alexis Duchateau perfected a set of porcelain dentures in 1770, it was common practice to use 'dead men's teeth' – particularly plentiful after the frequent wars at the time.

a) The contact lens – The first workable pair were produced in 1887 by F.E. Muller, a glassblower from Wiesbaden in Germany.

e) The safety razor – US citizen King Camp Gillette patented this in 1901. He believed his fortune lay in inventing something that people used once and then threw away. He wasn't wrong. Within the first year he sold over twelve million of his disposable blades.

c) The zip – There were several attempts at this before the Swedish engineer Gideon Sundback finally got the zipper to work in 1913. It was later claimed that by replacing the buttons on trousers the new device would eliminate any risk of embarrassment. Sadly …

10 Genius

Trivia pursuit – Genius edition

Team A questions

(The correct answers are in **bold**.)

Geography & travel

1 Is the driest inhabited place in the world a) Chile, b) Peru or c) **Egypt**?
2 The Sahara is the largest desert in the world. **True** or false?
3 Which is the deepest ocean: a) **the Pacific** or b) the Atlantic?
4 Australia ruled Papua New Guinea until its independence in 1975. **True** or false?
5 Is Reykjavik the capital of a) Romania, b) Hungary or c) **Iceland**?
6 Which was the first city in the world to reach a population of one million: a) New York, b) Paris or c) **Rome**?

Inventions

1 Marconi invented pasta. True or **false**? (He invented the radio.)
2 Who invented the electric battery. Was it a) Lucas, b) Eveready or c) **Volta**?
3 Marie Curie was Belgian. True or **false**? (She was Polish.)
4 The motorcycle was patented by Gottlieb Daimler in 1885. **True** or false?
5 Did Thomas Edison, the designer of the electric light-bulb, patent a) 13, b) 130 or c) **1,300** inventions?
6 The Romans invented the wheel. True or **false**? (The Mesopotamians around 3500 BC.)

Nature

1 Whales can communicate over vast distances. **True** or false?
2 Which elephants have small ears and high foreheads: a) African or b) **Indian**?

3 How much time do cats spend sleeping: a) one quarter, b) **one third** or c) half their lives?
4 Man-eating plants live in jungles. True or **false**? (There are no man-eating plants.)
5 Bamboo can grow as high as a twelve storey building. **True** or false?
6 A horse can reach a top speed of: a) **56 km/h**, b) 66 km/h or c) 76 km/h?

Culture

1 William Shakespeare wrote all his plays while standing up. True or **false**? (But Virginia Woolf did.)
2 When Franz Schubert died at the age of thirty-one, did he leave a) 234, b) 434 or c) **634** compositions?
3 Oscar Wilde's first and only novel was *The Picture of Dorian Gray*. **True** or false?
4 Michael Jackson had his first solo hit at the age of nineteen. True or **false**? (He was thirteen.)
5 Was the wife of Surrealist artist, Salvador Dali, called a) Zara, b) **Gala** or c) Tara?
6 The singer Björk comes from a) Norway, b) **Iceland** or c) Sweden?

Miscellaneous

1 Canoeing is an Olympic event. **True** or false?
2 Which city is known as the Eternal City: a) **Rome**, b) Venice or c) Florence?
3 How many languages are used in India: a) 58, b) 85 or c) **858**?
4 John F. Kennedy was the youngest US president to die. Was he a) 43, b) **46** or c) 48?
5 Tattooing was practised by the Egyptians as early as 2000 BC. **True** or false?
6 Which Apollo mission first put man on the moon: a) Apollo 13, b) **Apollo 11** or c) Apollo 9?

10 Genius

Trivia pursuit – Genius edition

Team B questions

(The correct answers are in **bold**.)

Geography & travel

1 Which is the most popular world holiday destination: a) the USA, b) **France** or c) Spain?
2 What is the official language of Brazil: is it a) Spanish, b) **Portuguese** or c) English?
3 Which river is longer: a) **the Volga**, b) the Danube or c) the Seine?
4 To which country do the Canary Islands belong: a) **Spain**, b) Morocco or c) Portugal?
5 The Pacific Ocean has 25,000 islands. **True** or false?
6 The population of the United Kingdom is more than double that of Australia. **True** or false?

Inventions

1 The Nobel Peace Prize is funded by the vast fortune Alfred Nobel made out of selling explosives. **True** or false?
2 The tin opener was invented a) 2, b) 27 or c) **45** years after the tin can.
3 John Boyd Dunlop, André Michelin and Charles Goodyear were all involved in developing the rubber tyre. **True** or False?
4 The fax machine was invented by Giovanni Caselli in a) **1865**, b) 1921 or c) 1967.
5 The first book printed in English came out in a) 1456, b) **1474** or c) 1507. (William Caxton.)
6 The person who invented champagne in 1690 was a monk called a) Pierre Chandon, b) Pierre Moët or c) **Pierre Pérignon**.

Nature

1 Chocolate is good for you because it's high in vitamins. True or **false**?
2 About a quarter of the world's coffee beans are grown in Brazil. **True** or false?
3 Only one continent on the planet has no spiders. Is it a) the Arctic or b) **Antarctica**?
4 Tigers have striped skin, not just striped fur. **True** or false?
5 The blue whale can live for six months without eating. **True** or false?
6 Were the first animals to be domesticated, a) **dogs** or b) cats?

Culture

1 The 18th century German born composer Handel became a British subject. **True** or false?
2 Richard Ashcroft was lead singer of which British band: a) Blur, b) Oasis or c) **The Verve**?
3 Which of the following is not a kind of dance music: a) trance, b) garage or c) **tip top**?
4 Who wrote Madame Butterfly? Was it a) Fellini, b) Armani or c) **Puccini**?
5 Who sang 'Smells like teen spirit' and died tragically a couple of years later? Was it a) **Kurt Cobain**, b) Jimmie Hendrix or c) Elvis Presley?
6 Michelangelo spent forty days on his back painting the ceiling of the Sistine Chapel in Rome. True or **false**? (It took over four years.)

Miscellaneous

1 What was the first animal in space: a) a monkey, b) a rabbit or c) **a dog**?
2 King Alexander of Greece died in 1920 after being bitten by his pet. Was it a) **a monkey**, b) a crocodile or c) a snake?
3 For which flowering tree is Japan famous: a) the Apple or b) **the Cherry**?
4 What colour is a New York taxi: a) blue, b) black or c) **yellow**?
5 For which country was André Agassi's father a boxer? Was it a) Canada, b) Italy or c) **Iran**?
6 In 1921, was a) **Germany** or b) America the first country to have a motorway?

12 Student

Job hunting. CVs, 4

Curriculum Vitae

Name	Ben Arnoldson
Address	311 Cowley Rd, Oxford
Telephone	01865 372 827 (mobile 0788 98878977)
E-mail	beautifulben@hotmail.com
Date of birth	12th August 1981
Education	June 1997
	8 GCSEs
	June 1999
	2 A-levels: English and Geography
Employment	July to December 1999
	Shop assistant. Gained experience of the retail trade
	January to March 2000
	Acquired interpersonal skills in the catering trade.
	April to September 2000
	Was involved in the music industry.
	September to December 2000
	Child-minding. Gained experience in working with children.
	January to March 2001
	Clerical assistant. Improved my word-processing skills.
Other skills	Word-processing
	Working knowledge of French, Spanish
Personal interests	Sport, music, working with children and foreign travel.
References	On request

Verb structures

Basic structures
See unit 1.

| ASPECT | VOICE | TENSES | | MODALS |
		Present	Past	*will (would, must ...)*
simple	active	He **writes** letters.	He **wrote** letters.	He **will write** letters.
	passive	Letters **are written**.	Letters **were written**.	Letters **will be written**.
continuous	active	He **is writing** letters.	He **was writing** letters.	He **will be writing** letters.
	passive	Letters **are being written**.	Letters **were being written**.	* Letters **will be being written**.
perfect	active	He **has written** letters.	He **had written** letters.	He **will have written** letters.
	passive	Letters **have been written**.	Letters **had been** written.	Letters **will have been written**.
perfect continuous	active	He **has been writing** letters.	He **had been writing** letters.	He **will have been writing** letters.

* Note: You usually avoid saying *be being* or *been being*. Therefore, the future continuous passive, and the present/past continuous passives are rare. For the same reason, the perfect continuous passive is almost never used.

Verbs with stative meanings
See unit 6.

The following verbs have stative meanings and are not usually used in the continuous form.

> believe, belong, consist of, contain, deserve, detest, dislike, doubt, envy, exist, forget, hate, hear, imagine, include, involve, know, like, love, own, possess, prefer, realize, recognize, resemble, see, seem, sound, suppose, suspect, understand, want, wish

I don't believe in ghosts. NOT *I am not believing in ghosts.*
I've known Jim for more than twenty years. NOT *I've been knowing Jim for more than twenty years.*

The following verbs have dynamic as well as stative meanings. The examples show the stative meanings.

appear (seem): *The region appears to be getting back to normal after the extensive flooding.*
be (permanent characteristic): *They are Spanish.*
feel (opinion): *I feel that footballers earn too much money.*
fit (correct size): *The trousers fit well, but the jacket is too small.*
have (possession): *I've had this watch since I was eighteen.*
smell (of something): *That smells delicious!*
taste (of something): *This wine tastes like vinegar. Let's ask for another bottle.*
think (opinion): *Do you think they'll come?*
weigh (weight): *This suitcase weighs a ton! What have you got in it?*

Reported speech with backshift
See unit 8.

Verbs in direct speech often move 'one tense back' when they are reported.

'We're going to Paris next weekend.' ➔ *He informed her that **they were going** to Paris the following weekend.*

'I inherited a sum of money.' ➔ *He claimed that **he had inherited** a sum of money.*

'I'm working for my father.' ➔ *He assured her that **he was working** for his father.*

Verb patterns: verbs followed by *to*-infinitive
See units 2 and 5.

verb + *to*-infinitive	
aim, arrange, attempt, can't afford, claim, decide, deserve, hope, intend, learn, long, manage, offer, plan, prepare, pretend, refuse, seem, tend, try, vote, wish	to go to come to stay

*We **aim to please**.*
*I **managed to beat** him at poker.*

verb + (object) + *to*-infinitive		
choose, expect, help, need, pay, prefer, want, would like	(me) (you) (her)	to come to go to stay

*She **wants to go** to the party.*
*She **wants me to go** with her.*

verb + object + *to*-infinitive		
allow, challenge, choose, dare, enable, encourage, force, inspire, invite, order, remind, teach, train, trust, urge, warned	me you her	to come to go to stay

*My parents **taught me to respect** other people.*
*They **allowed her to have** the afternoon off.*

Note: *Make* and *let* take an object followed by the infinitive without *to*.
*My parents always **made me do** all my homework before going out.*
*They never **let me go out** late at the weekends.*

Verb patterns: verbs followed by *-ing* form
See units 2 and 5.

verb + *-ing* form	
adore, avoid, can't stand, consider, delay, describe, detest, dislike, don't mind, dread, enjoy, fancy, finish, imagine, keep, miss, practise, resent, resist, risk, spend/waste time	coming going staying

*I never **waste time ironing** my clothes.*
*My family always **avoids talking** about politics.*

Note: *Begin, bother, continue* and *start* can be followed by the *to*-infinitive or the *-ing* form. There is very little change in meaning.

Verb patterns: reporting verbs

See unit 8.

verb + hearer + *to*-infinitive		
advise, ask, beg, convince, encourage, forbid, instruct, invite, order, persuade, remind, tell, urge, warned (not)	me you her	to come to go to stay

He *asked me to post* the letters.
She *invited Bob to go* skiing with her.

verb + hearer + *that* clause		
advise, assure, convince, inform, notify, persuade, promise, reassure, remind, tell	me you her	that ...

She *reassured them that* she was okay.
We regret to *inform passengers that* all flights are delayed.

verb + *to*-infinitive	
agree, ask, claim, demand, offer, promise, propose, refuse, threaten	to come to go to stay

She *refused to tell* the truth.
He *offered to pay* them in cash.

verb + *that* clause	
admit, agree, announce, claim, complain. confirm, explain, declare, deny, mention, propose, say, suggest	that ...

He *suggested that* I should go and see a doctor.
They *explained that* they wouldn't be coming to the party.

verb + *-ing* form	
admit, deny, mention, propose, report, suggest	coming going staying

They all *denied having seen* her.
She *reported seeing* a strange flashing light in the sky.

Phrasal verbs

See unit 4.

1 verb + particle
break down (*stop working*), come out (*be published*), draw up (*come to a stop*), fall out (*argue*), get away (*escape*), give in (*admit defeat*), go off (*explode*), go on (*happen*), go on (*continue*), set in (*begin and then continue*), show off (*behave to attract attention*), take off (*leave the ground*), turn up (*arrive unexpectedly*), wear off (*fade away*)

At the beginning of the holiday the bad weather *set in*. We didn't see the sun for three days!
The taxi *drew up* and four large men got out

2 verb + object + particle (SEPARABLE)
bring him up (*look after and educate him*), call it off (*cancel it*), give them up (*stop*), let them down (*disappoint them*), look it up (*locate it*), make it up (*invent it*), pick it up (*learn it*), put it off (*postpone it*), put you up (*provide you with accommodation*), take it up (*start a pastime*), think it over (*consider it*), try them out (*use for the first time*), turn it down (*refuse something*), wear her out (*make her tired*), work it out (*find a solution*)

The weather was so bad on the day of the game that they *called it off*.
I'm not sure whether I should accept or not. I'll *think it over*.

3 verb + particle + object (NOT SEPARABLE)
ask after you (*ask for news about you*), come across it (*find something by chance*), come into it (*inherit it*), count on him (*depend on him*), do without them (*manage without them*), get at something (*suggest something*), get over it (*recover from it*), look into it (*investigate it*), make for somewhere (*go in a particular direction*), run into her (*meet her by chance*), take after him (*have similar characteristics to him*)

After her father died she *came into* a lot of money.
'What are you *getting at*?' 'Well, to be frank, I'm not sure if I want to continue this relationship.'

4 verb + particle + particle + object (NOT SEPARABLE)
cut down on something (*reduce the amount of something*), come up with something (*think of something*), get away with it (*avoid discovery*), get round to it (*find time to do it*), get up to something (*do something – often something bad*), make up for it (*compensate for it*), put up with them (*tolerate them*), run out of them (*have no more of them*)

Have they *come up with* the answer yet?
She *ran out of* time and couldn't finish the last exam question.

Nouns

Uncountable nouns

See units 3 and 13.

The following nouns are uncountable in English but countable in some other languages. You use them with singular verb forms.

advice, baggage, behaviour, equipment, food, furniture, health, homework, information, knowledge, luggage, machinery, money, music, news, progress, research, toast, traffic, travel, weather, work

You can get lots of *information* and *advice* at the Tourist Office.
NOT *informations and advices*

The *traffic* is getting worse and worse.   NOT *The traffics are ...*

Plural nouns

See units 3 and 13.

The following plural nouns are uncountable. You use them with plural verb forms.

clothes, contents, glasses, goods, jeans, headphones, knickers, pants, pyjamas, scissors, shorts, stairs, trousers, wages

How much were those *jeans*?   NOT *How much was that jean?*
Where are the *scissors*?   NOT *Where is the scissors?*

Grammar glossary

```
                              modal
              main            auxiliary                                        main
  main        verb            verb                                             verb
  verb    adjective  conjunction        adverb    article       pronoun
    |         |         |         |        |         |             |            |
```
Learn these useful words and you can understand more about the language you are studying.
```
    |         |         |         |             |            |          |
determiner   noun    pronoun   main verb    preposition   noun    auxiliary
                                                                    verb
```

Agents are people or things that perform an action in a passive sentence.
For example: *He was brought up by **his aunt and uncle**.*

Back-shift is when a verb moves 'one tense back' in a conditional clause or reported statement.
For example: *If you **were** a woman you'd understand.*
'I can't come.' → *He said he **couldn't** come.*

Clauses are groups of words containing a subject and a verb.
```
              main clause    subordinate clause    main clause   time (subordinate) clause
```
For example: *I waited   but she didn't come   I'll phone   when I get there.*
Note: Subordinate clauses are introduced by conjunctions.

Collocation refers to words that frequently occur together
For example: *common sense   get on well   Merry Christmas*

Complements refer to adjective or noun phrases which give more information about the subject of a clause.
For example: *She was **very happy**.   It's **my fault**.   I feel **a complete idiot**.*
Note: Complements usually follow verbs like *be, seem, feel*.

Expressions are groups of words that belong together where the words and word order never or rarely change.
For example: *black and white   That reminds me, I must buy some toothpaste.   How do you do?*

Idioms are groups of words with a meaning which cannot be understood by taking the meaning of each individual word.
For example: *My father **footed the bill**.   Let's **play it by ear**, shall we?*

Intransitive verbs do not take an object.
For example: *He's **arrived**.   Is Marta still **sleeping**?   Stop **fidgeting**!*
Note: Many verbs can be either intransitive or transitive. It depends on the meaning or context.
For example: *I **can't stand** on one leg for very long.* (Intransitive)
*I **can't stand** modern jazz.* (Transitive)

Linkers are adverbs or adverb phrases which show a connection between one clause or sentence and another.
For example: ***Just as** we were leaving the restaurant, I spotted a friend.*
*Parents are worried about safety on the streets. **As a result**, they aren't allowing their children to play outside.*

Objects usually come after the verb and show who or what is affected by the verb.
For example: *She closed **the window**.   My neighbour hates **me**.   I've made **a cup of tea**.*
Note: Some verbs take a both direct object (DO) and an indirect object (IO).
For example: *She gave **him** (IO) **a kiss** (DO).   He sent **her** (IO) **some flowers** (DO).*
*I teach **students** (IO) **English** (DO).*

Particles are the adverbs or prepositions that form part of a phrasal verb.
For example: *turn it **on**   take **off**   get **on with** her*

Pronouns are words used in place of nouns or noun phrases. There are many classes of pronoun.
For example: Subject pronouns: *I, you, she,* etc.   Object pronouns: *me, you, her,* etc.
Possessive pronouns: *mine, yours, hers,* etc.   Demonstrative pronouns: *this, that, these, those*

Proper nouns are words that refer to a particular person, place or institution.
For example: *Janet, Madrid, the Internet*

Register describes a level and style of a piece of language which is appropriate for the circumstances in which it is used.
For example: *I am very grateful for your help.* (More formal)
Thanks a million for giving us a hand. (More informal)

Synonyms are words or expressions which mean the same as another word or expression.
For example: *They **did** the house **up** last year. / They **decorated** the house last year.*

Transitive verbs take an object.
For example: *You're wasting your **time**.   He's cut **his toe**.   I can't pronounce '**comfortable**'.*

Phonetic symbols

SINGLE VOWELS

/ɪ/	big fish	/bɪg fɪʃ/
/iː/	green beans	/griːn biːnz/
/ʊ/	should look	/ʃʊd lʊk/
/uː/	blue moon	/bluː muːn/
/e/	ten eggs	/ten egz/
/ə/	about mother	/əbaʊt mʌðə/
/ɜː/	learn words	/lɜːn wɜːdz/
/ɔː/	short talk	/ʃɔːt tɔːk/
/æ/	fat cat	/fæt kæt/
/ʌ/	must come	/mʌst kʌm/
/ɑː/	calm start	/kɑːm stɑːt/
/ɒ/	hot spot	/hɒt spɒt/

DIPHTHONGS

/ɪə/	ear	/ɪə/
/eɪ/	face	/feɪs/
/ʊə/	pure	/pjʊə/
/ɔɪ/	boy	/bɔɪ/
/əʊ/	nose	/nəʊz/
/eə/	hair	/heə/
/aɪ/	eye	/aɪ/
/aʊ/	mouth	/maʊθ/

CONSONANTS

/p/	pen	/pen/
/b/	bad	/bæd/
/t/	tea	/tiː/
/d/	dog	/dɒg/
/tʃ/	church	/tʃɜːtʃ/
/dʒ/	jazz	/dʒæz/
/k/	cost	/kɒst/
/g/	girl	/gɜːl/
/f/	far	/fɑː/
/v/	voice	/vɔɪs/
/θ/	thin	/θɪn/
/ð/	then	/ðen/
/s/	snake	/sneɪk/
/z/	noise	/nɔɪz/
/ʃ/	shop	/ʃɒp/
/ʒ/	measure	/meʒə/
/m/	make	/meɪk/
/n/	nine	/naɪn/
/ŋ/	sing	/sɪŋ/
/h/	house	/haʊs/
/l/	leg	/leg/
/r/	red	/red/
/w/	wet	/wet/
/j/	yes	/jes/

STRESS

In this book, word stress is shown by underlining the stressed syllable.
For example: <u>wa</u>ter; re<u>sult</u>; disa<u>ppoint</u>ing

LETTERS OF THE ALPHABET

/eɪ/	/iː/	/e/	/aɪ/	/əʊ/	/uː/	/ɑː/
Aa	Bb	Ff	Ii	Oo	Qq	Rr
Hh	Cc	Ll	Yy		Uu	
Jj	Dd	Mm			Ww	
Kk	Ee	Nn				
	Gg	Ss				
	Pp	Xx				
	Tt	Zz				
	Vv					

Irregular verbs

Infinitive	Past simple	Past participle
be	was/were	been
beat	beat	beaten
become	became	become
begin	began	begun
bend	bent	bent
bet	bet	bet
bite	bit	bitten
blow	blew	blown
break	broke	broken
bring	brought	brought
build	built	built
burn	burnt/burned	burnt/burned
burst	burst	burst
buy	bought	bought
can	could	(been able)
catch	caught	caught
choose	chose	chosen
come	came	come
cost	cost	cost
cut	cut	cut
deal	dealt	dealt
do	did	done
draw	drew	drawn
dream	dreamt/dreamed	dreamt/dreamed
drink	drank	drunk
drive	drove	driven
eat	ate	eaten
fall	fell	fallen
feed	fed	fed
feel	felt	felt
fight	fought	fought
find	found	found
fly	flew	flown
forget	forgot	forgotten
forgive	forgave	forgiven
freeze	froze	frozen
get	got	got
give	gave	given
go	went	gone/been
grow	grew	grown
hang	hung/hanged	hung/hanged
have	had	had
hear	heard	heard
hide	hid	hidden
hit	hit	hit
hold	held	held
hurt	hurt	hurt
keep	kept	kept
kneel	knelt/kneeled	knelt/kneeled
know	knew	known
lay	laid	laid
lead	led	led
learn	learnt	learnt
leave	left	left
lend	lent	lent
let	let	let

Infinitive	Past simple	Past participle
lie	lay	lain
light	lit/lighted	lit/lighted
lose	lost	lost
make	made	made
mean	meant	meant
meet	met	met
must	had to	(had to)
pay	paid	paid
put	put	put
read	read /red/	read /red/
ride	rode	ridden
ring	rang	rung
rise	rose	risen
run	ran	run
say	said	said
see	saw	seen
sell	sold	sold
send	sent	sent
set	set	set
shake	shook	shaken
shine	shone	shone
shoot	shot	shot
show	showed	shown
shrink	shrank	shrunk
shut	shut	shut
sing	sang	sung
sink	sank	sunk
sit	sat	sat
sleep	slept	slept
slide	slid	slid
smell	smelt/smelled	smelt/smelled
speak	spoke	spoken
spell	spelt/spelled	spelt/spelled
spend	spent	spent
spill	spilt/spilled	spilt/spilled
split	split	split
spoil	spoilt/spoiled	spoilt/spoiled
spread	spread	spread
stand	stood	stood
steal	stole	stolen
stick	stuck	stuck
swear	swore	sworn
swell	swelled	swollen/swelled
swim	swam	swum
take	took	taken
teach	taught	taught
tear	tore	torn
tell	told	told
think	thought	thought
throw	threw	thrown
understand	understood	understood
wake	woke	woken
wear	wore	worn
win	won	won
write	wrote	written

Tapescripts

1 Images

📼 01

Alex

It was the highlight of my whole life because, when I was a kid I always used to think – I hope I live long enough to see a man on the moon. So when it happened – I don't know how old my son was, but I said to him, 'Sit down and watch all of this – this is one of the most momentous things that will ever happen in your life.'

Beth

What annoys me is that people think punk was just a fashion. For me, it was much more than that – it was a way of life. I mean, how long do you think it took to do that make-up and hair? It used to take about four hours a day just getting dressed!

Chris

I'll never forget the day he came out of prison, partly because it was on my birthday, the 11th February, but mainly because it was such a happy event. What I found most amazing about that day was that he'd spent twenty-seven years in prison, and yet he looked as if he had just stepped out for a walk with his wife, as if it was something he'd been doing every day of his life. What an incredible man – and in spite of everything, he doesn't appear to carry any anger or bitterness.

Debra

I was only a kid and I was watching television, when a newsflash came on and I saw these crowds of people climbing on this wall. I had no idea what was going on and I actually thought something terrible had happened. Then I realised people were laughing and celebrating. I'd never heard of the Berlin Wall before that night.

📼 02

(W = Woman; M = Man)
W: Excuse me, is it okay if I sit here?
M: Sure, go ahead.
W: Thanks. Sorry, but you're American, right?
M: Right.
W: Oh, me too. Are you on vacation?
M: No, I'm working here for a few months.
W: You're kidding – so am I. What do you do?
M: I work for the American Central Bank. Pretty boring, huh?
W: Oh, no. I mean, a job's a job. … But you like London, right?
M: Er, to be honest, I can't stand it – especially the weather.

W: Oh yeah, the weather's terrible. But I love London.
M: How long have you been here?
W: Oh, not long – a few weeks. How about you?
M: The same. What are you doing here?
W: I'm an artist, and I was asked to bring over some of my work to a small gallery just near here. I've just had my first exhibition there.
M: Wow – that is impressive.
W: Thanks. So where are you from?
M: I'm from California – Santa Barbara.
W: You're kidding – so am I! Don't tell me you went to Rosefield High.
M: Yeah, I did – but I wasn't a very good student.
W: Me neither. What year did you graduate?
M: Um, 1989.
W: Oh, that's weird, me too. Do you remember Mrs Rivers?
M: Oh, the math teacher? Sure. She was horrible!
W: She's my mom.
M: Oh.

📼 03

a) Everybody's arrived, haven't they?
b) Nobody likes her, do they?
c) Just leave me alone, will you?
d) I'm late again, aren't I?
e) That's not really true, is it?
f) Let's have a drink, shall we?

📼 04

(See page 7.)

📼 05

Charles

(J = Journalist; C = Charles)
J: Excuse me! Hello.
C: Hello.
J: I work for *CHAPS* magazine, and we're doing a survey about men's self-image. Um, do you mind if I ask you a couple of questions?
C: Oh. No, no, go ahead. What do you want to know?
J: Well, um, I'd like to know what your clothes say about you.
C: What do my clothes say about me!? Gosh – I suppose they say that I'm meeting a client this afternoon, and that means I've got to make the right impression. So I have to wear a suit.
J: And would you say you care about your image?
C: Oh yes, I think I do. I like to look smart, even when I'm not working. Even when I wear jeans and a T-shirt, I like them to be clean and neat, and I think this says that I care about myself. It says that I've got good self-esteem.

Rick

(J = Journalist; R= Rick)
J: Excuse me.
R: Me?
J: Yes, hi there! I'm working on a feature for *CHAPS* magazine about men's personal style. Um, do you mind if I ask you some questions?
R: Er, no, I suppose not.
J: Could you tell me what image you're trying to achieve?
R: Image? I don't really have an image. I wear clothes I feel comfortable in – I suppose you'd call it a casual look.
J: Hm, and would you say that you're aware of fashion?
R: Er, probably not, no. My style hasn't changed for years.

Alan

(J = Journalist; A = Alan)
J: Excuse me, sir. Is it okay if I ask you a couple of questions for an article I'm doing for *CHAPS* magazine?
A: Yes, that's fine. Are you going to take photos?
J: Er, yes, if you don't mind. But first I'd like to know whether your appearance affects your life in any way.
A: Oh yes, totally. The way I dress *is* my life really. It hasn't really affected my career so far, but I'm hoping it will. Basically I want to be noticed, and the reason I want to be noticed is that I want to get on television.
J: Ah. And could you tell me what the last thing you bought was?
A: Oh yes, I adore shopping. Er, that would be the pink shirt I bought yesterday – oh, and the pink and black tie.

Matt

(J = Journalist; M = Matt)
J: Hello! I'm doing some research for an article about the way men dress. Er, can I ask you some questions?
M: Yeah, no problem.
J: Do you mind telling me what you wear to go out in the evening?
M: In the evening? What, you mean clubs and that sort of thing?
J: Yes, when you go clubbing.
M: Well, I dress exactly like this.
J: You don't dress up then?
M: Well, put it this way – I don't put a suit on. The clubs I go to don't let men in if they're wearing suits.
J: Really!? Well, how strange. Um, one more question? I'd just like to know if there's an item of clothing you couldn't live without.
M: Trainers. Definitely couldn't live without them. I've got about twenty-five pairs.

2 Family

🔊 06

Eva

I knew that there were a lot of things I would have to get used to when I decided to go to England and stay with a family. But I was looking forward to having egg and bacon for breakfast and tea at five o'clock. I was also dreaming of the charming English country cottage I would be staying in. I was a bit worried about the reserved British character. I'd heard that they objected to talking about anything personal but insisted on talking about the weather all the time. Nor did they approve of hugging or kissing, apparently. So imagine my surprise when my English family welcomed me with a big hug and then asked me about my family, my work and even my boyfriend. They didn't live in the country cottage I'd dreamt of, and we never had English breakfast or tea at five. But they succeeded in making me feel at home, and I felt as if I belonged to the family for the few weeks I was there.

🔊 07

(See page 18.)

🔊 08

(I = Interviewer; M = Mum; D = Dad)
I: So you're going to meet Sarah's boyfriend tomorrow?
M&D: That's right.
I: How do you feel about that?
M: Well, we're looking forward to meeting Andy at last – we've heard a lot about him, because Sarah's been going out with him for a while now. Several weeks, I believe.
I: Does Sarah usually bring her boyfriends home to meet you?
D: Well, it's difficult to know with Sarah really – she changes boyfriends like other people change their socks. We've met some of them.
M: Yes, I'd say we've met half a dozen over the years.
I: Have you liked most of her boyfriends?
M: No, not really. I'm always amazed at how awful they are. She goes for very strange types. There was just one we liked, wasn't there?
D: Oh, yes – you mean Jeremy. Lovely chap. We were impressed with him.
M: But he didn't last long. As soon as we told her we liked him, she dropped him.
I: What sort of person would you like Sarah to go out with?
M: Well, I think it's essential for him to come from the same kind of background.
D: Yes, and it's very important for him to have some kind of qualifications – you know, some ambition.
M: He needs to be a strong character to stand up to Sarah – she'd soon go off somebody who lets her do what she wants all the time.
D: Oh, anyway, we're not going to take it too seriously. She's far too young to get married or engaged or anything like that. And the poor chap is unlikely to last very long.

🔊 09

(I = Interviewer; A = Andy)
I: How do you feel about meeting Sarah's parents?
A: A bit nervous. I'm worried about making a bad impression because I'm quite shy. So I find it difficult to get on with people straight away.
I: But you're a DJ, aren't you?
A: Yeah, but it's easy for me to hide behind my music decks at work. I'm not very good at making conversation, especially with older people.
I: What are you most nervous about?
A: Well, I gave up studying to become a DJ, and I don't think Sarah's parents will be very impressed with that. Also, I dyed my hair last week, and they'll probably be a bit shocked by that.
I: How are you going to try and make a good impression?
A: Well, I'm going to wear clean clothes – not a suit or anything. I haven't got one. And I'll take her mum some flowers.
I: Why are you going to meet Sarah's parents?
A: Because Sarah fancies going to London for the day, and she feels like having Sunday lunch at home. And I always do what she wants.

🔊 10

Conversation 1
(S = Sarah; A = Andy)
S: Hello!
A: Hiya. The door's open!
S: Here, I remembered to bring you that CD.
A: Oh, cheers – that's great!
S: How's it going?
A: All right. I'm totally shattered.
S: Why? What've you been up to?
A: Nothing – it's just that I didn't finish work until five o'clock this morning.
S: Oh right. Well, you'd better just chill out this evening. Do you want to watch telly, or shall I go and get a video?
A: Whatever.
S: Do you know what's on telly tonight?
A: Oh, no idea. Rubbish as usual, I should think.
S: Oh dear, you're in a bad mood. You're not nervous about meeting my parents, are you?
A: No. Why should I be? But I am a bit worried about the long drive. My car's on its last legs.
S: Oh well, let's worry about that tomorrow. Come on – make me a nice cup of tea.

Conversation 2
(M = Mum; D = Dad; S = Sarah; A = Andy)
M: Hello. Welcome. Do come in.
S: Mum, Dad, this is Andy.
M&D: Nice to meet you.
A: Nice to meet you. These are for you – Sarah says they're your favourites.
M: Oh, thank you – that's very kind of you. And how are you, darling?
S: I'm absolutely exhausted, actually.
M: Oh dear. What's the matter? Have you been working too hard?
S: Oh no, nothing like that – it's just a long drive, isn't it?
M: Yes, of course. You must sit down and relax, both of you. Would you prefer coffee or tea, Andy?
A: I don't mind. Whatever's easiest.
D: How many miles is it exactly?
A: Oh, I'm afraid I don't know. The journey's taken us five and a half hours, but my car is rather old.
D: Oh yes, I always take the A420, followed by the A34, except during the summer when I tend to avoid motorways and go through Winchester on the backroads.
M: Well, we're not going to talk about roads all day, are we? Now Andy, what exactly do you do? Sarah tells us you're in the music industry …

3 Money

🔊 11

(See page 24.)

🔊 12

During the gold rush, Sam Brannan became one of the most successful businessmen in California. He arrived in California in 1846 with a group of two hundred Mormons who had left New York to escape religious persecution. They had made the journey by sea, and on arrival in San Francisco (then called Yerba Buena) they had tripled the city's tiny population.

When gold was discovered on John Sutter's land in 1848, Sam Brannan owned the only store between San Francisco and the gold fields. Quickly recognising a gap in the market, he bought up all the picks, shovels and pans he could find, and then ran up and down the streets of San Francisco shouting 'Gold, gold on the American River!'

He had no intention of digging for gold! No, he was planning to sell shovels. And having cornered the market, he ended up with a lot more gold than the person who had to dig for it.

This was a man who keenly understood the laws of supply and demand. A metal pan that sold for twenty cents a few days earlier, was now available from Brannan for fifteen dollars. In just nine weeks he made $36,000. He became the first gold rush millionaire within a few years.

In the end, though, Sam Brannan lost his fortune and his health, as did many of those who first benefited from the gold rush. Alcoholism finally led to his downfall, and California's first millionaire died an unnoticed death.

13

(M = Martha; D = Dad)

M: Morning!

D: You're in a good mood today. Any particular reason?

M: Yes, there is actually.

D: What – in love again?

M: No – I've decided to become a millionaire.

D: You've decided to become a millionaire. I see. And how exactly do you propose to do that?

M: Well, if you can spare a couple of minutes I'll tell you.

D: Martha, you know how valuable my time is …

M: Oh, Dad, I promise you it will be worth your while.

D: Okay – but just five minutes or else I'll be late for work.

M: Right. I've got this idea for a website …

D: Oh come on, you're wasting your time if you think you can make money out of the Internet. All the best ideas have been used up. You should be using your time more profitably getting a proper job …

M: All right, all right. Look, I promise you it's not some half-baked idea. It's something I've been chewing over for the last few weeks. Please just have a look at these plans, then tell me what you think.

D: Hm, hm, yes, interesting. There's certainly food for thought here. How are you going to find the money to do it?

M: Ah, well, er, I was rather hoping you might help me. Oh will you?

D: Well, I can't tell you until I've had time to digest all this information. But you've certainly got a good idea. It's very original.

M: But we're running out of time. If we don't do it very soon, somebody else will.

D: Yes, you could be right. Look, I've got to go now, but as soon as I get back from work I'll spend the rest of the evening looking at it. Have you told anybody else your idea?

M: No, not yet.

D: Well, don't … I think you've really got something here.

14

a

A tourist in Africa was walking by the sea when he saw a man in simple clothes dozing in a fishing boat. It was an idyllic picture, so he decided to take a photograph. The click of the camera woke the man up. The tourist offered him a cigarette.

'The weather is great. There are plenty of fish. Why are you lying around instead of going out and catching more?'

The fisherman replied: 'Because I caught enough this morning.'

'But just imagine,' the tourist said. 'If you went out there three times every day, you'd catch three times as much. After about a year you could buy yourself a motor-boat. After a few more years of hard work, you could have a fleet of boats working for you. And then …'

'And then?' asked the fisherman.

'And then,' the tourist continued triumphantly, 'you could be calmly sitting on the beach, dozing in the sun and looking at the beautiful ocean.'

b

There was a young lady from Niger,
Who smiled as she rode on a tiger.
They came back from the ride
With the lady inside
And the smile on the face of the tiger.

15

(See page 28.)

16

(I = Interviewer; P = Patti; E = Eric; L = Lee)

a

I: It's impossible to have too much money – do you agree with that, Patti?

P: Yes. If you have dreams, money makes them possible. Personally, I can't imagine having too much money. I'm always broke. Anyway, if I ever felt I had too much money, I'd give it away to charity.

b

I: And Patti, would you prefer fame or fortune?

P: Being practical, I'd say fortune, but if I were single with no kids and no responsibilities, I'd go for fame.

c

I: Eric, were you given or did you earn pocket money as a child?

E: I was given two shillings a week by my father, but on condition that I behaved myself. If I didn't behave well, I didn't receive it. Parents were much stricter in those days.

d

I: And Eric, what was the first thing you saved up for and bought yourself?

E: Oh, a set of toy soldiers. Not the plastic ones you get nowadays, but little metal ones, beautifully hand-painted. It took me nearly a year to save up for them. If I'd known that they would be valuable antiques today, I would've kept them. They'd probably be worth a fortune now.

e

I: Tell me, Lee, if you could buy yourself a skill, talent or change in your appearance, what would it be?

L: Well, there are lots of things I'd like to be better at, but if I had to choose one, it would have to be football – I'd like to be a brilliant football player!

f

I: And finally Lee, what can't money buy?

L: Happiness. I tend to think that once I have enough money to buy some new clothes or get a better car, then I'll be happy. But it never works out like that.

17

(I = Interviewer; P = Patti; E = Eric; L = Lee)

a

I: Does it matter if a wife earns more than her husband? How would you handle it?

P: It wouldn't matter to me, but it might matter to my husband. It shouldn't matter, but human nature being what it is, it probably would.

E: I would feel like a failure if my wife earned more than I did. It's a man's job to earn a living, and a woman's place is in the home.

L: It wouldn't worry me. I know loads of couples where the woman is the main breadwinner, and I think that's fine so long as both people enjoy what they're doing. In fact, it would be really good to have a wife who's earning a fortune. But actually, I'm probably not going to get married.

b

I: If you were given £1,000 to save, spend or invest in just one day, what would you do with it?

P: Um, the sensible thing to do would be to save it for a rainy day or pay off my overdraft, but I think I'd rather splash out on a family holiday. We need it.

E: Do you know what – I think I'd be tempted to get a new computer, because I spend quite a bit of my time on the Internet, and my computer's getting a bit slow. Yes, a new computer, that's what I'd spend £1,000 on.

L: Well, I certainly wouldn't save or invest it – I'd probably blow it on a new stereo system and some massive speakers.

a) Armando

It used to be my father's, and I learnt to write on it. Now it's a museum piece. My father thought I might become a musician. He was Daniel Almoia Robles, a famous Peruvian composer and storyteller who created *El Condor Pasa*. He gave it to me when he realised that I wasn't going to follow him into music. I value greatly other means of expression, like sound technology and cinematography, but when I write, I don't need anything else. When I lived alone in the Peruvian jungle for ten years, I took it with me, and I think that was the period when I wrote more than at any other time in my life.

b) Katie

My mother gave it to me rather than to one of my two sisters – maybe because she realised I was the least likely to get one of my own. I don't wear it because I'm afraid of losing it. I keep it on my bedside table. I see it when I wake up every morning. It's by far my most treasured possession. When I look at it, I remember my mum, who is living in England.

c) Heather

This is my most valuable possession because it saved my life when I got caught in an avalanche in Johnson Pass in Alaska's Chugach Mountain Range. It had been snowing for four days and the temperature rose that morning – perfect avalanche conditions. When the first person in our group of snowboarders leaped off the cornice, the rest of us decided to follow his tracks – no traversing and no hard turns, so as to not disturb the snow. When it was my turn, I made it down the first pitch safely and thought I was out of danger. But the person behind me started before I was at a safe distance and nervously made a hard right turn. I heard a loud crack, and then WHOMPH! The snow hit me really fast in the back of the neck. I pushed my neck-warmer over my face, which kept the snow out of my mouth and nose, allowing me to breathe as the avalanche swept me up. I began frantically swimming and tried to stay aware of which way was up. When the snow finally settled, I had managed to get part of my glove up through the surface. It took the others a few minutes to find me, but I knew they would. Luckily, my neck-warmer allowed me the extra air to wait out those few minutes.

d) Mike

I know it sounds a bit stupid, but this is the thing I'd least like to lose. It's not because it's worth anything, although it is quite an expensive one because it's got e-mail on it too. But the main thing is that if I lost this, I'd lose the addresses and numbers of practically everybody I know. It contains the details of about three hundred people.

4 Body

📼 19

(A = Ann; B = Bob; C = Chris; D = Dana; E = Ed; F = Fran; G = Greg; H = Helen; I = Ian; J = Jane; K = Keith; L = Lisa)

A

A: Oh dear – you look like death warmed up. Heavy night last night?
B: Yeah – good party, but I feel terrible.
A: Oh well, if you hadn't drunk so much you wouldn't be feeling so bad now, would you? Anyway, listen, I'll give you my secret cure: get a couple of raw eggs, mix them up in a cup, add a bit of chilli sauce and a pinch of salt, and drink it down in one go.
B: Ugh – that would just make me sick.
A: Yes, I know. But then you'd feel better, wouldn't you?

B

C: Why are you walking like that?
D: My ankle's killing me!
C: Oh dear, you poor thing! If you ask me, you need to lie down and put some ice on it to keep the swelling down.

C

E: Ugh! I can't swallow anything.
F: Oh yes, I know what you mean. I was the same last week. I could only eat ice cream!
E: So, what did you do?
F: Well, you could try this. Chop up some ginger and put it in boiling water with some honey and lemon. Drink it as hot as you can.
E: Does it work?
F: Well, it makes you feel better, but it's probably a good idea to take some aspirin too.

D

G: Don't touch my back!
H: Why? What's up?
G: I wanted to get a tan quickly so I didn't bother to put any suntan lotion on.
H: Oh well, it serves you right then, doesn't it?
G: It really stings.
H: Okay, take your shirt off. I'll put some after-sun lotion on it.

E

I: When did it start?
J: After I'd been playing computer games for about seven hours. I feel as if my head's going to explode!
I: Oh well, you've only got yourself to blame, haven't you?
J: I know, I know. But I've taken aspirin, and it hasn't worked.
I: Well, you could try putting your hands over your eyes and leaving them there for about five minutes. That usually works for me, particularly if it's been brought on by sitting in front of the computer for too long.

F

K: Have you got a cold?
L: No, I'm all right – I always get a streaming nose and red eyes at this time of the year.
K: That must be awful. If I were you, I'd try acupuncture. My sister used to suffer terribly, but then she had three sessions of acupuncture, and that was it.
L: Really? Can you find out who she saw?

📼 20

(See page 35.)

📼 21

Liz Hartley

Okay, let's see how you got on with the *Body knowledge quiz*.

Number 1, the aerobic system is the heart, lungs and blood circulation. It's important to do aerobic exercise regularly, because it gets more oxygen into your blood and gets your heart pumping.

Oh, yes, number two, the 'happy hormones'. These are endorphins and they're the reason you feel so high when you've had a good work-out. It's a good idea to do exercise when you're feeling run down or stressed. The exercise releases these endorphins and you end up feeling much better than before. It's the same feeling you get when you fall in love – but just doing exercise is probably less complicated.

A balanced diet, number three – um (b) is the correct answer here. You need to have a combination of carbohydrates, proteins and fats in your diet.

On the other hand, it's best *not* to include sugar and caffeine in your diet. They're just life's little luxuries, and they're not very good for you. You don't have to give them up completely, but you ought to cut down on them.

Okay, where were we? Ah yes, number 4 – for keeping supple, (a) is the correct answer. Obviously all these sports are really good for you, but if we're talking about improving the suppleness of your body, then you definitely need to do something like yoga, where you get a lot of stretching.

Right, number 5. If you exercise for twenty minutes three times a week, you're doing very well. One hour three times a week is fine, but you shouldn't overdo it – an hour every day is too much, except for professionals, of course. It's not a good idea to take it all too seriously, because that takes all the pleasure out of it.

And finally number 6. Stamina comes from practice, so you need to exercise regularly. Fruit's good for you, but it doesn't build up stamina – it has other benefits. Which is more than I can say for coffee – don't drink too much of it. It's poison!

Well that's it. But I'd just like to add a last piece of advice – try not to take it all too seriously. The more you enjoy what you're doing, the better you'll feel. So find the kind of exercise that suits you, and enjoy yourself!

22

(L = Laura; P = Phil)

L: Hey, Phil, how are you doing?

P: Oh hi, Laura – not too bad thanks. How are you?

L: Oh, up to my eyes in work as usual. I'm on my way to my third meeting today. How's that lovely girlfriend of yours?

P: Oh, we split up three weeks ago. She's on holiday with her new boyfriend.

L: Oh no – trust me to put my foot in it. I'm really sorry.

P: No, it's okay. I need to get it off my chest.

L: Who's her new boyfriend?

P: It's her boss. You wouldn't know him. He's not from this neck of the woods.

L: What kind of work does he do?

P: I don't know really. He seems to have his fingers in a lot of pies. He owns several companies anyway, including the one Mandy was working for.

L: Oh Phil, I don't know what to say.

P: Yeah – it's hard. I mean, we were supposed to be going on holiday together in a couple of weeks.

L: So, what are you going to do?

P: I don't know – I haven't made up my mind yet. I might go anyway, or I might not feel like it when the time comes. I don't know. I'll just have to play it by ear.

L: Look Phil, I'm afraid I've got to run – but if you need a shoulder to cry on, you know where to find me.

P: Thanks, Laura – I'll be fine.

23

Sam

(I = Interviewer; S = Sam)

I: Congratulations on winning the tournament, Sam. How do you feel?

S: Oh, great!

I: Are you going to celebrate?

S: Definitely. I've been training non-stop for ages and I need a good night out.

I: How do you train for a kick-boxing tournament like this?

S: Basically, you have to live like a monk for weeks …

I: Really? Aren't you allowed to go out?

S: Yes, actually you can go out, but you can't drink or smoke and you have to be in bed by midnight.

I: I guess that's quite difficult for a young guy like yourself. What other sacrifices do you have to make?

S: Well, obviously you have train every day, and the main thing for kick-boxing is to build up your stamina – so while I'm training I have to be quite strict with my diet.

I: So what do you eat?

S: Um, the first thing is cutting down on fat – no crisps or burgers. I'm not supposed to eat butter, but that's really hard because I really love it. Oh, and I mustn't drink too much caffeine.

I: And what sort of things are good for you?

S: High-fibre food, like brown rice and vegetables. Cranberry juice is good – loads and loads of fluid. That's really important.

I: What about protein?

S: Yeah, of course that's important, but meat tends to be very fatty – I try to stick to fish. Mushrooms are really good – I eat lots of mushrooms. But carbohydrates are as important as protein because I need the energy. I don't want to end up with enormous muscles.

I: Talking of muscles, do you work out?

S: Of course – that's part of the training. I work out every day, but I do quite a lot of aerobic exercise and not too much weight-lifting. For kick-boxing you have to increase your energy levels.

I: What are you going to have for dinner now the competition's over?

S: Steak and chips with loads of bread and butter, Coke to drink, followed by apple pie and cream. And a double expresso. No problem.

I: A well-earned treat. Enjoy it! Thank you, Sam Davidson, the new kick-boxing champion – and now back to the studio.

Catherine

(C = Catherine; M = Mike)

M: Catherine you look great in these photos.

C: Oh, thanks. I had to go through hell to get into that wedding dress.

M: What do you mean?

C: It was too small.

M: Why didn't you get one your size?

C: Oh, it was my grandmother's – my mother wore it on her wedding day, and I really wanted to wear it on mine.

M: Oh, I can see why – it's gorgeous. But the waist is minute!

C: Tell me about it. I suffered for six months so I could wear it.

M: How did you do it?

C: Oh, well, you know this diet that all the Hollywood actors are doing?

M: No – I thought they just had plastic surgery every time their body needed reshaping.

C: Well, they probably do that as well – but there's this new diet. I don't think it's very healthy if you do it for a long time, but it really works.

M: Is it the diet where you think of all the food you love and avoid it for six months?

C: No – actually, it's amazing. Believe it or not, you can eat things like, em,

roast chicken and steak and eggs and bacon, but you just can't eat any carbohydrates with it.

M: No bread.

C: No.

M: What about pasta?

C: No.

M: Oh, I couldn't live without pasta.

C: Mm, it was hard – I was dying for a nice plate of spaghetti.

M: Did you have to exercise?

C: Well, you know me – I'm not exactly sportswoman of the year. But I wanted to get rid of my stomach so I had to do sit-ups every morning. Nightmare!

M: How much did you lose?

C: To be honest, I have no idea – the important thing to me was that I could put that dress on and look good in it.

M: Are you still dieting then?

C: No way – I love my food and dieting is so boring. Hopefully, I won't need to wear the wedding dress again anyway!

5 Ritual

24

Terry, a Manchester United supporter
I remember watching Man Utd against Bayern Munich in the Champions League final. I'll never forget Sheringham equalising in the 89th minute. Then Solsjkar scored the winner two minutes later in injury time. It was incredible! With ten minutes to go I had already stopped believing it was possible to win, but Man Utd just never gave up!

Dawn, a Chelsea supporter
If I've forgotten to set the alarm clock, it's always a rush. I have breakfast quickly, put on my Chelsea shirt and leave the house. I can walk to the ground from where I live, and I always stop to buy a newspaper and get the latest team news. Three hours before kick-off and the atmosphere is already building. It's a great day out – the best moment in the week. If I remember to programme the video, then I can watch the whole match again when I get home. Magic!

25

Mark and Tim, Tottenham supporters
When I was about fourteen, I tried going to football matches for a while. All my friends did it, so I joined in just to be like them. I liked to think I was one of the lads – you know how it is. I loved being part of a big crowd, but apart from that I was never really that interested, and as I got older I remember thinking what a waste of time it all was. Anyway, after my third season I stopped going.

But now, my nine-year-old son is football mad, so I've started going again. He likes to arrive really early at the stadium to get a good place, so I'm spending more time there than ever! I love seeing his face when they score, but although I try to show how interested I am, it's no good. I can still think of a hundred things I'd rather be doing on a Saturday than standing around watching a football match.

▭ 26

My dad is the most ritualistic person I know, and many of his rituals involve his car.

5 We've never kept domestic animals in our house, but my father's car is as close as you'll get to the family pet. In fact, to be honest, the car probably gets better treatment and more affection than a

10 pet would.

Each night, the car is tucked up in its garage under a cosy blanket. Nobody – but nobody – is allowed in the garage in case they

15 accidentally brush against 'the precious one', causing who knows what damage.

When we were children, on the rare occasions when my dad would

20 get the car out of the garage (for births, deaths, marriages and national disasters – and then only if the buses weren't running), we would have to wear paper bags on

25 our feet in case we had a sudden urge to vandalise the seats with our school shoes.

We would never be allowed to shut the car doors ourselves … in

30 case we banged them too hard, I suppose. I mean, three, five and seven-year-old children can do untold damage to a car by banging the door shut.

35 Nowadays, we don't have to wear paper bags on our feet, but the 'Starting the car and setting off' ritual has never changed.

He'll start the engine and then

40 sit there for at least five minutes with the engine turning. As repulsive fumes pump out into the fresh country air, he'll take out his pipe, and start tapping out his last

45 smoke. Then he'll take a pinch of Players Medium Navy Cut (no other tobacco will do), stuff it in the bowl and spend a minute or two patting it down. Next, he'll get out his box

50 of matches and give it a shake. He always gives his matchbox a shake. The pipe won't light first go – he'll have several goes at it, and finally, when the tobacco takes, he'll puff

55 and puff until the car is full of smoke. With visibility dangerously reduced and a carful of choking passengers, he'll take the hand-brake off and reverse out of the

60 drive at hair-raising speed.

It isn't pleasant being a passenger, but we've always let him get away with this strange behaviour because he's the boss.

65 None of us would dare to complain.

My father used to be a pilot in the Royal Air Force, and I often wonder whether he would indulge in this kind of ritual before take-off

70 and whether his crew would let him get away with it because he was the boss. Probably.

▭ 27

a) I share an office with a woman who's forever talking to her boyfriend on the phone, blowing kisses and saying intimate things that I don't want to listen to. It really gets on my nerves!

b) She will insist on opening all the windows when she arrives in the morning, and then she complains it's freezing and puts the heating on full blast. The office is either freezing or boiling!

c) She's always leaving half finished cups of coffee around the desk – then I knock them over and it's my fault!

d) She will go on about her personal problems. Honestly, you'd think I was her therapist or something – I should charge her for my time!

e) She's always telling me what to do, which I resent. I mean, I was working here when she was still at school!

f) I've told her hundreds of times to get her own pencil sharpener and scissors, but she will keep using mine and not putting them back in their place. So when I need them I can never find them!

▭ 28

a) She's forever talking to her boyfriend on the phone.
b) She will insist on opening all the windows.
c) She's always leaving half-finished cups of coffee around the desk.
d) She will go on about her personal problems.
e) She's always telling me what to do.
f) She will keep using my pencil sharpener and scissors.

▭ 29

1
(I = Interviewer; B = Belen)
I: Tell me about weddings in your country.
B: Well, in Spain, where I'm from, there is this ritual, er, that, er, happens after the rings have been exchanged between groom and bride. It is called *las arras*, and it consists of thirteen gold coins which, er, the

groom puts in the bride's hands. Um, it symbolises their intention of, um, sharing everything: all the worldly goods they are going to receive together.

2
(I = Interviewer; N = Nerissa)
I: Tell me about weddings in your country.
N: Well, um, in Taiwan, um, we use a black umbrella to cover the bride's head, because we believe that it can protect the bride from the evil spirits. So normally there will be an elder person to hold the umbrella when she leaves her house to a groom's house.
I: And will this bring her good luck as well?
N: Yes, it will prevent bad luck.

3
(I = Interviewer; C = Carmel)
I: Tell me about wedding traditions in Turkey.
C: Um, I'm not actually Turkish, but I'm married to a Turk. And, er, the weddings in Turkey are quite different to how they are in the UK. Um, there are a lot of people at the wedding. There are sometimes as many as four or five hundred guests, and one of the most interesting things, I think, about Turkish weddings, er, is the fact that, er, the guests at the wedding pin, um, gold, money, banknotes, on the, er, bride's and groom's, er, costumes, on their, er, on the bridegroom's suit and on the bride's dress. Um, I think, as, from what I can understand, that this money and gold is used to, er, by the bride and groom, to, er, to set themselves up for their new life together, er, living in their, er, new house, their new home, to buy things like a fridge, and, er, and other things they might need for their future life together.

▭ 30

Student A's dialogues

a
A1: What have you been up to lately?
B1: Oh not much – the usual.

b
A2: Long time no see.
B2: Yes, it must be over a year.

c
A3: Alice sends her love.
B3: Thank you. Give her mine.

d
A4: How do you do.
B4: How do you do.

Student B's dialogues

a
A5: Keep in touch.
B5: I will.

b

A6: Thank you for a lovely evening.
B6: You're welcome. You must come again soon.

c

A7: Don't forget to phone me.
B7: I won't.

d

A8: How are you?
B8: Not so bad, thanks.

📼 **31**

The long goodbye
(A = Ann; B = Bob)
A: I'd better be going.
B: It's been lovely to see you.
A: Thank you for having me.
B: Thanks for coming.
A: I'll be off then.
B: Give my regards to your family.
A: I will.
B: Give me a ring.
A: Okay. I really must be off now.
B: Take it easy.
A: See you.
B: Look after yourself.
A: Bye for now.
B: Safe journey.
A: Love you.
B: Missing you already.

6 Digital

📼 **32**

(See page 54.)

📼 **33**

Interview with Lara Croft
(I = interviewer; LC = Lara Croft)
I: Lara, you've become very famous. Has this changed your life?
LC: Not very much really. I mean, people recognise me if I go shopping or something, but I don't actually go out very much. The extra money is nice, but that's never been much of a problem for me anyway.
I: What do you think is the secret of your success?
LC: Well, some people say I've only been successful because of the way I look. But it's not true – I've succeeded because I've never let anything stand in my way.
I: But you do look exceptionally fit.
LC: I'm 1 metre 70 and I weigh 57.2 kilos, if that's what you mean. But I don't have time for people who are only interested in my figure. I need to keep in shape for my job, so I've been working out practically all my life.
I: How did you first get involved in these missions?
LC: By accident – literally. When I was at school in Switzerland, I took up extreme skiing and spent a holiday searching for challenging terrain. When I was flying home the plane went down in the Himalayas. I was the only survivor, and it took me two weeks to reach civilisation. That was how I got a taste for adventure, and I've been going on missions ever since.
I: How long ago was that?
LC: Well, I've been doing this job since I was 21, and next Valentine's Day I'll be 32, so about eleven years.
I: How do your parents feel about your work?
LC: Well, they've been a bit frosty, since I started the job. They've also stopped my allowance because I tend to spend all my money on weapons.
I: Oh dear, how unreasonable. Lara, where do you live when you're not travelling?
LC: In a mansion in Surrey. I inherited it from my great-auntie about fifteen years ago and I love hunting in the woods.
I: Being a country girl, I suppose you like animals?
LC: Yes, they're delicious. I often bring my dinner in from the woods around my estate. I'm not a fussy eater though – I've tried all sorts of things in my time – smoked iguana, crispy tarantula and honeyed stick insects.
I: What do you do in your spare time?
LC: I spend any spare time at home cleaning my guns and preparing for the next adventure. Sometimes I get a film out – my favourite's *Aguirre, the Wrath of God*. Truth is, I've never been very good at relaxing.
I: What sort of car do you drive?
LC: I've had my trusty old Land Rover for years, though I prefer my Norton Streetfighter motorbike for popping into the village.
I: Are you involved with anyone at the moment?
LC: No, I haven't been seeing anyone recently. My parents were trying to get me to marry the Earl of Farringdon. But although I liked him, I wasn't ready to commit. I hear he's still waiting for me.
I: Who is your ideal man?
LC: My hero is Brian Blessed.
I: Who?
LC: He's a Shakespearean actor – you'd recognise him if you saw him. But what I admire about him is his perseverance. He's tried to climb Everest three times and he's written a book about his trip to Mount Roraima in Venezuela. My dream is to ski down Everest with Brian Blessed strapped to my back.
I: Good heavens. You are an unusual person. Thank you, Lara, and good luck with your next mission.

📼 **34**

a

'This crossword is the most difficult I've ever done. I've been trying to think of one word for two weeks.'
'How about "fortnight"?'

b

'Waiter! This lobster only has one claw.'
'I'm sorry, sir. He's been in a fight.'
'Well, bring me the winner then!'

c

'The invisible man has just arrived for his appointment, sir.'
'Well, tell him I can't see him today.'

d

I've received hundreds of replies to my ad for a husband. They all say the same thing: 'Take mine!'

e

'My girlfriend's gone on holiday to the West Indies.'
'Jamaica?'
'No, she went because she wanted to.'

📼 **35**

1

I love e-mail for speed and convenience, but I tend to write letters for pleasure. I love getting letters too. Hearing a letter drop through the letter box is much more exciting than getting an e-mail, even though it's usually a bill in my case.

2

I have mixed feelings about the Internet. Although I find it incredibly useful, I get fed up with it after about half an hour. There's a limit to how long I like to sit in front of a screen, whereas I can spend hours looking at books in the library.

3

Well, although I enjoy watching television, I actually think computer games are better because they're interactive.

4

It depends on what it is. I've booked flights online, and I've bought books and I'd probably buy boring stuff like washing powder and toilet rolls online. But I find shopping quite a social thing – I like to go round the shops with my friends, so I'd miss that if I did all my shopping on the Internet.

5

I think you can learn a lot from watching the right programmes on television, and it's a great way to relax as well. But I get far more out of reading a really good book.

7 Review 1

36

(C = Chris; D = Debbie)

C: I'm a bit worried about Ellie. She's nearly six and she still sucks her thumb!

D: Oh, I shouldn't worry too much about Ellie. I've got a friend who's been sucking her thumb for twenty-nine years!

C: You're kidding!

D: No, honestly. She only does it when she's really tired, but you can imagine how strange it looks on a grown woman.

C: Very strange. Has she ever tried to give up?

D: Of course. She's been trying to give up since somebody called her a baby when she was twelve. But she hasn't succeeded yet.

C: What methods has she used?

D: Well, for example, she's been having therapy for several years.

C: Has it helped?

D: Not really. Well, I think it's improved some aspects of her life, but she hasn't stopped sucking her thumb.

C: There must be something she can do.

D: I know, but she's tried everything. She's tried putting mustard on her thumb, but she just got used to the taste, and actually started liking it. Now she has mustard on everything! And apart from that, I've had hypnosis, I've taken up smoking a pipe, I've worn gloves, even in bed …

C: So do you suck your thumb too?

D: No!

C: You said 'I'.

D: Ah – no – I meant my friend … has … um …

8 Escape

37

(T = Tony; A = Angela)

T: Have you ever had a holiday romance, Angela?

A: I have actually. When I was twenty-six I went travelling to Australia. I went to Sydney – and while I was there I fell head over heels –

T: No!

A: No honestly, I really did. His name was Brad.

T: Brad?!!!

A: Yes, I know. Come to think of it, he did look a bit like Brad Pitt. Anyway, we met through a mutual friend, and to begin with I just worshipped him from afar – but then our mutual friend stepped in and arranged our first date. And that was it – the beginning of a beautiful relationship.

T: Ahh!

A: And actually, it's true – it was bliss. I was unbelievably happy. In fact, I really thought I'd met my soulmate – the person I would … and could … spend a lifetime with. Do you know what I mean? Anything ordinary we did felt extraordinary because we were together.

T: Yeah – I know what you mean.

A: I really did love him then … in spite of what happened later.

T: Oh dear – what happened?

A: Well, eventually I returned to London. We spent six months on the phone. We swapped love letters, and parcels. He was the one who had never travelled, who didn't like his job, so it made sense that he should come here. Finally, the great day came, and I sat in Arrivals for ages, wondering what was holding him up. Meanwhile, he was being held by Customs because immigration officers suspected that he had plans to work and hadn't just come here on holiday.

T: Oh no!

A: Anyway, I finally got to see him, but I realised almost immediately that for me at least, it was over.

T: Oh no, why?

A: Well, basically, it wasn't the best of beginnings, was it?

T: No, I suppose not.

A: And to be honest, I don't think our relationship was strong enough for real life problems.

T: So what happened to him?

A: Well, in the end he was deported back to Australia, and that was the last I heard of him.

38

(T = Tony; G = Gill)

T: You're not the type to have a holiday romance, are you, Gill?

G: Actually, I am. In fact, I met my husband on holiday.

T: No!

G: Yes, it's true. I went on a camping holiday in Scandinavia with some university friends, and Ash came along at the last minute.

T: Camping in Scandinavia? Not exactly tropical …

G: No, come to think of it, it was a bit cold at times. Anyway, as soon as I saw him I thought, 'Yes, this one's for me.' Do you know what I mean?

T: Oh yes, I know what you mean.

G: But then I found out he had a girlfriend back home.

T: Oh no!

G: Basically I had two weeks to impress him – so I used my best weapon: I put on my little black dress …

T: I thought you said it was cold …

G: Yes, it was, but, to be honest, I didn't notice the temperature. And anyway, it was worth it because it

worked – he resisted for a few days, which felt like years! But eventually he surrendered, and we spent the rest of the holiday together. In fact, we were inseparable.

T: What happened when you got home?

G: It was a horrible time because we knew we wanted to be together, but we both had other relationships to sort out.

T: That must have been difficult.

G: It was, but it all worked out well in the end. I mean, it's our fifth wedding anniversary in June.

9 Attraction

(I = Interviewer; W = woman; M = Man)

1

I: What do you think makes a face attractive?

W1: Er, smooth skin, perfect teeth and sparkling eyes.

2

I: What do you think makes a face attractive?

M1: Ooh, big eyes, full lips, oh, and a big smile.

I: Like Julia Roberts?

M1: Exactly.

3

I: What do you think makes a face attractive?

W2: It's probably easier to say what I don't like. On a man, I don't like a small nose – it doesn't have to be enormous, but a little turned-up nose on a man looks silly.

I: So you don't like Brad Pitt then?

W2: Well, I like everything about him except his nose!

4

I: What do you think makes a face attractive?

M2: Good bone structure. High cheekbones. For a woman, a small chin, and for a man, a square jaw.

5

I: What do you think makes a face attractive?

W3: Oh, I love dimples.

I: Dimples?

W3: Yeah. They're so cute.

I: Where do you like them?

W3: Oooh!

I: No, I mean where on the face – you know, do you like a dimple in the chin?

W3: Yeah, I quite like that, but I meant dimples in the cheeks when somebody smiles – oh, it's so cute.

(JO = Jean Oldham; RT = Rita Taylor; MH = Michael Hirst)

JO: Well, I work on a women's magazine, so you can imagine how many beautiful models I've met. But I'm also in daily contact with women who are not physically perfect, and I have to say that the most beautiful women I know are not the models – they are the intelligent, interesting women whose inner beauty shines out. I believe that true beauty comes from within, and no amount of cosmetic surgery can give you that.

RT: Yes, I agree with you, Jean, but not everybody has the confidence to let their inner beauty shine out. Plastic surgery can actually give people that confidence. I really don't think there's anything wrong with trying to improve on what nature has given you.

MH: Ah well, that's where I disagree with you, Rita. I think we should be grateful for what God has given us. The point is, it's selfish and indulgent of people to spend vast amounts of money on superficial improvements when there's so much poverty and sickness in the world.

RT: Actually, it's not that expensive, you know, Michael. I mean having your nose done only costs the price of a vacation frankly, cosmetic surgery can do more for you than a vacation, because the benefits last longer.

JO: Well, I don't know about that. I agree with Michael. I think that we should accept ourselves as we are and refuse to be influenced by stereotypical ideas of beauty.

RT: I'm sorry, but I don't think you're being very honest, Jean. I read your magazine and I frequently read articles encouraging women to have their hair dyed or highlighted. And do you ever go to the dentist, Michael? What do you think about people who have their teeth straightened? If you ask me, it's no different from having cosmetic surgery.

MH: No, hang on, Rita. I think we have to make the distinction here between having something done for health reasons and having some part of your body changed simply because you don't like it …

JO: Or because you want to stay young. Of course it's good to keep healthy, do sport, use sunscreen, that kind of thing, but I love to see life experience showing on people's faces. These aging film-stars who've had so much cosmetic surgery … they all look the same.

RT: It's easy for you to say that, Jean, because you're lucky enough to be a good-looking woman. But if you're honest, I'm sure you will admit that your looks had something to do with you getting the job you have.

JO: Rita, are you suggesting …

MH: Oh, this is rubbish, Rita. You're talking about a very different world from the one I know.

RT: Look, you two may not agree with it, but it's a fact of life. People who feel good about the way they look are more likely to do well in their career – good looks open doors.

(See page 84.)

(See page 84.)

(C = Cilla; J = James)

C: So what's your first question, James?

J: They say that the way to a man's heart is through his stomach, and I must say, I do like my food. If you were to cook me a meal, how would you impress me? … And that question goes to Number 1.

No 1: Actually, I'm not a very good cook. But when you choose Number 1 tonight, the only tasty thing on your mind will be me.

J: Number 2?

No 2: Hello, James.

J: Hello.

No 2: My speciality is chocolate mousse – it's sweet, dark, delicious and bubbly – just like me.

J: Okay. And finally to Number 3.

No 3: Well, James, I'd make sure you ate plenty of spinach, 'cause like Popeye, you'll need all your strength to keep up with me!

C: And your second question, James?

J: I've got two pet frogs which my friends say are like me – a good set of legs, like a drink and come alive in the evening. Imagine you had a pet that reflected your personality, and what would it be? … That question for Number 2.

No 2: Well, I'd have to be a koala bear – my enormous brown eyes make me irresistible, and you'll want to cuddle me all night.

J: … and Number 3 .

No 3: I don't want to frighten you, but I have earned the reputation for being a bit of a man-eater. So I'd have to describe myself as a man-eating tiger, because when I go after something, there is no escape.

J: Number 1.

No 1: It would have to be a fox, 'cause I'm sly, cunning and naturally foxy. So you're going to have to chase me if you want to catch me.

C: It's time for your last question, Chuck. I hope it's a good one.

J: I'm a very superstitious sort of person and I believe that wishes can come true. If one of your wishes were to come true, what would it be? And that goes to Number 3.

No 3: Well, James, I wish that Numbers 1 and 2 would disappear, so that you and I could start our date right now.

J: And Number 1, please.

No 1: I had my palm read by a gypsy recently, and she told me that I would meet a tall, dark, handsome stranger before my next birthday. Guess what – it's my birthday tomorrow.

J: And finally to Number 2.

No 2: James – I wish the screen between us was transparent – because if you could see me, you'd know that I was the only one for you.

44

(J = James; M = Melanie)

M: When the screen went back, I was expecting a tall, dark, handsome man. But what I saw was tall, dark and not very handsome.

J: I think Mel loved my eyebrows. I think she fell in love with them as soon as she saw them. Everybody else does.

M: I didn't fancy James, and it was probably partly because of his eyebrows. He's extremely proud of them, but I think they look like a couple of caterpillars.

J: During the date, I talked about myself, my character, my personality, my job, because I really wanted Melanie to get to know me. Melanie is actually quite serious and rather difficult to get to know. She wasn't very talkative and she didn't tell me much about herself. But I think she liked all my jokes.

M: During the date, James talked about himself non-stop, and it was quite clear that he wasn't interested in getting to know me at all. He's very talkative. In fact, I didn't get a chance to say anything really. He laughed a lot at his own jokes too. At first, I thought he was really funny, but then I got a bit tired of his jokes and I wanted to talk about more serious things – you know, get to know him a bit better.

J: Mel is a total flirt – she was all over me like a rash.

M: I'm an affectionate sort of person, but there was no kissing on the date. It would have been like kissing my brother.

J: I think Mel fancied me more than I fancied her – basically her body language gave it away. Although I think Mel is pretty, I think she should work out a bit more and maybe lose a few kilos.

M: During the date, James said that he would give me eight out of ten if I lost four or five kilos. At the time, I thought the only weight I needed to lose was the man sitting next to me.

J: I thought the date went really well and I'm looking forward to seeing Melanie again. She says she's busy for the next three months, but I'll call her then and hopefully, something will develop between us.

M: James is not my type at all. He's big-headed, self-obsessed and immature. Frankly, I feel sorry for the woman who ends up with him.

📼 45

Never Ever by All Saints

A few questions that I need to know.
How you could ever hurt me so?
I need to know what I've done wrong,
And how long it's been going on.

Was it that I never paid enough attention?
Or did I not give enough affection?
Not only will your answers keep me sane,
But I'll know never to make the same mistake again.

You can tell me to my face,
Or even on the phone.
You can write it in a letter.
Either way I have to know.

Did I never treat you right?
Did I always start the fight?
Either way I'm going out of my mind.
All the answers to my questions I have to find.

📼 46

Never Ever by All Saints (continued)

My head's spinning.
Boy, I'm in a daze.
I feel isolated.
Don't wanna communicate.

I take a shower.
I will scour.
I will roam.
Find peace of mind.
The happy mind,
I once owned, yeah.

Flexing vocabulary runs right through me.
The alphabet runs right from A to Zee.
Conversations, hesitations in my mind.
You got my conscience asking questions that I can't find.
I'm not crazy. I'm sure I ain't done nothin' wrong.
No, I'm just waiting, cos I heard that this feeling won't last that long.

Never ever have I ever felt so low.
When you gonna take me out of this black hole?
Never ever have I ever felt so sad.
The way I'm feeling, yeah, you got me feeling really bad.

Never ever have I had to find.
I've had to dig a way to find my own piece of mind.
I've never ever had my conscience to fight.
The way I'm feeling, yeah. It just don't feel right.

(Never ever have I ever felt so low …)

I'll keep searching deep within my soul
For all the answers – don't wanna hurt no more.
I need peace, got to feel at ease.
Need to be free from pain,
Go insane.
My heart aches, yeah.

Sometimes vocabulary runs through my head.
The alphabet runs right from A to Zed.
Conversations, hesitations in my mind.
You got my conscience asking questions that I can't find.
I'm not crazy. I'm sure I ain't done nothing wrong.
Now I'm just waiting, cos I heard that this feeling won't last that long.

(Never ever have I ever felt so low …)

You can tell me to my face.
You can tell me on the phone.
Ooh, you can write it in a letter, babe,
Cos I really need to know.

10 Genius

📼 47

(A = Andy; B = Beth; C = Chris)
A: So this is her husband – Diego Rivera. She can't have fallen in love with him for his looks, can she? Ha ha.
B: No, I reckon he must have been either very rich or very intelligent.
C: Actually, he was both highly intelligent and very rich. At first, Frida's father was against her marrying Diego because he was a Communist, but he finally agreed to it because he couldn't pay his daughter's medical expenses any more. Frida must have spent a fortune on doctors and operations over the years.
B: Oh, yes, what a terrible life – first polio and then that awful accident. It's amazing she produced so many paintings, isn't it?
A: Yes, she must have been an incredibly brave woman.
B: But the marriage didn't work out too well, did it?
C: Well, it had its ups and downs.
B: She painted this one with the cropped hair while they were

separated, didn't she?
C: Yes, that's right.
B: She really looks like a man here. In fact, she looks as if she's got a moustache! And why was she dressed in a man's suit?
A: I thought it might have had something to do with women's liberation. You know – she cut off her hair to symbolise equality or something.
C: Er, no – the reason she cut off her hair and put on a man's suit is because Diego Rivera loved her long hair, and also loved the traditional women's Mexican dresses she used to wear. She did it to hurt him.
B: And why did they divorce?
C: Er, nobody really knows. Diego may have found out about Frida's affair with Leon Trotsky, or it could have been Frida who was unhappy about Diego's affair with an American film star. What we are sure about is that Frida was very unhappy about the divorce.
A: But they were back together by the time she painted *Roots*.
C: Yes, they remarried a year after they separated. She painted this one when her health was beginning to deteriorate. She must have been in a lot of pain.
B: I find this one rather depressing. The rocks she's lying don't look very comfortable – I suppose they represent her pain.
C: Probably, but actually, if you look at the expression on her face, she looks quite calm. I think the green leaves suggest hope. In spite of everything, she was a very optimistic person. The last painting she did was called *Viva la vida* – long live life.

📼 48

(A = Alice; B = Bob)
A: What can you tell me about this picture then?
B: Well, I dunno. It looks a bit strange to me. It must be a fairly modern picture. I suppose it might be a Picasso. Wasn't his style something like that? I dunno. To be honest, I don't know a lot about art. Could it be by oh, wassisname, Salvo Dali, or something?
A: All right, what do you think it's about then?
B: Who knows! It's a bit hard to make out, isn't it? Is it a man or a woman? OK, say a man. I guess he could be in a prison. Is that a prison bar above his head? I think he may be crying – no, hang on, those funny things there must be his nose. Anyway, it's not much good, is it? He can't be much of a painter. Either that, or he must have been in a bit of a hurry. Not my kind of thing, I'm afraid.

📼 49

(See page 92.)

📼 50

Interview with Trevor Baylis
(I = Interviewer; TB = Trevor Baylis)

I: Trevor, let me, er, start by asking you what gave you the idea for the clockwork radio?

TB: Well, I was sitting where I am now looking at that television over there, and I was, um, actually watching a programme about the spread of AIDS in Africa, and they said the only way they could stop this dreadful disease cutting its way through Africa was with the power of information and education. But there was a problem. Most of Africa doesn't have electricity. The only form of electricity available to them was in the form of batteries, which were horrendously expensive. And so I said to myself, hang on, hang on. Now, this is where dreams play an important part in everybody's life. You got to explain what a dream is all about. Um, the beautiful thing about a dream is you can do anything you like in your dreams, right? Now why I am saying this to you is because I could see myself somewhere in the jungle, right? And I can see myself with a pith helmet, a monocle, a gin and tonic in my left hand and one of those fly swatting things, listening to some raunchy number by Dame Nellie Melba on my wind-up gramophone, mmm? And then I am thinking to myself, blimey, if you can get all that noise by dragging a rusty nail around a piece of old bakelite using a spring, surely there's enough power in that spring to drive a small dynamo which in turn will drive my radio, and so I was stirred enough to get off my backside and go to my, my shed, my studio, which sounds so much nicer, my graveyard of a thousand domestic appliances, and actually find enough parts to actually start doing those first primitive experiments …

I: And, um, how long did it take you to design a prototype?

TB: Well, from the actual, from the concept to, er, having the first in-a-box model out there it would have taken me two to three months, I guess, so, yes, it took about two or three months.

I: So you got, you got the prototype, um, how easy was it from that point on? How easy was it to find a backer and set up production?

TB: Well, first things first. I did know that there are these thieves about that will steal your idea. Because I had a whole range of products for the disabled that were stolen from me at an earlier time. So I did know about patents and how important

they were. So I found a lady called Jackie Needle, a patent attorney, and I said to her 'Jackie, I want to write up a patent, can you help me?' So we did a search and couldn't find any clockwork radios of the kind that I had done, and she filed for a patent to me, for me, and therefore then I had a starting date, as it were. Now I knew that nobody pays you for a good idea, but they could pay you for that piece of paper, so then I went round every British company I could think of with a confidentiality agreement, and they all talked down to me. 'Oh yes, I think we're, I think that we are working on something like this, aren't we Johnny?' You know all that old sausage. Um, I mean it was so humiliating … and in the end, quite frankly after about three or four years of this, I thought, I have had enough of this. Why do I need this? I was fifty-six or something when this happened. So I was given a chance through the BBC World Service to meet up with the guys from the BBC *Tomorrow's World* programme, and they said, 'Come on, we'll do the story.'

I: So the whole thing got off the ground. How long was it then before the production of them started?

TB: Well, the important thing was funding. Um, the *Tomorrow's World* programme was seen by a fellow in South Africa, a chap from a company called Liberty Life. He came to my house here, and we sat out there, and he said, 'Look, um, we can help you make this happen, provided we can share in its success.' I said of course, and so we formed a company called Baygen, Baylis Generators, and he wrote a cheque for three-quarters of a million pounds whilst I was in this room.

I: And how many radios are produced each month?

TB: Well, I'm sure they might tell me differently, but I'm sure they must be doing 200,000 a month.

I: And in what ways has the clockwork radio changed your life?

TB: Well, not, not significantly. I mean my lifestyle hasn't changed. The house hasn't, has remained more or less the same, but I do get involved with lots more television and radio. I like people, so I'm doing fundamentally what I like doing anyway, communicating.

I: And finally what advice would you give to someone who had a good idea?

TB: Don't go down the pub and tell everyone about it. That's the first thing, right? Get on to the Patent Office. Get their literature, and read all about it, right? Nobody pays you for a good idea, but they might pay you for a piece of paper which says

you own that idea. But remember, somebody might already own that idea, so you must do a search first. There's no excuse afterwards.

11 Sell

📼 51

(P = Perry; M = Mum)

P: Mum, I need a new pair of trainers.

M: Okay, I'll give you £20, and you can go and get some.

P: £20!!!!! I can't get a pair of trainers for £20!

M: Your last pair cost less than that.

P: I know, and everybody made fun of me. It's not nice being the odd one out.

M: Don't be silly.

P: You don't understand. I need Nikes.

M: What's so special about Nikes?

P: All my friends've got them.

M: What, even Jamie?

P: Mum, Jamie's pathetic. I mean all my cool friends have got them. And Michael Jordan wears them.

M: Who's Michael Jordan?

P: Oh honestly, he's only the most famous basketball player ever.

M: I am not paying £50 for a pair of trainers.

P: £69.99.

M: What! I've never spent that much on a pair of shoes.

P: Yeah, but you don't care how you look.

M: Perry!

P: I promise I won't be rude any more, and I'll keep my room tidy, and I won't want anything else for my next birthday or Christmas.

M: I'm not spending £70 on a pair of trainers.

P: You want me to look stupid, don't you? I hate you.

📼 52

Joe Smedley, marketing executive
Children are much easier to reach with advertising than adults are – they like it and they pick up on it really fast. So, it's the advertiser's job to capitalise on this.

We have a term, 'pester-power', which means the marketing potential of children nagging their parents to spend money. And I'm not just talking about toys here – our aim is getting children to pester parents to buy something for the whole family, like a holiday or car. The trick is to produce adverts that appeal to both children and adults – to split the message in two.

Another key concept for advertisers is 'the playground pound'. Children want what their friends have – playground credibility is very important. In other words, brands give children a sense of identity and help them fit in with a peer group. For instance, if you have the wrong brand of trainers, you're excluded. Brands have the power to show that you're the right sort of kid. If you get it a little bit wrong, it's completely wrong.

So you can see children are a very important market for us, and in return, we like to promote education. In fact we're looking into promoting our products directly in the classroom. This is something that's already happening in America. Companies donate free computers and other school equipment in exchange for advertising their brands on exercise book covers, posters and that sort of thing. I think it's fantastic – the kids benefit, and the companies get brand loyalty from a very early age.

I'd love to be a child today. They really know what they want and they have so many more choices. Advertisers respect children's opinions.

Sally McIlveen, headteacher

Basically, children nowadays are being constantly brainwashed by all the advertising that goes on around them. I tell you what – if the children in my school remembered any of their school work as well as they remember the advertising jingles they hear on television, my job would be a pleasure.

Usually the pupils at our school wear uniforms, but Friday is a non-uniform day, and that's when you really see the power of advertising. The kids are dressed from head to toe in labels, mainly sports stuff like Adidas, Nike, that sort of thing. And they all look the same!

There's a great deal of pressure on parents to buy children all these labels and gadgets. They call it 'pester power' – children nag their parents until they give in. I feel sorry for the families who don't have much money, because the pressure is just the same.

I really believe it's time the government put a stop to all this aggressive television advertising.

Mind you, it's worse in America apparently. Schools are actually being subsidised by companies like McDonalds and Pepsi. Okay, the school gets free equipment from these big companies, but then the children have to add up burgers or multiply cans of Pepsi in their maths lessons. I think it's terrible to think that the schools end up promoting a product that's not even good for the children. I mean, where will it end? Will we see the day when kids are required to wear Nikes before they're allowed to go to school?

Companies like to say they're promoting education and school-business partnerships, but what they're really doing is going after the kids' market wherever they can.

I think it's really sad that children are being forced to be consumers from such an early age. I don't think all this choice is liberating for children – it just means that they're getting older younger, and that's a shame.

📼 53

Alison

My favourite one is the one where this guy invites his girlfriend back to his flat for a drink. He's a typical lazy slob, and the flat is a right mess as they walk in, and he tries to tidy up a few things. Erm, then, he, he goes into the kitchen but he finds he's run out, except for a jar of instant. So he starts making funny noises, like, er, ssh, sshh, brrr, sshh. He opens up cupboards and closes them, pretending he's really busy. After a few minutes he comes out, and she believes it's the real thing. Mind you, if she's stupid enough to be going out with a guy like that, she'd probably believe anything.

Ben

I saw one the other day that I really liked. It was a sunny day in a park, and there's this kind of angel character flying around all over the place. You know, a sort of Cupid with a bow and arrow. He keeps firing arrows at people but he keeps missing, or he shoots a dog which falls in love with an old lady or something. And he's getting really dejected 'cos he's getting it all wrong, when this other Cupid turns up, but instead of shooting love arrows, he fires these vanilla cones at people. So, there's a couple on the bench having an argument, when all of a sudden, they're both holding cones and all in love with each other. I scream when I see that one … Get it? I scream … Oh, never mind.

Celia

There was another one years ago that was really good. It was always the same bloke, and, erm, terrible things kept happening to him. Like, em, he'd be in a sinking ship and the water would be coming up to his knees, or he was painting a room and he finds he's painted himself into a corner and can't move. Oh, I don't know, there were loads of different situations, and each time it was really terrible. But instead of getting depressed, he'd take one look at the situation and he'd put his hand in his pocket, take one out and light up. Then he would blow out the smoke and smile, looking really relaxed.

Dan

Do you remember that one with a sort of James Bond kind of character who parachutes onto the roof of a skyscraper? He's got a coil of rope over one shoulder and a package strapped to his back. Then he jumps over the edge of the roof and abseils down the building. Then, when he's gone down ten floors or so he smashes through the window with his feet. Then what? Oh, yeah, there's this beautiful woman in the room, who looks up at him, but without being too surprised. He takes the package off his back and gets down on his knees. He opens it up and hands it over to the gorgeous woman. Er, that's it, I think. Do you remember that one?

📼 54

(P = Presenter; S = Shelley Russell; J = Jim Falmer)

P: Good evening and welcome to *Talkback*. Recently, the tabloid press have been under fire yet again, this time for their apparent disregard for truth and accuracy.
In the studio tonight we would like to welcome Shelley Russell, Oscar-winning actress, and Jim Falmer, editor of *The Daily Post*.
Shelley Russell, let's start with you. Do you think there should be greater restrictions placed on the press and the stories they print?

S: Yes, absolutely. I can't open a newspaper or magazine without reading stories full of false information about myself or people I know. It's getting …

J: Sorry, but I can't believe that you're actually complaining about free publicity. I mean, I remember, Shelley, before you were famous, you were begging us to write features about you … anything …

S: If you would just let me finish – of course the press have been important. I'm an actress and I understand the power of the press. But the thing is, I rarely seem to read anything true about myself these days. Take last week – your paper wrote this story about me and my co-star, who incidentally happens to be married to a very good friend of mine – taking a bath together in my hotel room.

J: Oh that. That was …

S: Hang on, I haven't finished. You went on to say that the bath was filled with $5,000 worth of champagne. Now, …

J: Well, that was just a bit of fun. I don't think you should take that too seriously.

S: Oh really! You don't think that it's at all serious that my co-star's children woke up to the headline: SHELLEY GETS BUBBLY WITH SHAUN IN CHAMPAGNE BATH, or that his wife is now filing for a divorce …

J: Look, I don't know whether …

S: Anyway, to get back to what I was saying … The point I'm trying to make here is that famous people have families with feelings. I am sick of the gutter-press making up stories just so that they can splash sensational headlines across the front page and sell more newspapers – it's irresponsible and it messes up people's lives.

J: Look love, you're just angry about that particular article because the photos we printed of you weren't very flattering. Anyway, we made a public apology and said that there'd been some inaccuracies in the article.

S: Yes, but what you didn't do was say what the inaccuracies were, so …

P: If I could just come in here. I think we need to address the root of the problem. Jim Falmer, why do certain newspapers continue to print these stories when it's obvious that they're not true?

S: To increase circulation and make more money.

J: If you would let me answer the question – I think we have to look at the relationship between fame, the public and the press. The public are fascinated by fame and scandal, and they love to read about their favourite stars. The problem is, it's not always clear what's true and what isn't. I mean, if a newspaper prints something scandalous or embarrassing about a famous person, they're bound to deny it, but that doesn't mean it's not true.

S: Are you trying to say …

J: No smoke without fire, if you ask me.

P: Well, I'm sorry to interrupt you, but we'll carry on after this short break for some travel news …

🔊 55

(See page 106.)

🔊 56

Before seeing *The Blair Witch Project*
(I = Interviewer; W = Woman; M = Man)

a
I: Excuse me. Do you mind if I ask you how you feel about seeing this movie?

W1: Um, a bit nervous, actually. I don't know quite what to expect, but I think I'm going to be scared.

b
I: Excuse me – are you feeling nervous about seeing *The Blair Witch Project*?

M1: Yeah, a little uneasy, I must admit … but I've brought my girlfriend, so I can hold her hand if I get scared.

c
I: How do you feel about seeing this movie?

M2: I'm looking forward to being frightened to death.

d
I: What are you expecting from this film?

W2: To be scared stiff – hopefully.

e
I: Do you think you're going to enjoy *The Blair Witch Project*?

W3: Er, no – I don't think 'enjoy' is the right word. But I've heard so much about it that I can't wait to find out what it's all about. In fact, I feel quite apprehensive, but I love horror films, and this one sounds as if it's going to be really scary.

f
I: Any expectations?

M3: Well, I've been visiting the website for a while now and I'm really looking forward to finding out what happens. I expect to be absolutely terrified!

🔊 57

After seeing *The Blair Witch Project*
(I = Interviewer; W = Woman; M = Man)

I: So, how was it for you?

W1: Extremely disappointing. I wasn't the least bit scared, and, and you know from the start that everybody dies, so there's no suspense. Anyway, the characters are so annoying that I felt like killing them myself. It does not live up to the hype.

I: What did you think of it then?

M1: Absolute rubbish. My girlfriend fell asleep, and I spent the last half of the movie with my eyes shut – not because it was scary – but because the camera angles made me feel sick. Don't see it if you suffer from motion sickness. In fact, just don't see it.

I: So were you frightened to death?

M2: No way. After all the hype, it was a massive letdown.

I: What did you think?

W2: Over-hyped nonsense. I spent most of the time waiting for something to happen. I feel completely disillusioned.

I: Did the film live up to your expectations?

W3: No, it didn't. I don't think I've ever been so bored in my entire life, and I still haven't got a clue what it's about. In fact, there's no story to speak of. This film is a perfect example of hype over substance.

I: Your verdict?

M3: A total waste of time. I was bored out of my mind. The website was much more entertaining than the film.

12 Student

🔊 58

John
Ah, Madame Lorenzo! How could I ever forget? It was my last year at school, and she took us for French, which I was hopeless at. I remember the first time she walked into the room. She stood at the front, put her bag down on the teacher's desk and looked around the room. Then she pointed at me and said 'You, boy, take that imbécilic grin off your face. The only thing that's funny is your score in the French exam last year.'

Then she started looking around in her big bag and eventually produced a little compact mirror and a lipstick. She held up the mirror, and we could see her long, long fingernails which were the same blood red as the lipstick she started to put on.' She must have been near to retirement, but she was incredibly elegant. She was slim and petite with blond hair tied in a tight bun – all the guys in the class were completely fascinated by her. But she was vicious. She had this way of criticising you that made everyone else in the class laugh at you. I can't remember the number of times she reduced me to tears. Every time I hear the word 'imbecile' I still think of her. It was her catchphrase. 'You are an im-bé-cile, boy. I 'ave more brains in my little finger than you have in your 'ole 'ead. You are like my Marcel. You will never amount to much. You are an imbecile.' We all knew that Marcel was her husband, and everyone giggled. I was terrified of going to her classes, but in a funny sort of way I really loved being there.

Clare
Mr Tucker is the one I remember best. The sergeant, we called him, because he used to wear his military medals to school every day. In fact he always wore the same jacket – in two years I never saw him wear anything else. He had a big moustache and a nervous tic with his eye which twitched really fast when he got angry. He was always shouting as if we were deaf or something. 'You'll learn,' he used to shout. 'You'll learn when you've settled down and started a family. It's not all rubbish that we teach you here, you know.' Another one of his sayings was 'In my day …' 'In my day, young people had to join the army. That used to knock some sense into them. My generation never had the chance to go to university like you lot.' I reckon he was probably too stupid to get into university anyway. A bit sad really. I wonder what he's doing now?

🔊 59

(I = Interviewer;
Mrs B = Mrs Barrington;
Mr B = Mr Barrington)

I: What's Saffron going to do when she leaves school?

Mrs B: Until a few months ago, she was going to go to university, but she's changed her mind. Now she reckons she's going to make it in the pop world.

I: And how do you feel about that?

Mr B: We think she's making an enormous mistake.

I: But surely she can go back to her studies if her music career fails.

Mr B: That's true, but once she gets a taste of freedom, she'll find it more difficult to go back to college. I just think it's such a waste – in three years' time, she'll have got her degree and she'll still be young enough to try out the music business. At least if it doesn't work out she'll have a qualification behind her.

I: Have you discussed this with her?

Mrs B: Of course, but she's made up her mind. We're just hoping that she'll get it out of her system and then come to her senses and go back to her studies. When I left school I didn't go on to university, and I've regretted it ever since. I just don't want her to make the same mistake as I did.

I: Will you support her while she's trying to be a pop singer?

Mr B: You mean financially? No. She won't be living at home, and we can't afford to pay for her to live in London, so it's up to her to make it work.

🔊 60

(I = Interviewer; S = Saffron)

I: You're leaving school soon, aren't you?

S: Yes, my A-levels start next week, but I'm not too bothered about the results, because when I leave school I'm going to concentrate on my music career. I'm lead singer in a band and I don't need any qualifications to be a pop star. I see my future very clearly – I'm going to be incredibly famous and fabulously rich.

I: So you've already got a contract then?

S: Er, no, not as such. Actually, we haven't got a manager yet, but the minute I've taken my last exam, I'm going to find a really good one.

I: So, do you intend to continue living at home?

S: No way. I'm moving to London just as soon as I've left school. London's where it all happens in the music industry.

I: Do you think you'll be able to live off your music right from the start?

S: Well, if we don't make it straight away we might have to get part-time jobs for a few months or something. I know it's going to be hard at first, but I bet you, by this time next year, we'll have had a record in the charts.

I: And where do you see yourself in five years from now?

S: In five years' time I'll be staying in posh hotels and won't be able to walk down the street without being recognised. In fact, I'll give you my autograph now if you like – it'll be worth a fortune in a few years' time!

🔊 61

Tom's second story

While I was travelling, I got an incredibly painful tropical ear infection after I fell into a stinking latrine. Feeling like death, I lay in bed with a raging fever for what felt like a lifetime. Wracked with pain, I couldn't face eating anything and I lost so much weight that I looked like a skeleton. Eventually, I managed to get hold of some antibiotics which brought me back from death's door.

🔊 62

(P = Pete; K = Kate)

P: Come in!

K: Hi Pete – I just wondered if you fancied coming out for a coffee.

P: Oh, I was just writing a letter.

K: Writing a letter! Is your phone out of order?

P: No – well, not exactly a letter. Ben's applied for a job at a children's summer camp, and they've asked me for a character reference. He must have put me down as one of his referees.

K: Oh dear – you're not going to tell them the truth, are you?

P: What do you mean?

K: Well, that he's a big-headed show-off who goes out every night and never does a day's work.

P: Oh, come on, he's not that bad – I mean, kids love him. He's always entertaining his little brother's friends with his magic tricks and silly jokes.

K: Oh yes, he's great with children – but he's a big kid himself, isn't he?

P: Yes, I suppose he is a bit immature.

K: And I hope they don't expect him to work before four o'clock in the afternoon. You know what he's like – he needs a bomb under him to get him up in the morning.

P: Mm.

K: Also, he hates taking orders from anybody. Do you remember that job he had last summer in a restaurant? He ended up throwing a bucket of water over the chef when she asked him to wash the kitchen floor.

P: Oh no, don't remind me. He won't do anything he doesn't enjoy, will he? Mind you, he did run that restaurant single-handed when the chef and two of the waiters were off sick with food poisoning.

K: That's true. He's good in a crisis. But having said that, he's good at causing a crisis as well – I mean, you know the food poisoning was his fault, don't you?

P: Oh, yes – oh dear, this isn't helping.

K: Hey, do you think he's still got blue hair?

P: Come on. Let's go and get that coffee.

🔊 63

Angels **by Robbie Williams**

I sit and wait.
Does an angel contemplate my fate?
And do they know,
The places where we go
When we're grey and old?
'Cos I have been told
That salvation lets their wings unfold.
So when I'm lying in my bed,
Thoughts running through my head,
And I feel that love is dead,
I'm loving angels instead.

And through it all
She offers me protection,
A lot of love and affection,
Whether I'm right or wrong.
And down the waterfall,
Wherever it may take me,
I know that life won't break me,
When I come to call, she won't forsake me,
I'm loving angels instead.

When I'm feeling weak,
And my pain walks down a one way street,
I look above,
And I know I'll always be blessed with love.
And as the feeling grows,
She breathes flesh to my bones.
And when love is dead,
I'm loving angels instead.

(And through it all …)

13 Home

🔊 64

Room 1

At first sight this room looks a bit of a mess. A real eccentric lives here. You can tell it's a woman because there are piles of cushions everywhere – men don't like cushions. Cushions may look attractive, but nine times out of ten, they don't make seats more comfortable. But that's typical of the different ways men and women approach homes – men tend to be more practical, whilst women are more concerned with aesthetics.

The room is extremely cluttered – there's far too much stuff, and every surface is covered. There isn't really enough furniture here – she could do with a few shelves or cupboards to put all this stuff in. But this is not a practical person. This is somebody who lives in the world of imagination – perhaps a children's book writer.

There's nothing calming about this room – there are loads of bright colours, but no pastels at all. Also, there's very little natural light and not many indoor plants. More green would help bring this person down to earth. But the bright colours definitely suggest a person who is warm-hearted and sociable. In fact, judging by the number of candles and full ashtrays, I'd say she's a bit of a party animal.

Room 2

This one's more difficult because there are very few clues here about the type of person who lives in it. I think it's a man because there are hardly any personal objects on display – for instance, there aren't any family photos around the place.

But there's plenty of evidence to suggest that he's a successful career man, someone who spends most of his time travelling. There are a couple of oriental rugs which are probably worth a lot of money, and a few other ornaments which suggest that he travels to the Far East.

Most of the furniture is functional rather than decorative. I think this is somebody who doesn't actually spend much time at home, and when he does, he's obsessively tidy. The lack of decoration suggests that he wants to be ready to pack his bags and leave at short notice.

He has little time to socialise, except in a working context, and probably never entertains at home. He's single, and may be the sort of person who has problems with commitment in personal relationships.

📼 65

Lizanne

(I = Interviewer; L = Lizanne)

I: Lizanne, you're from America. What do you have for breakfast?

L: Er, eggs, bacon, pancakes, and a bit of toast on the side.

I: And what to drink?

L: Usually we start with orange juice and have lots and lots of coffee.

I: And your eggs – how do you like to have them done?

L: Sunny side up.

I: What does that mean?

L: That means that the yolk is facing upward – it's not been turned over.

I: Thank you.

Nicola

(I = Interviewer; N = Nicola)

I: Nicola, you're from Germany. Tell me about breakfast. What do you have for breakfast?

N: Well, in Germany it's different. Some people like jam or cereals, but the typical breakfast is, of course, with cold meat like salami, bacon or ham, and cheese. And we always have hot bread rolls and coffee. But I don't like coffee very much. And, of course, boiled eggs – they are very important in Germany and very typical, with salt or pepper.

I: You don't drink coffee for breakfast. What do you like?

N: I like to drink tea.

Michiko

(I = Interviewer; M = Michiko)

I: Michiko. What do you have for breakfast? What do you have to drink for breakfast?

M: We drink green tea for breakfast.

I: OK, and what about, what do you eat?

M: We eat rice, miso soup, pickled vegetables, er, grilled fish – like salmon, and Japanese omelette, and seaweed.

I: What, what do you have in the Japanese omelette? What does that …

M: Japanese omelette is sweet taste, and it's different from the western omelette.

I: And miso soup. What is in that?

M: Miso soup is a salty soup, which often has seaweed, vegetables and tofu.

14 Review 2

📼 66

a

A student at Oxford was sitting an exam when he asked a supervisor for a glass of red wine and a plate of scones, correctly adding that this tradition had been the right of Oxford scholars dating back to medieval times. The wine and the scones were brought to the exam room, and the student enjoyed the lot before finishing his exam. A few weeks later, the student was shocked to find that he'd failed the exam, not because he had performed badly, but because he hadn't been wearing his sword as he sat the exam.

b

A student who was sitting an exam continued to write a full five minutes after the professor had told everyone to stop. When the student tried to hand in his paper, the professor told him not to bother, as he had already failed. 'Do you know who I am?' the student angrily asked the professor. When the professor replied that he had never seen the student before, the student pushed his paper into the middle of the pile of other papers and quickly ran out of the room.

Macmillan Heinemann English Language Teaching
Between Towns Road, Oxford OX4 3PP
A division of Macmillan Publishers Limited
Companies and representatives throughout the world

ISBN 0 333 75760 2

Project management by Desmond O'Sullivan, ELT Publishing Services.
Designed by Jackie Hill, 320 Design.
Illustrated by Martin Chatterton pp51, 54, 58, 81, 122; Martina
Farrow pp28, 124; Rebecca Halls pp13, 63, 66, 77, 97; Jelly pp121,
124; Ed McLachlan pp16, 27, 60, 93, 110; Julian Mosedale pp7, 62, 63,
65, 67, 115, 116, 131, 133, 134; Nicola Slater p100; Spark p126;
Alastair Taylor p132.
Cover design by Andrew Oliver.
Cover painting *In Coconut Grove* © Howard Hodgkin.

Authors' acknowledgements
We would like to thank all our colleagues at the Lake School,
Oxford, for their help and continued support; in particular, Peter
Maggs, whose thoughtful comments on work in progress and whose
help on the Teacher's Book were much appreciated. Thanks also goes
to our upper intermediate students who have kept us focused at all
times on what works in the classroom (and made sure that we
disregarded everything else).
We are especially grateful to Philip Kerr, who, as well as writing the
Inside Out Workbook, made several inspired contributions to the
Student's Book. Similarly, we would like to thank Jon Hird for the
Student's Book review units, Helena Gomm for the *Inside Out*
Teacher's Book, and everybody involved in the *Inside Out* Resource
Pack: a great team!
At Macmillan Heinemann ELT we would like to thank Sue Bale
(publishing director), David Riley (publisher), and Pippa McNee
(picture researcher). We would also like to thank Jackie Hill
(freelance designer), Edith Boreham (freelance permissions editor),
and James Richardson (freelance audio producer). Thanks also go to
the production and marketing teams who have worked so hard to
make *Inside Out* what it is.
However, we reserve the biggest thank you of all for Desmond
O'Sullivan (freelance project manager). It has been a rare privilege to
work with such a talented and committed professional. Thanks for
everything, Des.
In addition, we must thank our families, without whose support and
understanding none of this would have been possible.
We would also like to thank teachers and staff at the Escuelas Oficial
de Idiomas of Spain for their help in the early stages of the project,
in particular at A Coruña, Alcala de Guadaira-Seville, Alcorcón,
Barcelona 1, Barcelona 2, Bilbao, Cartagena, Ciudad Lineal,
Fuenlabrada, Gandía, Getafe, Jesus Maestro-Madrid, Mostoles,
Pamplona, San Blas, San Sebastián de los Reyes and Santander.
Thanks also to Mary Pickett (International House, London) and Jenny
Johnson (International House, Barcelona) for their very helpful
comments.

The authors and publishers would like to thank the following for
permission to reproduce their material:
Atlantic Syndication Partners on behalf of *The Mail on Sunday* for
extract based on 'How Madonna went from a Material girl to Geisha
girl' by Caroline Hendrie, (11th April, 1999); Syndication International
on behalf of *The Sunday Mirror* for extract adapted from
'Embarrassing parents' by Denna Allen (*The Sunday Mirror
Magazine*, 16th May, 1999); Sasha Abransky for extract based on his
article 'Yellow Fever' (*The Independent on Sunday*, 5th September,
1999); News International Syndication for adapted quotations from
'What's your most treasured possession?' copyright © Times
Newspapers Limited (*The Times Millennium*, 18th September, 1999);
The Observer Syndication on behalf of Esther Addley for extract
from an article (*The Guardian*, 15th November, 1999); *Men's Health
Magazine* for adapted text from 'I smoke ... and I work for *Men's
Health*' by Greg Gutfeld, (December, 1999); HarperCollins Publishers
Ltd for extracts from *Collins COBUILD English Dictionary*
© HarperCollins Publishers Ltd 1995; Penguin UK and Peters Fraser
and Dunlop Group for an adapted extract from *Fever Pitch* by Nick
Hornby (Victor Gollancz, 1992) copyright © Nick Hornby, 1992; The
Observer Syndication on behalf of Richard Benson for information
from 'Joy of Text' (*The Guardian*, 3rd June, 2000); The Observer
Syndication on behalf of Hamish Mackintosh for extract based on
'Single White E-mail' (*The Guardian*, 10th June, 2000); News
International Syndication for questionnaire based on 'A Day in the
Life of Lara Croft' © Richard Johnson/Times Newspapers Limited,
(19th December, 1999); The Independent Syndication for extract
based on 'Our Generation of Couch Potato Kids, Stuck in their
Rooms and Glued to TV', by Rhys Williams and Andrew Buncombe,
(*The Independent*, 19th March, 1999); Association for Computing
Machinery, Inc. for extract based on 'Go To Your Bedroom',
(*The Guardian*, 21st January, 2000) first published as 'The Digital
Hug' ACM's *interactions* magazine (Nov/Dec, 1999 special issue)
© 1999 Association for Computing for Machinery, Inc.; *The Week* for
use of extract based on an article (22nd July, 2000); Atlantic
Syndication Partners on behalf of *The Daily Mail* for extract based on
'The leaping lettuce' (1st October, 1998); Atlantic Syndication
Partners on behalf of *The Mail on Sunday Night and Day Magazine*
for adapted extract from 'Notes from a Big Country' by Bill Bryson
(3rd August, 1997); Atlantic Syndication Partners on behalf of *The
Daily Mail* for text based on 'You did what?' by Michael Harvey
(31st July, 1997); Curtis Brown Ltd, London on behalf of Danny
Danziger for text based on 'Best of Times, Worst of Times' (*Sunday
Times Magazine*, 26th September, 1999) copyright © Danny Danziger,
1999; Syndication International on behalf of the Mirror Group for
adapted text from '8 Minutes to get yourself a date' by Jane Ridley,
(*The Mirror*, 26th April, 2000); Lyrics of *Never Ever* by All Saints:
Words and Music by Sean Mather, Robert Jazayeri and Shaznay Lewis
Copyright © Rickidy Raw Music/BMG Music Publishing Ltd/Universal
MCA Music Ltd/Music Sales Limited. All rights reserved. Used by
permission. Recording courtesy of Warner Music UK Ltd; *The
Observer* for extract based on 'Where to go to see a Masterpiece' by
Robert McCrum (*Observer Life*, 12th October, 1997); *Brill's Content
Magazine* for use of material from 'The truth about life with Sharon
Stone' by Phil Bronstein (*The Observer Review*, 11th April, 1999:
article first appeared in *Brill's Content Magazine*, April 1999)
Reprinted with permission; Screen Press Books for information from
Into the Woods (The definitive story of The Blair Witch Project) by Ed
Potton and Amber Cowan first available through Screen Press Books
and Times Newspapers; Macmillan Publishers Limited for adapted
extract from *Take That: our story* as told to Piers Morgan, originally
published by Boxtree Limited; Telegraph Group Limited for extract
based on 'Why students love a long-haul to hell' by Helen Chappell
(*The Sunday Telegraph Review*, 29th March 1998; Lyric of *Angels* by
Robbie Williams: Words and Music by Robert Williams and Guy
Chambers Copyright © 1997 EMI Virgin Music Ltd/BMG Music
Publishing Ltd (50%) EMI Virgin Music Ltd, London WC2H OQY. All
rights reserved. Reproduced by permission of International Music
Publications Ltd. Recording ℗ 1997 courtesy of EMI Records Ltd;
COLORS for quotations from *COLORS Magazine: Home*
(August/September 1998); Oxford University Press for the definition
of Feng Shui from *Oxford Advanced Learner's Dictionary of Current
English* 6th Edition by AS Hornby © Oxford University Press 2000;
Syndication International on behalf of Mirror Group for extract
based on 'Start your day the Feng Shui Way' by Rachel Dobson
(*Sunday Mirror Magazine*, 16th May, 1999); News International
Syndication for text based on 'Titanic tax haven to sail with 65,000'
by Mark Austin copyright © Times Newspapers Limited (15th March
1998); Rough Guides Ltd, Travel Guide and Reference Book
Publishers, London and New York for their website home page
(www.roughguides.com).
Whilst every effort has been made to locate the owners of copyright,
in some cases this has been unsuccessful. The publishers apologise
for any infringement or failure to acknowledge the original sources
and will be glad to include any necessary correction in subsequent
printings.

The publishers wish to thank Gavin Aherne, Cathren Allan, Willy
Bowman, Michelle Egan, Gee's Restaurant, Oxford (01865 553540),
Barry Hopkins a.k.a. Mr Wiggy, Helen Kunzemann, Jamie Luke,
Monica Perez, Don Reed, Diane and Kaleigh Rolls, Greg Sweetnam,
Alan Thompson, and Karen Warner.